Servant
Vs.
Bond servant

What is the difference?

Contents

Chapter 1

What is a servant?

Have you ever seen the drawing of Jesus Christ with a baby lamb draped across His shoulders? In ancient Hebrew times the shepherds would break the legs of a rebellious lamb, and drape it over their shoulders, and keep it with them at all times, so that while the lamb's legs are healing, it would become accustomed to hearing the shepherd's voice. The lamb would then become sensitive to the scent and the feel of the shepherd. Therefore, when the lamb was fully healed, it would not be rebellious. It would not stray far and when the lamb heard the shepherd's voice it would come running.

Jesus might be alluding to this fact when he said, "*My sheep hear My voice*". The Amplified Bible reads in John 10:27, "*the sheep that are My own hear and are listening to My voice, and I know them and they follow Me*". Clearly this shows that God has chosen His sheep, His people. Many persons in the Old Testament are called servants among them Abraham, Jacob, Joshua, Samuel, and Daniel. Moses is designated as such about 40 times and David more than 50 times. The servants know God by the gospel, they are accepted and loved by Him, they hear His voice through faith, and they follow Him. God has given those who follow and obey to the Lord Jesus, and they can never be removed from Him or His love. Those who follow and obey are called servants of Christ.

Christ took upon Himself the form of a servant. As the Son of Man, Jesus did not come to be served but to serve and to give His life as a ransom for many, as Jesus said in Matthew 20:28, "*Just as the Son of Man did not come to be served, but to serve, and to give His life a ransom for many*", also in Mark 10:45, "*For even the Son of Man did not come to be served, but to serve, and to give His life a ransom for many*". The New Testament term for serve is *Diakonos* which means "*to wait at tables, to serve*". A waitress or a waiter might be considered a modern day *Diakonon*. The *Diakonon* gives hospitality, distributes food, sets a table, does the work of a deacon, or exercises spiritual gifts. In the New Testament the idea of *diakoneo* or serving is extended to the saint or followers of Christ, or in other words the servants of Christ, you and me. It is so very awesome to be a servant of Christ, to do His will. When you put Christ first in your service and do your work as to the Lord you not only do more and do your best, but the burden is light. Our Lord Jesus Christ refers to this in Matthew 11:30,"*For my yoke is easy and my burden is light*".

However, Christian service should not be entered into lightly, or carelessly, but must be entered into affectionately, considerately, devotedly, and soberly, and in the fear of God. If at any time you consider going into some type of service, you should first pray to God and ask Him if this is what He would like you to do, and when you get a clear answer from God then you can proceed. Your abilities and interests are an important part of the will of God for your life. In your service you must be yourself, too many people are trying to imitate others instead of being themselves, and serving God the way God wants them to serve Him and others. You are unique. Your uniqueness is what God instilled in you to cause you stand out amongst a crowd, you are one *in* a million not one *of* a million. God gave you a special talent, special abilities, and special capabilities. God matches Spiritual gifts with natural abilities so that you can fill a special place, do a specific job that only you can do. There may be more than one person doing a job or working in some kind of service but only you can do it the way God made you to do it. God has created the other people who are serving and working with you and gave them their special gifts and talents, and only they can do the work the way God made them to do it. The wonderful aspect of this is that God made them with their gifts and made you and I with our gifts so that we all can work together in a God given, awe-inspiring plan. All of the servants of the Most High God, all the true followers of Christ, shall serve God. Each of the servants of God, from the ministering angels, to the ministers of the Gospel shall be where God is, and serve Him. We not only will serve God on earth but we are told that we will serve God in heaven. Revelation 7:15, mentions serving God in heaven, *"For this reason they are before the throne of God and they serve Him day and night in His temple and He who sits on the throne will spread his tabernacle over them."* This refers to the heavenly throne of God where His servants serve him day and night in His temple. Not in any material temple but in the New Jerusalem and general assembly and the church, the Temple of the Living God. In this state there will be no material temple or place of worship but God and the Lamb will be the temple. There will not be any night there; this phrase, "day and night", shows there is no interruption of their service. There will be nothing to obstruct them. They will be busy praising God, singing Hallelujah's to Him, adoring the perfections of His nature, admiring the wonderful works of providence and grace and ascribing the glory of salvation to Him and to the Lamb. This will be the service of the children of God. They are happy in their heavenly employment. Heaven is a state of service though not of suffering, it is a state of rest but not sloth, and it is a praising and delightful rest. All the redeemed owe their happiness to God's sovereign mercy. His presence and favor complete their happiness and joy. May all God's people come to Him and receive every needed grace and offer all praise and glory! I recently received the book "Heaven" by Randy Alcorn, from a friend that actually opened my eyes as to what to expect when we receive our heavenly reward. In the book Randy Alcorn says, "Service is active not passive. It involves fulfilling responsibilities in which we expend energy. Work in heaven will not be frustrating or fruitless, instead it will involve lasting accomplishments, unhindered by decay and fatigue, enhanced by unlimited resources. We will approach our work with the enthusiasm we bring to our favorite sports or hobby." Work in heaven will not be frustrating. It will be fulfilling, we will have a sense of accomplishment. We will be happy in our employment.

We also will serve God on earth by serving His body, His church, and His people. We are all of the body of Christ. We all have special abilities that God gave us which only we can do, that special task that God gave us to do, the way God made us to do it. In 1 Corinthians 12:12-26 the apostle Paul speaks of the human body and applies it to the body of Christ. *"For as the body is one and hath many members and all the members of that one body being many is one body. So also is Christ. For by one Spirit we were all baptized into one body, whether Jew or Greek, whether slaves or free, and we were all made to drink of one Spirit. For the body is not one member but many. If the foot says because I am not a hand I am not part of the body it is not for this reason any the less a part of the body. And if the ear says because I am not an eye I am not part of the body, it is not for this reason any the less a part of the body. If the whole body were an eye, where would the hearing be? If the whole were hearing where would the sense of smell be? But now God has placed the members, each one of them, in the body, just as he desired. If they were all one member where would the body be? But now there are many members but one body. And the eye can not say to the hand I have no need of you or again the head to the feet I have no need of you. On the contrary it is much truer that the members of the body which seem to be weaker are necessary, and those members of the body which we deem less honorable on those we bestow more abundant honor and our less presentable members become much more presentable. Whereas our more presentable members have no need of it, but God has so composed the body giving more abundant honor to that member which lacked. So that there maybe no division in the body but that the members may have the same care for one another. And if one member suffers, all the members suffer with it, if one member is honored all the members rejoice with it".* In this comparison of the human body we are shown by the apostle Paul that the human body is but one body. As numerous as the body parts are, they all belong to, and make up, one body performing different tasks for the good of the whole, for which they were created. As compared to the human body, Christ's servant, the church body, is made up of many parts. All are united and make up one complete body. The church body is made up of one head, Christ, where the servants are made to drink into one Spirit, or to become of one heart and soul with one another being knit together in love. Not any one member is the whole body, nor does it consist of one sort of person. There are many members, many personalities, many gifts, yet all are one in Christ and all are related to each other. Could that be one reason why Christians call each other brothers and sisters? Without each of them the body of Christ would not be what God intended it to be. Christ strengthens them all, in the exercise of grace and in the discharge of duties. All are needed. Not one person in the church should say because he is not as handy and useful as another, cannot give or do as well or as much as another. God has deemed it necessary to call even the weak and feeble by His grace, and place them in His body that His strength shall be made perfect in their weakness. The week and feeble saints whose hearts and hands are to be strengthened by prayer, whose infirmities we are to bear, have their usefulness. Christ has a particular charge for us that we should take care of the week and feeble. Every member of the body is useful and necessary. Christ admires the beauty of His body, His church. He regards their prayers; He takes notice of their service and accepts it as a gift from His servants to Him. The members of the body of Christ, are made, fashioned, and set in the places that are according to His sovereign will. Each member equally stands in the best situation and position to be used in the greatest service and usefulness for Christ, and the body. God, not man, has positioned every member of his body in a place where He saw fit that would best serve the whole body with their own unique gifts, talents, and capabilities. There are many members of the body, we are all baptized in the Holy Spirit, we all have a job to do that Christ chose for us to do Each member is placed by God, so each member should be content with his place, gifts, talents, abilities, and usefulness since it is the sovereign God who works all things to His own will, who put them there. The servants of Christ have different powers and different places. We should do the duties of our own place and not argue or fight with others. All the members of the body are useful and necessary to each other. All Christians are dependant upon one another. Each is to expect and receive help from the others. Let us then have a spirit of unity in our service!

There are many members in the body of Christ, some give others receive, but all make up one body with Christ as the head. No one person can be spared. If one person is spared there is a break in the system, there is a deficiency, and the body would not experience the fullness of Christ that fills it. God has composed the body, appointed in such an order, mixed it and united all its parts in such a way as they are favorable to each other, and in this way it is a beautiful structure. Unity is an essential need in the church, and divinely provided variety within the unity is also necessary. This is a call to mutual love and concern in the fellowship of believers which maintain the unity that honors the Lord. This is the one body in which all serve yet never do they loose their personal identity and service that God has designed them to do. We all have a job to do that Christ chose for us to do. All parts of the body should defend the unity of the body being linked together to serve one another.

To be a servant you need to have a willing heart, a servant's heart, a servant's attitude. Bakers Evangelical Dictionary reported that the word *servant, service*, or *serve* in its various forms occur well over 1,100 times in the New International Version of the Holy Bible. Doesn't that show how important service is to God? The Message Bible says in 2 Corinthians 9:7-8 that, "*God loves it when the giver delights in the giving. God can pour on the blessings in astonishing ways so that you're ready for anything and everything more than just ready to do what needs to be done.*" People are servants to other human beings and servants of God. In the Old Testament the Hebrew word for servant is *EBED*. Ebed has 2 key components; *action* (the servant as a worker) and *obedience.* Servants belong to each other to perform a variety of work, and rely on God for their strength. The tree is known by its fruit, may the word of Christ be so grafted in our hearts, that we may be fruitful in every good word and work. What the mouth commonly speaks, generally agrees with what is most in the heart which should think, speak, and act, according to the words of Christ. Those who found their hope upon Christ, who is the Rock of Ages, are safe, being kept by the power of Christ through faith unto salvation, and they shall never perish. Jesus Christ is the great shepherd; He will shortly distinguish between those that are His and those that are not. All other distinctions will be done away, but the great one between saints and sinner, holy and unholy, will remain forever. The happiness the saints shall possess is very great. It is a kingdom prepared that the Father provided. God is looking for workers. There are places in service to fill, and the angels can not take our place. You will be amazed at how God can use you to reach others. No matter what task God has called you to do, always remember that your ministry touches the whole world, if you are truly serving the Lord. In Matthew 25:34-40 (NASB), it talks about our service to our Heavenly Father and the kingdom we are going to inherit, "*Then the king will say to those on His right, come you who are blessed of my Father, inherit the kingdom prepared for you from the foundation of the world, for I was hungry and you gave me something to eat, I was thirsty and you gave me something to drink, I was a stranger and you invited me in, naked and you clothed me, I was sick and you visited me, I was in prison and you came to me, then the righteous will answer Him, Lord when did we see You hungry and fed You, and thirsty and gave You something to drink and when did we see You a stranger and invite you in, or naked and cloth you, when did we see you sick or in prison and come to you. The King will answer and say to them, "Truly I say to you to the extent that you did it to one of these brothers of mine, even the least of them, you did it to me."* "For I was hungry and you gave me something to eat". This is not the cause of the kingdom being prepared for them or of their being entitled to it or of their being put into the possession of it but as description of their character and as a testimony and evidence of grace in them by which it appeared that they were the blessed of the Father. Our Master has left us an example that we may learn to do the will of God as He did with delight and pleasure. When particular difficulties occur it is good to satisfy ourselves with what Jesus Christ says and does. Obedience to the Father and dependence upon, Gods will sum up Jesus' whole life. At different times in Jesus' ministry He used object lessons to teach with, such as harvest time, as in John 4:34-38 (NASB), *"Jesus said to them, "my food is to do the will of Him who sent me and to accomplish His work. Do you not say, there are yet four months and then comes the harvest? Behold I say to you lift up your eyes and look on the fields that they are white for harvest. Already he who reaps is receiving wages and is gathering fruit for life eternal so that he who sows and he who reap may rejoice together. For in this case the saying is true, "one sows and the other reaps." I sent you to reap that for which you have not labored, others have labored and you have entered into their labor."* Jesus was performing the will of the Father and thereby received greater sustenance and satisfaction than any mere physical food could offer Him. Jesus used the fact that they were surrounded by crops growing in the field and waiting to be harvested as an object lesson to illustrate His urgency about reaching the lost which was "harvest" symbolized. Jesus knows the hearts of all, so He is able to state their readiness for salvation. The Lords call to His disciples to do the work of evangelism contains promises of rewards that bring eternal joy and the mutual partnership of shared privileges. Jesus said to His disciples, His food is to do the will of the Father. Now as food is pleasant and delightful and refreshing to the body of man, so doing the will of God was as delightful and refreshing to the soul of Christ. He took as much pleasure in it as a hungry man does in eating and drinking. As 1 Corinthians 10:31 (NASB) makes reference to giving glory to God in everything, *"Whether, then you eat or drink or whatever you do, do it all for the glory of God."* In eating and drinking, and in all we do, our aim should be the glory of God. We should be trying to please and honor Him.

An evangelist once described his mother as a woman characterized by great love for people. As an example he recalled the childhood memory of finding her serving a meal to an old tramp. She had gone shopping and encountered the unfortunate man and invited him home for a warm meal. As he was enjoying his lunch, her guest looked at his hostess and said, "I wish there were more people like you in the world". The evangelist's mother answered, "Oh, there are, you just have to look for them". The man shook his head at her remark; "But lady, I didn't need to look for you. You looked for me".

The duty of servants is summed up in one word, obedience. They are to be sincere, not pretending to be obedient, and they are to serve faithfully. In Luke 5:4-6 (NASB) the author recalls how Jesus was teaching the people and preaching the word of GOD. JESUS was in a boat out on the water, and the people who were listening to Him were on shore. Jesus spoke to Simon Peter, being the master of the vessel and asked him to venture deeper out in the water to catch more fish. Jesus gave orders to Simon Peter to cast his net into the sea in order to draw up a quantity of fish. Though Simon Peter knew Jesus to be the Messiah, the King of Israel, and the teacher sent from God, he protested, *"When He (Jesus) had finished speaking, He said to Simon Peter, "put out into the deep water and let down your nets for a catch". Simon answered and said, "Master, we worked hard all night and caught nothing, but I will do as you say and let down the nets". When they had done this they enclosed a great quantity of fish and their nets began to break."* Simon Peter no doubt thought Jesus' directive made no sense but he obeyed anyway and was rewarded for his obedience. Simon Peter was objecting to what Christ advised and directed. They showed faith and obedience in Christ, even though they had been fishing for hours, they were working hard; they were tired and worn out. They were discouraged that with all their work their labors were in vain, they hadn't caught any fish, not one fish. Learning to work together with the Lord will make your service more prosperous. The disciples were fishing for many hour and caught no fish, when Jesus told them to cast your nets, and they *obeyed* they drew in so much fish that the nets began to break! It actually required 2 boats to retrieve all of the fish! There is a difference between serving and serving at the direction of the Lord. When the Lord is in it He can fill the nets. When the Lord is in it He can make it prosperous. Christ came into the world, not only to restore but to preserve and nourish spiritual life, in Him there is enough for all that come to Him. You can do the same thing in the same way however, apart from the Lord you are going to keep pulling up empty nets because you are working under your own accord and strength, but as soon as the Lord joins you, it makes a difference. The key to the secret to all Christian service is in the verse, *"I will do as you say"*, to recognize that you can't do it by yourself and to depend upon the presence of the Lord. His presence is with you in all that you do for Him. No matter how difficult your place of service might be or how discouraging the situation, adopt and attitude of Simon Peter and God will do wonders for you. That obedience of faith makes the difference between success and failure. You can trust in the truth that 1 Kings 8:56 (NASB) speaks of, *"Blessed be the Lord who has given rest to His people Israel according to all that He promised, not one word has failed of all His good promises which He promised, through Moses, His servant."*

Jesus, who sits on the right hand of the Father, who has the name above every name, and His angels, authorities, and power subject to Him, is the exalted mediator, greatly illustrates His humility in showing us how exactly to serve others, in His washing of the disciples feet. Jesus did this as an example so that He might help us understand that serving others in this way is not "beneath our dignity", and so we may promote God's glory and the good of others. The Holy Scriptures tells the story of Jesus washing the feet of the disciples in John 13:3-17 (NASB), *"Jesus, knowing that the Father had given all things into His hands and that He had come forth from God and was going back to God, got up from supper and laid aside His garments and taking a towel He girded Himself. Then He poured water into a basin and began to wash the disciple's feet and to wipe them with the towel with which He was girded. So He came to Simon Peter, he said to Him, 'Lord, do you wash my feet?' Jesus answered and said to him 'what I do you do not realize now, but you will understand hereafter'. Peter said to Him, 'Never shall you wash my feet!' Jesus answered him, 'If I do not wash you, you have no part with me.' Simon Peter said to Him, 'Lord, then wash not only my feet but also my hands and my head.'*

Jesus said to him, 'He who has bathed needs only to wash his feet, but is completely clean and you are clean, but not all of you'. For He knew the one who was betraying Him for this reason He said, 'not all of you are clean'. So when He had washed their feet and taken His garment and reclined at the table again He said to them, 'Do you know what I have done to you? You call me Teacher and Lord and you are right for so I am. If I then, the Lord and teacher washed your feet you also ought to wash one another's feet. For I gave you an example that you also should do as I did to you. Truly, truly I say to you a slave is not greater than his master nor is one who is sent greater than the one who sent him. If you know these things you are blessed if you do them'."

During the time of Jesus, in ancient society, foot washing was reserved for the lowliest servants. Peers did not wash the feet of another's except for rare occasions and as a mark of great love. This custom was performed by lowly servants to the reception of strangers or travelers whom just returned from a journey during which they had contracted dirt and filth. The dusty and dirty conditions of the region made it necessary for feet to be washed customarily. Although the disciples most likely would have been happy to wash the feet of Jesus, they could not conceive of washing each others feet. They would not "stoop" to washing feet. When they saw Jesus actually washing their feet they were shocked. His actions serve as a symbolic of spiritual cleansing and a model of Christian humility. Through this action Jesus taught the lesson of selfless service that was superbly demonstrated by His death on the cross. Jesus was making a point in this symbolic action of foot washing, that unless the Lamb of God cleanses the sins of humans, then their sins can have no part with Him. The purpose in His action was to establish the model of loving humility. Joy is always tied to obedience. The master should serve his servant. What a surprising instance of humility in this, that Christ the Lord and Master should wash the feet of His disciples. Christ argued that what He had done to them, though He stood in such a superior relation to them, displayed that they should perform this action one to another. With this action, He taught them to behave in a spirit of humility to one another, to be kind, to love, and to serve one another in all things. Christ is an example to His people in many things, in the exercise of grace, in meekness, humility, love, patience, and in the discharge of duty. Jesus Christ proclaimed that the disciples should wash one another's feet as He had washed theirs which is not to be taken literally by this action, as though this was an ordinance binding upon all persons in all places and to be done at certain times. Our Lord's meaning of foot washing is that He has given it as an example of humility and love. We must lay aside everything that hinders us in what we have to do. Jesus was showing us that we should always have a heart and willingness to be a servant and not when it is convenient to us. Even though He was and is God, He performed a task that only slaves did at that time. It gives us an example how to be a servant that will do anything to help others no matter how offensive. Jesus wanted to show the full extent of His love. Do you? In Matthew 20: 26-28 (NASB), the Lord was teaching the disciples the style of greatness and leadership when He said," *It is not this way among you, but whomever wishes to become great among you shall be your servant and whoever wished to be first among you shall be your slave, just as the Son of Man did not come to be served, but to serve, and to give His life as a ransom for many."* The Gentile leaders dominate in domineering fashion, using carnal power and authority. Believers are to do the opposite; they lead by being servants and giving themselves away for others, as Jesus did. As in the example of 2 Corinthians 5:14-15 (NASB), *"for the love of Christ controls us having concluded this, that one died for all therefore all died, and He died for all so that they who live might no longer live for themselves but for Him who died and rose again on their behalf"*. The word translated "for" means "in the place of" emphasizing the substitutionary nature of Christ's sacrifice. One died for all, expresses the truth of Christ's substitutionary death. A ransom is a price paid to redeem a slave or a prisoner. Redemption does not involve a price paid to Satan, rather the ransom is offered to God, to satisfy His justice and wrath against sin. The price paid was Christ's own life, as blood atonement. This then is the meaning of the cross. Christ subjected Himself to the divine punishment against sin on our behalf, suffering the brunt of divine wrath in the place of sinners was the "cup" He spoke of having to drink. God is more concerned about the servant than He is about the service. To be a servant is a wonderful opportunity to be like the Lord Jesus Christ. We live in a world filled with people who have incredible needs of all kinds and we can relate to these needs. The attitude Jesus showed in washing His disciples' feet is the same attitude that enabled Him to give up the power and glory of being God and became a man. Here we see that our Creator, the Almighty Powerful God, is first and foremost a servant. He is willing to serve His own servants! When we come to the point that we are able to do everything in an attitude of service and humility, we are truly following Jesus Christ! Whoever would be considered a great man in the kingdom of Christ, must be a minister to others, if he desires to be truly great in the eyes of God. He must do great service for Christ and to the souls of men, and seek to bring great glory to God, by faithfully ministering the word and ordinances and by denying him worldly honor and glory, and by serving others. Whoever is first in the kingdom of the Messiah, shall be a servant, not only a minister, but a servant, not a servant of some but of all. This was verified in the apostle Paul who became a servant to all men. Paul teaches that we have to look for and seek higher things, and that our conduct must be worthy of the gospel that we say that we believe in. Our love of God must be sincere, not in words only. All our love is too little to bestow upon God, therefore all the powers of the heart, soul, mind, and strength must be engaged to God. In Matthew 22:37-40 (NASB) it explains how our love should be, "And He said to him *"you shall love the Lord your God with all your heart, and with all your soul, and with all your mind. This is the great and foremost commandment, the second is like it, you shall love your neighbor as yourself. On these two commandments depend the whole law and the prophets."* In the gospel of Mark 12:30 the word "strength" is added. Some translations say heart....soul....strength. Some translations even added the word mind. The use of the various terms is not meant to represent distinct human faculties but to emphasize the completeness of the kind of love that is called for. Thou shall love the Lord your God with all your heart, and with all your soul and with all your mind, that is, with all the powers and abilities of the soul, of the will, of the understanding, and of the affections, in the most sincere, upright and perfect manner. People are utterly unable to achieve these qualities without the grace of God. They do not have true love for God in their heart, soul and mind. All a person can achieve on their own with their own carnal mind is enmity against God, and everything that is divine and good, and that belongs unto him. When the Spirit of God does produce the grace and fruit of love in a person's soul he ends up producing love for the Lord, When the unspeakable gift of Christ's love, and His affections are bestowed on the ones that God loves and who loves Him, then the servant is sensitive to God's everlasting and unchangeable love toward him, as it says in 1 John 4:19 (NASB), "*we love because He first loved us*". We are to love God "*with all thy mind*" as it says in Deuteronomy 6:5 (NASB), "*love the Lord your God with all your heart and with all your soul and with all your strength*", also in Mark 12:30 (NASB), "*love the Lord your God with all your heart and with all your soul and with all your mind and with all your strength. This is the first and great commandment. It is the major principle from where all actions of men should flow. The first command is to love God, who is the source of all love. We are to love God, and love our neighbor as it says in Leviticus 19:18 (NASB), "*do not seek revenge or bear a grudge against one of your people, but love your neighbor as yourself. I am the Lord*", also "*Thou shall love thy neighbor as thy self*". A person would desire to be loved by his neighbor and do well to him as he would want the neighbor do to him. This assumes men love themselves, or otherwise they can not love their neighbor. It is not talking about a person loving themselves in a sinful way, by indulging themselves in carnal lusts and pleasures, even though some are lovers of pleasures more than lovers of God. They are to love themselves and their neighbor in a natural way, and in a spiritual way, so as to be concerned for their souls, and their everlasting happiness. On these two commands hang all the laws of the prophets. The love of God is the first and the greatest commandment and to love our neighbor as ourselves is the second great commandment. We must love our neighbors as truly and sincerely as we love ourselves in many cases we must deny ourselves for the good of others.

A servant who is called does not refer to the general invitation to salvation, but to Gods wonderful call to serve Him. This call produces:

1.) Fellowship with Christ

1 Corinthians 1:9 (NASB), "*God is faithful, through whom you were called into fellowship with His son, Jesus Christ our Lord*".

2.) Peace in our hearts

1 Corinthians 7:15 (NASB), "*yet if the unbelieving one leaves let him leave, the brother or the sister is not under bondage in such cases but God has called us to peace*",

3.) Freedom from sin

Galatians 5:13 (NASB), "*for you were called to freedom, brethren, only do not turn your freedom into an opportunity for the flesh but through love serve one another*".

4.) A worthy walk

Ephesian 4:1(NASB), "*Therefore I, the prisoner of the Lord implore you to walk in a manner worthy of the calling with which you have been called with all humility and gentleness with patience showing tolerance for one another in love*".

5.) Hope

Ephesians 4:4 (NASB), "*there is one body and one spirit, just as also you were called in one hope of your calling*".

6.) Holiness

1 Peter 1:15 (NASB), "*but like the Holy One, who called you, be holy yourselves also in all your behavior*".

7.) Blessings

> 1 Peter 3:9 (NASB), "*not returning evil for evil, or insult for insult, but giving a blessing instead for you were called for the very purpose that you might inherit a blessing*".

8.) Eternal glory

> 1 Peter 5:10 (NASB), "*after you have suffered for a little while the God of all grace who called you to His eternal glory in Christ, will Himself perfect, confirm, strengthen, and establish you*".

Serving the Lord Jesus Christ is the greatest work in the world. No matter how difficult the work or how many times we feel like quitting we can keep going and growing in the way we serve, the way God tells us to in His word. Although the believer is responsible for the work, the Lord actually produces the good works and the spiritual fruit in the lives of believers. This is accomplished because He works through us by the indwelling Spirit. God energizes both the believer's desires and his actions. When God is glorified, his Spirit can work to bring Christ to those who need to know Him. The faithful ambassador of Christ does nothing to discredit his ministry, but everything he can to protect its integrity, the gospels integrity, and Gods integrity. Paul lived and walked by the power of the Holy Spirit which shows in 2 Corinthians 6:1-10 (NASB), "*And working together with Him we also urge you not to receive the grace of God in vain – for He says "at the acceptable time I listened to you, and on the day of salvation I helped you. Behold now is "the acceptable time" behold now is "the day of salvation" giving no cause for offense in anything so that the ministry will not be discredited but in everything commending ourselves as servants of God in much endurance, in afflictions, in hardship, in distress, in beatings, in imprisonment, in tumults, in labors, in sleeplessness, in hunger, in purity, in knowledge, in patients, in kindness, in the Holy Spirit, in genuine love, in the word of truth, in the power of God, by the weapons of righteousness for the right hand and the left, by glory and dishonor, by evil report and good report, regarded as deceivers and yet true, as unknown yet well known, as dying, yet behold we live, as punished yet not put to death, as sorrowful yet always rejoicing yet poor yet making many rich as having nothing yet possessing all things*" There is a time in Gods economy when He listens to sinners and responds to those who are repentant, and it was and is that time. However there will also be an end to that time, which is why Paul's exhortation was so passionate. Like Paul any believer who engages in a faithful ministry of reconciliation should expect to be rejected, and accepted, to be hated and loved, to encounter joy and hardship, this is what Jesus had already taught his disciples. The most convincing proof that Paul is a servant of God is the patient endurance of his character reflected in Paul's hardship, and the nature of his ministry. Paul showed his dedication to service to them by mentioning his faithfulness in enduring persecution, his calling, his diligence in ministry, and his labors to the point of anguish. Paul listed the important elements of the righteousness God had granted to him. It was the central reason that all the other positive elements of his endurance were a reality. During his entire ministry Paul never operated beyond the boundaries of the direction and guidance of Divine revelation. Paul did not rely on his own strength when he ministered. Paul did not fight Satan's kingdom with human resources but with spiritual virtue. Paul had both offensive tools, such as the sword of the spirit and defensive tools such as the shield of faith and the helmet of salvation at his disposal.

December 13, 1862 was one of the bloodiest days in the civil war. Wave after wave of union troops were injured or killed as they assaulted the virtually impregnable confederate town of Fredericksburg Virginia. So many men cried for help and for water that a continuous moan seemed to move across the field. Secure behind strong breastworks, Sergeant Richard Kirkland of the second South Carolina regiment listened with increasing sympathy. Kirkland was a new Christian having received Jesus Christ as his Savior as the results of evangelistic efforts among the confederate troops. He approached his commanding officer and said," all day I have heard these poor people crying for water, and I can't stand it no longer. I come to ask permission to go and give them water". When permission was granted, Kirkland took all the canteens he could carry, slowly crawled over the barrier, and began to move among the pitiful men. The union troops quickly saw what he was doing and held their fire. For several hours he ministered doing what he could to ease the agony of the suffering, and as a result became known as to military historians as the "angel of Fredericksburg".

The servants of Christ know His voice, and know His gospel, so you figure that they should not argue or bicker amongst each other, right? Wrong! Let's explore some of the reasons why servants might argue.

Some servants are selfish. They are discontent with the gifts that God gave them. They want the gifts that they have not been given, they want the gifts that God gave to someone else. With that attitude they in effect question God's wisdom and imply He made a mistake in assignments. So they see the gifts that they want in others and they stew and churn and then when they see the other person who has the gifts that they want, they make the other persons service more difficult for them by arguing with them and bickering with them about how they serve, where they serve, when they serve and anything else they can think of. They seek showy public gifts that God knows they can not handle and can become vulnerable to carnal demonically counterfeited gifts. They have a hard time realizing that God is working with each one of us on earth, and equipping us from heaven. In Hebrews 13:20-21 (NASB) it talks about us being equipped," *Now the God of peace who brought up from the dead the Great Shepherd of the sheep through the blood of the eternal covenant even Jesus our Lord, equipping you in every good thing to do His will working in us that which is pleasing in His sight through Jesus Christ to whom be the glory forever and ever amen*". God's gifts are sovereign. They are distributed for the education and edification of the church and the glory of the Lord. One who is adequate is one who is capable of doing everything one is called to do. Equipped is someone who is enabled to meet all the demands of godly ministry and righteous living. As 2 Timothy 3:17 (NASB) talks about, "*So that the man of God may be adequate, equipped, for every good work.*" The word not only accomplishes this in the life of the man of God but in all who follow him. God has designed visible public gifts to have a crucial place, but equally designed and more vital to life are the hidden gifts that maintain a perspective of unity. God would much rather unity and peace between his servants. All gifts are imperative to maintaining the perspective of unity and peace. Christ salvation provision is perfect and He calls for only obedience and trust in what he has already been given

Some servants may be discouraged. When the servant starts working they have high hopes, they have plans, and they think they know what God wants. They work hard, toil long hours and after a time they see things not working out the way they think it should, they try hard to make it work out. Even if God doesn't want it the way they want it, the servant keeps trying to make it the way that they think God wants it. So God stands back, with His arms crossed, leaning against the wall, with one leg bent with His foot against the wall, saying, "go ahead, you know better than Me, finish". Instead of the servant stopping and asking God what He wants, the servant keeps toiling and working until the servant gets fatigued, worn out, depressed, discouraged, with little or no success. Then with all the stress mounting on top of the servant, something brings the servant to their breaking point and he snaps and fights and argues with everyone about everything. Until that servant stops laboring in their own power, and lets our Lord come up to the servant, puts His arm over their shoulder and whisper in their ear, "now lets try it My way" they are going to keep falling deeper and deeper in discouragement and depression, and they are going to keep snapping at everyone. In situations like this, Psalms 100:2 (NASB) requests us to, "*Serve the Lord with gladness; come before Him with joyful singing*". In this request the Lord says to come before His presence with singing, the throne of His grace with thankfulness for mercies received. He implores all of us into public worship and singing. We are to serve the Lord with gladness, not with fear, not under a spirit of bondage. We are to worship with spiritual joy and freedom of soul, willingly, and cheerfully. When God speaks, that word has power, and when we believe that word and act on it, the power goes to work. Christians who live in the word are used of God to get His work done in this world. Your place of service may not be a big one but it's an important one and God put you there because you are the right person for the job right now. He wants to work through you to get some things accomplished for His glory, and He will do it if you will "let the word of Christ dwell in you richly in all wisdom". In Colossians 3:16 (NASB) it talks about Christ's power in us," *Let the word of Christ richly dwell within you, with all wisdom, teaching, and admonishing one another with psalms, and hymns and spiritual songs, singing with thankfulness in your hearts to God.*" The word richly may be more fully meant by "abundantly, or extravagantly rich", and dwell means to live in, or to be at home. The Holy Scriptures should permeate every aspect of the believer's life and control every thought, word and deed. This concept is parallel to being filled with the Spirit since the results are the same. The Holy Spirit fills the life that is controlled by Gods word. This emphasizes that the filling of the spirit is not some ecstatic or emotional experience but a steady controlling of the life by obedience to the truth of Gods word. The soul prospers when we are full of the scriptures and of the grace of Christ.

Some servants might think of themselves greater than the other. They may have ambitious views of superiority. As in Luke 22:24-27 (NASB), when the disciples were arguing over whom is greater, "*and there arose also a dispute among them as to which one of them was regarded to be the greatest. And He said to them, "The kings of the Gentiles lord it over them and those who have authority over them are called benefactors" but it is not this way with you, but the one who is the greatest among you must become like the youngest and the leader like the servant. For who is greater the one who reclines at the table or the one who serves? Is it not the one who reclines at the table? But I am among you as the one who serves"*. This reveals how large an issue this was in the minds of the disciples, and let's faces it, in our minds also. This reveals how far they were from grasping all that Jesus had taught them. Are we any different? How unbecoming in the worldly ambition of becoming the greatest is this to the character of the servant of Christ. Christ took upon Him the form of a servant and instead of being ministered unto, ministered to others, where two days before, put on the towel, took a basin and washed the feet of the disciples. Our Lord, by His own example would rather His servants deter from their ambitions views of superiority over each other and learn from Him, who was meek and lowly and by love, serve one another. There should be no complaint of one member against another, as useless and unnecessary, no rioting, no rebellion or insurrection of one against another, no dissention, and no division. The members of Christ's body is tempered and mixed together and are in such close union and have such a dependence on each other that they are necessarily obliged to take care of each others good and welfare. We are to be Christ-like, to be like-minded, and lowly-minded according to the example of the Lord Jesus Christ. Kindness is the law of Christ's' kingdom, and the lessons of His school. If you expect or experience the benefits of Gods' compassion for yourselves you must be compassionate one to another. It is the joy of leaders to see people like-minded. Christ came to humble us, let there not be among us a spirit of pride. We must be watchful of our own faults and defects, but ready to make favorable allowances for others. We must patiently care for others, but not be busy bodies in other people's matters. Peace can not be enjoyed without lowliness of mind. The example of our Lord Jesus Christ is set before us. In our lives we must resemble Him.

Another way an argument might arise is Satan sticking his ugly little head in the midst of God's work. In the way to eternal happiness, we must expect to be assaulted and sifted by our enemy Satan. If he can not destroy he will try to disgrace and distress us. Nothing is more certain of a fall in the professed follower of Christ. Unless we watch and pray always, we may be drawn into those sins which we are most resolved against. If believers were left to themselves they would fall but they are kept by the power of God, and the prayers of Christ. Theses things are not brought to pass by anything done by us therefore all boasting is shut out. As the attempt to disgrace us increase, we need to grow stronger in our faith, our resolution must get stronger, and our love for God and Christ must get deeper and stronger. This is not to encourage us to be strong in our own strength. All Christians must be faithful to their Lord, and determined in His cause. Christian must take great care to please Christ. We must strive to do well then we shall be crowned with the fruits of our labor. To win the prize, we must run the race. We must do the will of God before we receive the prize. The word hardship or afflictions is used to signify "suffer evil" and means the evil of afflictions and persecution of every kind, loss, imprisonment, death or many other kinds of hardships and afflictions. Christ is the captain of salvation, the leader and commander of the people, who are made a willing people in the day of His power. When He raises His forces and muster His armies, these are volunteers, soldiers for Christ, who willingly enlist themselves into His service and under His banner to fight His battles, and who fight against sin. They are all true believers in Christ and are ministers of the word, who fight the good fight of faith, which they have in common with other saints. The servants of Christ have to fight against conflict as 2 Timothy 2:3 (NASB) talk about, *"Suffer hardships with me as a good soldier of Christ Jesus. So then each of us shall give an account of himself to God"*. Christian service isn't based on feelings, it's based on obedience. It's a matter of the will and not the feelings. Christian service that's based only on feelings will be a rollercoaster kind of experience, up one day and down the next. It will also lead to a shallow ministry that thinks more about pleasing ourselves than helping others. Service that is motivated only by our good feelings is likely to be undependable, selfish, and inconsiderate. In 1 Thessalonians 4:1 (NASB) tells us how our service should be, *"Finally, then, brethren we request and exhort you in the Lord Jesus that as you receive from us instructions as to how you ought to walk and please God (just as you actually do walk) that you excel still more"*. To please God is done by obedience to the word of God. The apostle does not lay his commands upon them as he might have done previously; he pleads by saying, furthermore brethren, or request of you in the most kind and tender manner. He had real hearty love and affection for them. He shows it in a most moving and powerful manner. The walk of believers is twofold, internal or external. Their internal walk is by faith, which is the faith in Christ. Their external walk is not as it was before conversion; it is the renewal of their souls under the influence of the Holy Spirit and the will of God. To abide in the faith of the gospel is not enough; we must abound in the works of faith. The rule according to which all ought to walk and act is the commandments given by the Lord Jesus Christ. Sanctification in the renewal of their souls under the influence of the Holy Spirit and attention to appointed duties, constituted the will of God respecting them. Unless joy is balanced with Godly fear our service may not amount to very much. All responsibility without joy will crush a person and turn Christian service into slavery, but all joy without Godly fear will make that servant shallow and immature. Jesus calls us both friends and servants.

If you're serving in the will of God, you are like Esther: you have come to the kingdom for such a time as this. In Esther 4:14 (NASB) she was warned, *"For if you remain silent at this time, relief and deliverance will arise for the Jews from another place and you and your fathers house will perish, and who knows whether you have not attained royalty for such a time as this?"* What God starts He finishes, as it says in Philippians 1:6 (NASB),*"For I am confident of this very thing that He who began a good work in you will perfect it until the day of Christ Jesus.* If you decide to quit He will lovingly discipline you until you are willing to obey, if you persist in your rebellion He may put you on the shelf and label you "disqualified!" as it warns in 1 Corinthians 9:27 (NASB), *"but I discipline my body and make it my slave so that after I have preached to others, I myself will not be disqualified.* God will get the work done either with or without you but either way His will, will be done, and if you quit you will be the loser because you will not get the blessing. God's purpose and promises will not fail. You and I are God's instrument, a chosen vessel to be molded and used by the hand of God. When God is using you as a vessel, when God is sending you, when God is with you, you can storm the gates of hell with a squirt gun and you will have great success and you will be victorious. The servants of the Lord are always standing on holy ground and had better behave accordingly. If nobody else is watching, God is, and He will be our judge. God's goal for our lives is not money but maturity, not happiness but holiness, not getting but giving. God is at work making people more like His Son, and that's what Christian service is all about, showing people the love of Jesus Christ, leading people to Jesus

Christ by actions. Your purpose is to build people of Christian character, people with virtue, whom God can bless and use to build others. The word of Christ is spoken to all believers and there is a cleansing virtue in that word. The more we abound in what is good, the more our Lord is glorified. We must abide in Christ; we must have union with Him by faith as it says in, John 15:5 (NASB),"*I am the vine you are the branches, he who abides in me and I in him, he bears much fruit, for apart from me you can do nothing.*" The word abides means to remain or stay around. The remaining is evidence that salvation has already taken place. The fruit or evidence of salvation is continuance in service to Him and in His teaching. The abiding believer is the only legitimate believer. Abiding and believing are actually evidence of genuine salvation. Jesus Christ is the vine, the true vine; believers are the branches of this vine. From a vine we look for grapes and from a Christian we look for Christian temperament, and a Godly disposition in life. We must honor God and do well, this is bearing fruit. HE that abide in me and I in him, are the ones that are in Christ and He in them. They bring forth much fruit, in the exercise of grace and performance of good works and continue to do so not by virtue of the servants own free will, power and strength, but by grace continually received from Christ. For without Christ you can do nothing spiritually good. They can do nothing little or great, easy or difficult. They can not think a good thought, speak a good word, or do a good action. Nothing can be done "without Christ", without His spirit, grace, strength, or presence, or as separate from Him. If it would be possible for the branches that are truly in Him, to be removed, they could not bring forth fruit or good works, any more than a branch separated from the vine can bring forth grapes, so all the fruitfulness of a believer is due to Christ, and His grace, and not to the free will and power of man.

Do an assessment of the level of your personal giving to the Lord.
Do an assessment of your time and abilities.
Make changes as needed.
When is the best time to serve?
Do you find the best time to serve is selective?
Do you look at how comfortable you will be serving?
Do you want to be seen?
Do you want to do something big?
Is God calling you to do something?
A lot of people need their attitude adjusted. They need a servant's attitude.
Are you going to let God's will be done in your life?
What I do effects the way people view me. I want to be a soldier I want to be a servant.

Chapter 2
What does a servant look like?

In the previous chapter we looked at what a servant is, now let's dig in and discover what a servant looks like.

Every man is a servant of the master to whose commands he yields himself, whether it be the sinful disposition of his heart, in actions which lead to death or the new and spiritual obedience implanted by salvation. As the same metal becomes a new vessel when melted and recast into another mould, so the believer has become a new creature, 2 Timothy 2:21 *"Therefore if anyone cleanses himself from these things he will be a vessel for honor, sanctified, useful to the Master, prepared for every good work".* If a man cleanses himself, and keeps himself clear from such men who are dishonorable, if he shuns their defiling ways and polluting principles, if he keeps clear of their heresies, and is not carried away with the errors of these wicked men, is not drawn aside by them into Immoral practices but stands fast in the faith and depart from iniquity; he shall be a vessel onto honor. He will be made a vessel of honor and will be honored by Christ. He will appear to be one that is set apart by God the Father and whose sins are cast away by the blood of Christ and who is sanctified internally by the Spirit of God. External holiness springs from internal holiness. We must see to it that we are holy vessels. Everyone in the church, whom God approves, will be devoted to the Master's service, and thus fitted for His use. We must be that vessel that is honored, that is sanctified, and useful for the Master and is prepared for every good work. It is possible for God's servant to resist God so willfully that they cease to be vessels. Pray that does not happen to you!

The servant who yields themselves to sin in any way that would enter their heart or in any way that the arch enemy would whisper in their ear, they were a slave to that sin, as it speaks of in Roman 6:19 *"I am speaking in human terms because of the weakness of your flesh, for just as you presented your members as slaves to impurity and to lawlessness resulting in further lawlessness so now present your members as slaves to righteousness resulting in sanctification".* Paul was speaking this way using the illustration of slave and master because it is easy to understand. You once let yourselves be slaves to impurity and lawlessness now you must choose to be slaves to righteousness so that you will be Holy. In 1 Peter 2:16, it talks about being free, *"you are not slaves you are free, but your freedom is not an excuse to do evil you are free to live as Gods slaves."* Someone who is now a slave of righteousness ought to be more diligent, ambitious, industrious, persevering, zealous, and tenacious in the service of God than they had been in the service of sin. They were once servants of sin, now they are servants of righteousness. Let the same servants that have been employed in the service of sin, be made use of in the service of righteousness. Let your eyes be employed in looking and diligently searching into the scriptures of truth, your ears in hearing the gospel preached, your lips, mouth, and tongue in expressing the praises of God for what He has done for you, your hands in distributing to the interest of Christ and the necessities of the saints, and your feet in hastening to attend on public worship and observe the testimonies of the Lord. Let them be employed under the same form and character as servants, waiting upon the Lord ready to fulfill His will and in the same manner, freely, willingly, and cheerfully, in all acts of righteousness and holiness. The believer who have become a new creature, there is a great difference in the liberty of mind and spirit so opposite to the state of slavery, which the true Christian has in the service of his rightful Lord whom is his Father, by the adoption of grace. We are called by grace in the condition of a servant. Do not be troubled or anxious, or uneasy with it. We must patiently and cheerfully serve our Master faithfully. Choose to serve Master Jesus! Christ's servant is bought by Christ with His own money, with the price of His own blood. The servant becomes a volunteer to Christ, through the power of Christ's grace upon the servant, and though he serves His Lord Christ freely, readily, and cheerfully from a principal of love and gratitude he shall not fail of a reward of grace, he shall be honored of God, approved of men and shall receive the reward of an inheritance. Serve God acceptably with reverence and Godly fear. We ought to serve God whether or not our labors are ever recognized. What grace that God not only gives us work to do and the ability to do it, but then He rewards us for what He enabled us to accomplish.

Servants are to dedicate themselves to God, to be humble and faithful and to use their spiritual gifts in their respective ways. Since all things are of God, and by Him, and to Him, then the saints ought to present their bodies to Christ, and to know and approve and to do His will. Since they have nothing but what they have received from God they should not think too highly or glory in their attainments. They are to present their bodies as living sacrifices to God, Romans 12:1 is a powerful appeal, *"Therefore, I urge you, brethren; by the mercies of God to present your bodies a living and holy sacrifice acceptable to God which is your spiritual service or worship"*. All things are of God and by Him, and servants ought to present their bodies to God, to know, approve and to do His will. Servants who have their being from and in God, and are blessed by God with all spiritual blessing in Christ should give up themselves and cheerfully serve God. Your service for Christ will last eternally. Most of the people you meet day after day are either wasting their lives or merely spending their lives, but God's servants have the privilege of investing their lives in what is eternal. No matter what type of service God assigns you, you can not succeed apart from the word of God. The word of God reveals the God of the word, His character, His attributes, and the servants must know the Master, if we are to serve Him acceptably. We have to know the heart and mind of God to understand Him more and to comprehend why He put us in the form of service that He did. The better we know God the better we can enjoy Him and serve Him. God never acts in violation of His character. That character is revealed in the bible. If we are to serve God in ways worthy of Him we must spend time reading His word. The measure of our faith and service is the result of quality time spent in the word of God. Unless what we do is based on what God says, and what God is, we will find ourselves failing. What we think determines what we are and what we do. As servants of the Lord, we have problems to solve, plans to make, people to help, and purposes to achieve and we simply can not do it in our own wisdom and strength. But the word of God equips us to live for Him and work for Him. God doesn't call the equipped, He equips the called. GOD is working with you on earth, and equipping you from heaven. Equip you is not the Greek word for "perfect" or "perfection" used through out Hebrews to indicate salvation but is a word that is translated "prepared", it refers to believers being edified. The verb has the idea of equipping by means of adjusting, shaping, mending, restoring, or preparing. By trusting alone in Jesus, looking at him alone for peace, pardon, justification, sanctification, and eternal life, glory should be ascribed continually, forever and ever, to Him, as it will be by angels and saints, to all eternity.

 Spiritual service is required of all Christian's not just leaders. Godly service results from each servant of Christ fully using their spiritual gift in submission to the Holy Spirit and in cooperation with other believers such as it says in Ephesians 4:11-16 "*He gave some apostles, and some as prophets, and some as evangelists and some as pastors and teachers, for the equipping of the saints for the work of service to the building up of the body of Christ until we all attain to the unity of the faith and of the knowledge of the Son of God, to a mature man, to the measure of the stature which belongs to the fullness of Christ. As a result we are no longer to be children tossed here and there by waves and carried about by every wind of doctrine by the trickery of men, by craftiness, in deceitful scheming, but speaking the truth in love, we are to grow up in all aspects into Him who is the head even Christ, from whom the whole body being fitted and held together by what every joint supplies, according to the proper working of each individual part causes the growth of the body for the building up of itself in love*". Servants should present their bodies as living sacrifices in their service to God. Unto every believer is given some gift of grace. All is given as seems best to Christ. He gave to them, a large measure of gifts and graces; particularly the gift of the Holy Spirit that brings trust and obedience. There is fullness in Christ and a measure of that fullness is given in the counsel of God to every believer. We never come to the perfect measure till we enter into heaven. God's children are growing, as long as they are in this world. Christian's growth leads to the glory of Christ. The more a man finds himself wanting to improve, according to the measure he received from Christ; he may believe that he has the grace of sincere love and charity rooted in his heart. God gave them gifts by which they were qualified to be apostles. They were called by Christ, had their doctrine in Him, and their commission to preach it, and were guided by the Holy Spirit. Some were called to be prophets, who are extraordinary ministers of the word who had a gift of interpreting the scriptures. Some were called to be evangelists, who were distinct from ordinary ministers of the word. They were below the apostles yet above the pastors and teachers. They were companions and assistants to the apostles. Some were called to be pastors and teachers. Pastors are called to shepherd the flock, to oversee the church, and the teacher is the gifted servant in the church, who assists the pastor in teaching. Gifts are distributed to men by Christ to qualify them for it. The preaching of God's word is a laborious one, and no man has enough sufficiency in himself to do it alone, it requires faithfulness. Those who are preachers of God's word are worthy of respect, esteem, and honor, it is a service not a dominion.

Servants of God know God's word, know God's voice, and hear God's calling. The Old Testament Prophet Samuel was given to the temple priest Eli and to the temple by His mother, Hannah, as an infant. For a long time Hannah could not conceive a child, she made a promise to God that if He would give her a child that she would give the child back to Him. God gave her Samuel. After she finished nursing Samuel, she gave him to Eli, to the temple, and most of all back to God. So Eli proceeded to teach Samuel about God's word, God's ways, and God's work. One night as Samuel was laying in his bed, God called him. Samuel rises and goes to Eli and asked did you call me, Eli replied no, go back to bed. Samuel complied. When Samuel went back to sleep he was awoken again by God calling him. He didn't know it was God, so he rose and went to Eli again. Eli told him the same as he told him the first time, that he did not call Samuel and to go back to bed. Three times this happened. In 1 Samuel 3:9 tells the response that Eli gave to Samuel. "*And Eli said to Samuel, go lie down and it shall be if He calls you, that you shall say; speak Lord for your servant is listening. So Samuel went and lay down in his place*". The meaning is that Samuel should not rise and go to Eli as he did previous times that he should continue laying in his bed, on hearing the voice of God, Samuel should desire that the Lord speak to him and be ready to attend. Eli, perceiving that it was the voice of God that Samuel heard, instructed him what to say. Though it was a disgrace to Eli, for God's call to be directed to Samuel and not to him, yet Eli told Samuel how to answer God's call. Thus the more experienced servant should do their utmost to assist and improve the less experienced servant that is rising up. Let us never fail to teach those who are coming after us. In John 1:30, John the Baptist says "*this is the one I mean when I said, a man who comes after me has surpassed me because he was before me*" Good words should be told to children which they may be prepared to learn Divine things, and be trained up to regard them. Jesus calls children to Him in, Matthew 19:13-15,"*Then some children were brought to Him so that He might lay His hands on them, and pray and the disciples rebuked them. But Jesus said "let the children alone, and do not hinder them from coming to me for the kingdom of heaven belongs to such as these". After laying His hands on them, He departed from there*". Jesus is saying do not drive away these children from my presence, they are the emblems of the kingdom of heaven. Through these children, I will instruct and point out to you how converted persons should represent the faith, which have a place in my church below and expect to enter into my kingdom and glory above. They are, or ought to be, like such children, harmless and inoffensive; free from malice, meek, modest, and humble. They should be without pride, self-conceit, ambitious views, and desire of grandeur and superiority.

God provides our every need, so it should stand to reason that He should expect something from us in return. God wants and asks us to please Him at the core of our lives. We make God our core value by obeying Deuteronomy 10:12-14 "*Now, Israel, what does the LORD your God require from you, but to fear the Lord your God, to walk in all His ways and love Him and to serve the Lord you God with all your heart and with all your soul, and to keep the Lord's commandments and His statutes which I am commanding for you today for your good. Behold to the Lord your God belong heaven and the highest heavens, the earth and all that is in it*". This rhetorical question leads to 5 basic requirements that God expects of his servants.

1.) To hold God in awe and submit to Him
2.) To conduct life in accordance with the will of God
3.) To choose to set ones affections on the Lord, and on Him alone
4.) To have the worship of the Lord and the central focus of life
5.) To obey the requirements the Lord has imposed

God's servants should fear Him, walk in all His ways, love Him, serve Him wholeheartedly and observe His commands. He asks us for our heart. . Since we owe

Yahweh our very lives His request seems little to ask, especially since the commands He has gives us are designed for our good. There is never a conflict of interest when it comes to Godly living. God asks nothing of anyone that would require them to act contrary to their belief system. Even those who are asked in the course of things to give their physical lives for their beliefs are trading physical comforts for an eternity of joy. As Paul says in Philippians 1:20-21 in the Amplified Bible, "*This is in keeping with my own eager desire and persistence, expectations and hope, that I shall not disgrace myself or be put to shame in anything, but that with the utmost freedom of speech and unfailing courage, now as always heretofore, Christ (the Messiah) will be magnified and get glory and praise in this body of mine and be boldly exalted in my person whether through (by) life or through (by) death. For me to live is Christ (His life in me) and to die is gain (the gain of the glory of eternity)*". Paul was very confident and excited about Christ's' promise. For Paul life is summed up in Jesus Christ. Christ was his reason for being. Death would relieve him of earthly burdens and let him focus totally on glorifying God. We here are taught our duty to God is in our righteous acts, our devotion, in our pure morals, in our principles and our practices. We must fear the Lord our God. We must love Him and delight in communion with Him; we must walk in the ways in which He has appointed us to walk. We must serve Him with all of our heart and soul. What we do in His service we must do cheerfully and with good will. We must keep His commandments. Our obedience should be praiseworthy and respectable. We must give honor to God and to Him we must remain, as one we love and delight in, trust in, and from whom we have great expectations. We must love, serve, and obey Jesus Christ and daily be changed into His image, from glory to glory by the Spirit of the Lord. We receive from the Lord everyday the fruits of His mercy. Let us present ourselves, all we are, all we have, and all we can do.

The average person in the western world knows the name of Dr. David Livingstone only because of Henry Stanley's famous statement,"Dr. Livingstone, I presume". During his lifetime, however, Livingstone was arguably the world's best known missionary. By the time Stanley caught up with Livingstone, he had been in Africa for many years and had known a life full of hardship. A lion had attacked him, leaving his left arm virtually useless. He had been through countless confrontations with hostile tribes, had lost his wife to a fever, in fact, he had lost mostly everything that a man can lose while serving Christ. While on a brief visit to England, he was once asked by a group of students to reflect on his losses. He answered; "for my own part, I have never ceased to rejoice that God has appointed me to such an office. People talk of the sacrifice I have made in spending so much of my life in Africa..... is that a sacrifice which brings its own blest reward in healthful activity, the consciousness of doing good, peace of mind, and a bright hope of glorious destiny hereafter? Away with such a thought, it is emphatically no sacrifice. Say rather it is a privilege. Anxiety, sickness, suffering, or danger, now and then, with a forgoing of the common conveniences and charities of this life, may make us pause, and cause the spirit to waver, and the soul to sink; but let this only be for a moment. All these are nothing when compared with the glory which shall be revealed in and for us. I never made a sacrifice." The heart that delights in God and longs only to see His glory advanced will hardly ever be concerned with sacrifice. God in his vast and awesome wisdom asks that we first love Him and then live in keeping of that core value.

He does not want his followers to think that what they do is sacrificial, even though from the world point of view it is. Being grateful to the grace of God will always be found near the center of the servants most powerful motivation.

Christ's servant prays for the gracious presence of God, the manifestation of God unto himself, the discoveries of God's love, the enjoyment of him in Christ, communion with God, comforts of God's Spirit, and the joy of his salvation. The servant makes a personal request for blessing as it says in the Amplified Bible in Psalms 31:16 "*Let your face shine upon your servant; save me for your mercy's sake and in your loving kindness*", and in Numbers 6:25-26,"*The Lord make His face shine upon you, and be gracious to you, the Lord lift up His countenance on you, and give you peace*". The scripture says save me for your mercy's sake, which actually means not for any righteousness of his own but for the sake of the grace and goodness of the Lord; which is putting salvation upon its sure foundation according to the grace and mercy of God. We have a friend in heaven who will not fail us if we commit our spirit into His hands.

A servant of Christ is humble, not humble in appearance only, or merely in words, having a show of humility. Deep in their hearts they have a spirit of humbleness and contriteness. Proverbs 29:23 says, "*A man's pride will bring him low, but a humble spirit will obtain honor*". Honor shall uphold the humble in spirit. The servants of God are made humble by the Spirit of God in all spiritual things. They know their own weakness in doing anything that is spiritually good, they give all glory, honor, and salvation to the grace of God. In 1 Peter 5:6, the Holy Scriptures says, "*Humble yourselves therefore under the mighty hand of God, that he may exalt you in due time*". When a servant is humble before God, and in His sight, they quietly submit to His will, patiently bearing every affliction without argument. Sooner or later such who are humbled shall be exalted; it is the usual way and method which God takes to demean the proud, and exalt the humble; for humble souls honor him, and therefore such as honor him he will honor; and this he does in his own time, in a time that makes most for his glory, and their good. Where God gives grace to the humble, he will give wisdom, faith, and holiness. To be humble, and subject to our God, will bring greater comfort to the soul than the gratification of pride and ambition. But it is to be in God's own wisely appointed time. Cast all your personal cares, family care, cares for the present, and cares for the future, for yourselves, for others, for the church, on God. Cast our care upon God, and leave every event to his wise and gracious will. Firm belief in that the will and counsel of God is right, calms the spirit of a man.

A servant of Christ not only loves God whole-heartedly without holding back, but also loves others. They are not self-seekers, or self-pleasers. They are to love and please God, to love and please God they serve others As in Luke 6:38 says, "*Give, and it will be given to you. They will pour into your lap a good measure – pressed down, shaken together, and running over. For by your standard of measure it will be measured to you in return*" Give liberally according to your ability, and it will be returned. By serving God and others we store up heavenly treasures. Matthew 6:19-21 says "*Do not store up for yourselves treasures on earth where moths and rust destroy and where thieves break in and steal but store up for yourselves treasures in heaven where neither moths or rust destroy and where thieves do not break in or steal, for where your treasure is there your heart will be also"* Do not store up for yourselves treasures on earth, is meant by treasures of an earthly kind, worldly wealth and riches. Christ is not saying not to have any of these. It's an attitude of the heart. Christ discourages us from covetousness, and worldly mindedness. He discourages us from hoarding plenty of worldly things for ourselves, making no use of them for the good of others. Worldly riches such as clothes, gold, silver, jewelry, precious stones, and money, we should not covet, or hoard, it is foolishness to trust in it, and depend on it. We are to store up for ourselves treasures as in the treasures of life, and treasures of peace, and treasures of blessing, and the souls of the righteous and the spirits and souls that shall be created in the years to come. Which infinitely surpass everything that is valuable on earth and which can never be corrupted or taken away, lay up your earthly treasures in heaven, put them into the hands of God in heaven. The Holy Scriptures talk a lot about laying up heavenly treasures, Luke 12:33 *"sell your possessions and give to the poor. Provide purses for yourselves that will not wear out, a treasure in heaven that will not be exhausted where no thief comes near and no moth destroys"*. 1 Timothy 6:18-19 *"command them to do good to be rich in good deeds and to be generous and willing to share. In this way they will lay up treasures for themselves as a firm foundation for the coming age so that they may take hold of the life that is truly life"*. Matthew 19:21, *"Jesus answered if you want to be perfect go sell your possessions and give to the poor and you will have treasure in heaven then come and follow me"*. Treasures are safer in God's hands than in our own. Where your treasure is there your heart will be also diverts from worldly mindedness that your treasure is on earth and lies on earthly things. If your treasure is put into the hands of God, your heart will be with Him, and be settled on Him and your desires will be after heavenly things. Your affections will be set on heavenly things.

People do not have the natural will to come to Christ, or to have him reign over them. They have no desire, no hunger and thirst after his righteousness and salvation, where there are any such desires; they are distributed by God unto men. God works upon the stubborn and inflexible will and makes the soul willing to be saved by Christ and submit to His righteousness and do His will. It speaks of this in Philippians 2:13, in the Amplified Bible, "*(Not in your own strength) for it is God who is all the while effectually at work in you (energizing and creating in you the power and desire) both to will and to work for His good pleasure and satisfaction and delight"*. He sweetly and powerfully draws the cords of love to Himself and to His Son and influences by His grace and Spirit. He works in the servants hearts. There is, in all believers, a will, and a power of doing. God therefore both implants in them principles of action to work from, a faith and love, a regard for His glory and gives them grace and strength to work with, without which they can do nothing. The Greek word for "will" indicates that He is not focusing on mere desires or emotions but on intent to fulfill a planned purpose. God's power makes His church willing to live Godly lives. God wants Christians to do what satisfies Him.

A servant, who is willing to serve Jesus Christ, the way He wants us to serve Him, must
  1.) Know the divine resources personally
  2.) See the human needs compassionately
  3.) Become channels of God's mighty resources

4.)   God alone is glorified.

When God is glorified, His Spirit can work to bring Christ to those who need to know Him. God alone has the resources to meet human needs all we can do is receive His riches and share them with others as Peter and John did in Acts 3:1-9, *"Now Peter and John was going up to the temple at the ninth hour, the hour of prayer, and a man who had been lame from his mothers womb was being carried along whom they used to set down every day at the gate of the temple which is called beautiful in order to beg alms of those who were entering the temple. When he saw Peter and John about to go into the temple he began asking to receive alms. But Peter, along with John fixed his gaze on him and said "look at us!" and he began to give them his attention expecting to receive something from them. But Peter said "I do not possess silver or gold but what I do have I give to you. In the name of Jesus Christ the Nazarene – walk!" and seizing him by the right hand, he raised him up and immediately his feet and his ankles were strengthened. With a leap he stood upright and began to walk and he entered the temple with them, walking and leaping and praising God, and all the people saw him walking and praising God"* The ninth hour is three o'clock pm. The Jews had three daily times of prayer; the other two were nine o'clock am, and twelve o'clock pm. The gate named beautiful, is a large and extravagant gate inside the temple mount on the eastern side, separating the Court of the Gentiles, from the Court of the women. Beggars, who begged for money, consider the temple the best site to do their begging because the daily temple worshipers came to impress God with their pious good works including offerings at the temple treasury. Peter and John were intimate companions and had great respect for each other and they were often together. Some think that they were together at the high priest palace at the trial of Christ. They ran together to Christ's tomb. They now went together to the temple, not to attend the daily sacrifice, which was cancelled due to the sacrifice Christ made, but to attend the duty of prayer, which was still enforced. They also looked at this as possibly an opportunity to preach Christ. This man's lameness came not through any disease or fall, or any external hurt but from birth, from a defect in nature, in one of his limbs or more, which made the events after the miracle more extraordinary. He was so lame that he could not walk by himself or go to the temple by himself; he had to be lead or be carried. They laid him at the gate of the temple, it has been a common practice, it may be for years past, to bring him every day at prayer time, and lay him at the gate of the temple where the people went in, so he was well known by the people, that he has been a lame for a long time, ever since he was born so that there could be no imposture in this case. Just as Peter and John were entering the temple through the gate at which the lame man lay. The man looked at them and though they were strangers to him, he figured they were Israelites, by their going into the temple at that time, asked for an offering, and begged them to give him something for his relief and support. Peter fastened his eyes upon him, or looking intently at him, being no doubt under some uncommon impulse of the Spirit of GOD to take notice of him and cure him of his disease. John was also under a same impulse at the exact time and who was equally concerned in his cure. Peter and John seem to have been lead by a divine direction to work a miracle on a man above forty years old who had been crippled from his birth. Peter said look at us, which raise this lame man's attention to them. He looked at them, as they asked him, he directed his eyes toward them and he looked at them. The man was expecting to receive something from them but not a cure for his lameness, which he little thought of, but some money. Then

Peter said "*silver and gold have I none*", they had no money either of gold or silver coin, "but *such as I have I give thee*", meaning the gift of healing not that he communicated that to him, but exercised the gift upon him by curing him of his lameness. In the name of Jesus Christ of Nazareth, signifying that it was by the command of Christ, he said what follows and by his power he brought by the authority and virtue of Christ Who was treated with so much contempt by the Jews and had lately been crucified by them, in Christ's name he bid him rise up and walk without making any use of medicine or applying anything to him, but believing that power would go along with the words, and strength would be communicated to him in whose name he spoke, and here lies the difference between the miracles brought by Christ and by His disciples, those that were done by Him were done in His own name and by His own power, and those that were performed by His disciples were done in the name of Christ and by His power alone. The lame man stood firm upon his feet and walked about by which it was abundantly manifest to him and others that he had a perfect cure. He joined the divine worship to acknowledge the goodness of God. If Peter and John, would do the good deed of healing the man, we must go forth in the name and the power of Jesus Christ, and call on helpless sinners to rise and walk in the way of holiness by faith in Christ alone. How sweet the thought that with our fallen nature, the name of Jesus Christ of Nazareth can make us whole!

A servant of God is a giver. They give of their time, their gifts, their abilities, their energy, their money, they give anything they have. They give of their own free will, in the heart of a servant. The Holy Scriptures speak of this in 2 Corinthians 9:7-8 in the Amplified Bible, "*Let each one (give) as he has made up his own mind and purposed in his heart not reluctantly or sorrowful or under compulsion for God loves (He takes pleasure in prized above other things and is unwilling to abandon or do without) a cheerful (joyous, prompt to do it) giver (whose heart is in his giving). And God is able to make all grace (every favor and earthly blessing) come to you in abundance so that you may always and under all circumstances and whatever the need be self sufficient (possessing enough to require no aid or support and furnished in abundance for every good work and charitable donation*". True, most people relate these verses to giving of money, but along with money there is more to giving. The term purposed occurs only here in the New Testament, it indicates a premeditated, predetermined plan of action that is done from the heart voluntarily. It is giving without grief, sorrow, sadness, depression, regret, or reluctances. There is joy in giving of what you have. God loves a cheerful giver. God has a unique, special love for those who are happily committed to generous giving. The Greek word for cheerful is the word from which we get hilarious, which suggests that God loves a heart that is enthusiastically thrilled with the pleasure of giving of what they have, or of giving of themselves. God, no man, will supply everything needed for real happiness and contentment. God gives back lavishly to generous, cheerful givers not so they may satisfy selfish, nonessential desires but so they may meet the variety of needs others have. God gives not only enough for ourselves, but that also, we may supply the wants and needs of others. Let us be bold enough to copy the example of Christ, showing it as, it is more blessed to give than to receive. Blessed be to God for the unspeakable gift of his grace whereby he enables and inclines some of his people to lavish upon others, and others to be grateful for it, and blessed be His glorious name to all eternity, for Jesus, Christ, that inestimable gift of his love, through whom this and every other good thing pertaining to life and godliness are freely given to us, beyond all expression, measure and bounds. God gives us a picture of his good, Godly, and lavish gifts in the story of Him feeding the multitude with five loaves of barley bread and two fish in Matthew 14:15-21 *"when it was evening, the disciples came to Him and said, "this place is desolate and the hour is already late so send the crowds away that they may go into the villages and buy food for themselves". But Jesus said to them, "they do not need to go away you give them something to eat". They said to Him, "we have here only five loaves and two fish" and He said "bring them here to me", ordering the people to sit down on the grass, He looking up toward heaven, He blessed the food, and breaking the loaves He gave them to the disciples and the disciples gave them to the crowds and they all ate and were satisfied. They picked up what was left over of the broken pieces, twelve full baskets. There were about five thousand men who ate, besides women and children".* Jesus knew they did not have enough food to feed the crowd. He wanted the disciples to state it plainly so that the record would show that a miracle has occurred by the power of Christ. The best way to have an increase is to bring what we have, our gifts, our abilities, whatever we have, and put it into Christ's hands, whereby not only good is done to others, but the giver is blessed as well. The people sought the spiritual food of Christ's word and then he took care that they should not want bodily food. The people followed Jesus, and He gave them what they came for. He spoke to them and told them of His kingdom. He healed those who had need of healing. His servants who fear Him, and serve Him faithfully will not go without any good thing. When we receive creature-comforts we must acknowledge that we receive them from God and that we are unworthy to receive them, that we owe them all, and all the comfort we have in them, to Christ. The blessing of Christ will make a little go a great way. He fills every hungry soul, and abundantly satisfies it with goodness.

When you are a servant you are not a manufacturer, but you are a distributor. Once you accept yourself as a distributor of Gods' riches and not a manufacture, you will experience a wonderful new freedom and joy in service. You won't be afraid of new challenges because you know God has the resources to meet them. You need to receive it, share it, and let God have all the glory in your service. We are channels of Gods' resources. As Gods' children and Gods' servants we can draw upon the riches of His grace. Whether we loose our wealth, our health, or our loved ones, as in the story of Job, God is alive forever more and His promise to take care of us in any and every circumstance abide forever. We can glory in our humiliation, in our losses, because when all our riches are gone we will still belong to the God of the universe. We will still be His beloved child, blessed in every spiritual blessing in heavenly places in Christ. In Ephesians 1:3-7 in the Message bible, it speaks of this blessing, *"How blessed is God! And what a blessing He is! He is the Father of our Master Jesus Christ and takes us to the high places of blessing in Him!! Long before He laid down earths foundation, He had us in mind, had settled on us as the focus of His love, to be made whole and holy by His love. Long, long ago He decided to adopt us into His family through Jesus Christ. (What pleasure He took in planning this!) He wanted us to enter into the celebration of His lavish gift-giving by the hand of His beloved Son. Because of the sacrifice of the Messiah, His blood poured out on the alter of the Cross – we're a free people, free of penalties and punishments chalked up by all our misdeeds".* Blessed is derived from the same Greek word as Eulogy which means to praise or commend. This is the supreme duty of all creatures. In His providential grace, God has already given believers total blessing. Spiritual refers to the work of God who is the divine and spiritual source of all blessings. In heaven, refers to the realm of Gods' complete heavenly domain from which all His blessings come. Gods' abundant blessings belong only to believers who are His children by faith in Christ so that what He has is theirs, including His righteousness, resources, privileges, position and power. Gods' election or predestination does not operate apart from or nullify man's responsibility to believe in Jesus Christ as Lord and Savior. Through Gods' sovereign will before the creation of the world and therefore obviously independent of human influence and apart from any human merit, those who are saved have become eternally united with Christ Jesus. This describes both a purpose and a result of God choosing those who are to be saved. Unrighteous persons are declared righteous, unworthy sinners are declared worthy of salvation all because they are chosen in Him (Christ). This refers to Christ imputed righteousness granted to us, a perfect righteousness which places believers in a holy and blameless position before God.

As God's children and God's servants we can draw upon the riches of His glory. With their new identity in Christ believers are spiritually alive; they are united into Gods household. As the church they are the dwelling place of God, built on the words and work of the apostles and prophets, as Paul speaks about in Ephesians 3:14-16 *"For this reason I bow my knees before the Father, from whom every family in heaven and on earth derive its name, that He would grant you according to the riches of His glory to be strengthened with power through His spirit in the inner man"*. I bow my knees is not an instruction only for physical posture during prayer but also suggested and attitude of submission, reverence, and intense passion. When Paul said every family in heaven and on earth, Paul was not only teaching the universal Fatherhood of God and the universal brotherhood of man, but was also referring to believers from every era of history, those who are dead (in heaven) and those who are alive (on earth). Paul's prayers are almost always for the spiritual welfare of others. They are limitless and available to every believer. Spiritual power is the mark of every Christian who submits to God's word and spirit. It is not reserved for some special class of Christians, but for all those who are always disciplining their minds and spirits to constantly study the word, understand it, and live by it wholeheartedly. As Paul refers to in Philippians 4:19, *"And my God will supply all your needs according to His riches in glory in Christ Jesus"*. Although the outer physical person becomes weaker with age, the inner spiritual person should grow stronger through the Holy Spirit who will energize, revitalize, and empower the obedient committed Christian. Believers in Christ need a fresh supply of strength to enable them to exercise grace, to perform duties, to resist satan, and his temptations, to oppose their corruption, and to bear the cross and undergo afflictions cheerfully and to hold on to the end. This is a blessing that comes from God, and is a gift of His free grace, a grant from Him. He is the strength of the lives of His people, of their salvation, of their hearts, and of the work of grace in their hearts. The process in which the saints are strengthen by God is His spirit, who strengthen them by leading them to the fullness of grace and strength in Christ by the love of God in their hearts, by applying the promises of the gospel to them, and by making the gospel and the ordinances of it, useful to them, will enables them to go from strength to strength and glory to glory. If the law of Christ is written in our hearts and the love of Christ is there, then Christ dwells there. How powerfully the apostle speaks of the love of Christ! The breadth of the love of Christ shows its extent to all nations, the length that it continues from everlasting to everlasting, the depth it saving those who are sunk in the depth of sin and misery, the height it rising them up to heavenly happiness and glory. Those who receive grace from Christ may be said to be filled to the fullness of God. Should this not satisfy man? God, who is also their God, is able and willing to supply their wants, and He does so. HE withholds no good thing from them, for He supplies all their needs. God is the God of all grace, and a fullness of grace is in His Son, and this grace is sufficient for them. God is abundantly rich in the perfection of His nature. According to the riches of His goodness He supplies the needs of everything living. He is also rich in His grace. He supplies the spiritual needs of His people, according to the riches He has. He gives all things richly, plenteously, and abundantly to enjoy. He reveals Himself glorious, and makes His people glorious. God gives all things pertaining to life and Godliness for the sake of Christ Jesus, in whom they are accepted. Let us pray for patient submission and hope. Let us pray for humility and a heavenly mind when exalted. It is a special grace to always have a mind of Christ. Do not to loose your comfort in God, or distrust His providence. Do not to be proud, or secure, or worldly, when God prospers you. This is a harder lesson than any of the others. Through Christ we have grace to do what is good, and through Him we must expect the reward, and we have all things by Him, let us do all things through Him, and to His glory.

 As Gods children, and Gods servants we can draw upon the unsearchable riches of His grace. A sinner lives a life of holiness after being born of God. He is delivered from the guilt of sin, by pardoning and justifying grace. Ephesians 2:8-9 talks about this grace, "For *by grace you have been saved through faith and that not of yourselves it is the gift of God not as a result of works so that no one may boast."* How highly the apostle speaks of the unsearchable riches of the grace of Jesus Christ! Those whom God advances to honorable employments He humbles in their own eyes. Generally speaking, the greatest saints are, the most humble souls, as in the case of Abraham, Jacob, Moses, David, and others, these have the best thoughts of others, and not of themselves. They rejoice greatly when the manifestation of the grace of God is revealed in others. They have the lowest opinion of their own works, and are the greatest admirers of the grace of God. They humbly submit to the sovereign will of God; the reason of their great humility. Paul talks about this grace in Ephesians 3:8, in the Amplified Bible, *"To me, though I am the very least of the saints, (Gods consecrated people) this grace, (favor, privilege) was granted and graciously entrusted to proclaim to the Gentiles the unending (boundless, fathomless, incalculable, and inexhaustless) riches of Christ (wealth which no human being could have searched out)".* In light of Gods perfect righteousness, Paul's assessment of himself was not false humility but simple honesty. He knew his unworthiness. The reason of their great humility is because they are aware of their own sinfulness, vileness, and unworthiness, which keeps them humble in their own sight. One of the first steps we must take before our service can be used by God is to confess our bankruptcy and receive by faith the grace that we need for acceptable service. What does it mean when you mention grace? So many people don't seem to understand what grace is. The word is charis. It comes from the word chairo which means rejoice, to rejoice. People listen when you start understanding what grace is, it'll turn something on inside of you. You have to rejoice. It is wonderful to understand what grace is, it's not what man can do, it is what God would do.

As Gods children and Gods servants we are to draw upon the riches of His mercy. Gods eternal love and good-will toward His servants, is the fountain where all His mercies flow to us, and that love of God is great love, and that mercy is rich mercy, which it talks about in Ephesians 2:4 "*But God, being rich in mercy because of His great love with which He loved us*". Mercy is a perfection of the divine nature, and is essential to God, mercy is His nature. The act of Christ's will and abundant mercy, with all the blessings and benefits of it, is only exhibited in God the Father and Christ Jesus. It is said to be rich in mercy. He is free and liberal in dispensing it to a large number of persons in great abundance and variety. For Christ's love to His chosen people is very great. If they would only consider who it is that has loved them! God is infinite, unchangeable, and sovereign. God admits to no variation or alteration in His mercy. What does mercy mean? In the ancient Greek the word mercy is the word eleos, it refers to Gods compassion. In the phrase "The Lord Jesus Christ", the word "Lord", kurios, was never used of a person that wasn't already known to have compassion and concern for everyone around them. The word kurios had built in it the fact that He was and is, a compassionate caring Lord. Grace is what deals with our sin. Mercy is what deals with the consequence of our sin. "Rich" is the word plousios, it means abundance of wealth. In other words if you want to talk about riches, you go to God. The first thing you will find is that He is rich in mercy. Our God abounds in mercy. Paul is showing us that God has already proved that He loves us, out of His love He shows mercy to us.

As Gods children and Gods servants we can draw upon the riches of Gods wisdom. The apostle Paul knew the mysteries of the kingdom of God as well as any man, yet he was at a loss, and despairing to find the bottom and the answers to the mysteries of God, he humbly sat down at the brink and adores the depth. Paul then says in Romans 11:33, "*Oh the depth, of the riches, both of the wisdom and knowledge of God! How unsearchable are His judgments and unfathomable are His ways.*" There is not only depth to the Divine counsel of God, but abundant riches of that which is precious and valuable. The Divine counsels are complete; not only do they have depth and height, but also breadth and length. God's counsels are beyond knowing. There is a vast distance of inadequacy between God and man, between the Creator and the creature, which forever shuts us off from knowledge of His ways. What man shall teach God how to reign over the world? All things in heaven and in earth, which relate to our salvation that belong to our peace, are all of Him by way of creation, and through Him by way of providence. This includes Gods relationship with His creatures. There is an unfathomable depth of riches, wisdom and knowledge in Gods counsel. With regard to unbelievers how unsearchable are His judgments; with regard to believers how unsearchable are His ways. His ways we can not trace. The apostle gives himself up to the awareness of that divine plan which he had drawn out of the riches both of the wisdom and knowledge of God. God alone has the resources to meet human needs, all we can do is receive His riches and share them with others.

There is joy when you grow more and more in the image of Christ, as you serve Him, and do His will. Every Christian should strive to become "conformed to the image of His

Son" and those who serve Him have a wonderful opportunity to learn from Him and become more like Him. As in Romans 8:29 talks about, *"For those whom He foreknew He also predestined to become conformed to the image of His Son so that He would be the firstborn among many brethren"*. This is not a reference simply to Gods omniscience – that in eternity past He would know who would come to Christ. Rather it speaks of a deliberate choice to set His love on us and establish an intimate relationship. Predestined is meant to mark out, appoint, or determine beforehand those God chooses. The goal of Gods predestined purpose for His own people is that they would be made in the likeness of Jesus Christ. This is the prize of the upward call. The foreknowledge of God by which He foreknows and foretells things to come, with whom all things are present which is eternal, universal, certain, and infallible. He foreknew all men, so that all men would be predestined, and conformed to the image of Christ. They are called by grace, and justified by glory, they are a special people, whom God has foreknown. The cause of predestination which was done before and without any consideration of good or evil is entirely owing to the free grace of God, and is the foundation of good works, faith, holiness, and preservation. This regards the everlasting love of God to His own people, His delight in them, and holds them in high esteem. He foreknew them from everlasting, affectionately loved them, and took infinite delight and pleasure in them. This is the foundation of their predestination and election of their obedience to Christ, of their calling, justification, and glorification. He also predestined them to be conformed to the image of His Son. He has perfect, distinct, and special knowledge of them, and He loves them with an everlasting love. He predetermined them to His everlasting and unchangeable purpose and decrees, and conform them to the image of Christ. Gods elect are chosen to be holy through the sanctification of the Holy Spirit.

There is joy in serving Jesus, no matter what kind of service He has called you to do. Don't ever loose this joy. If you do your service will start to become a burden and you will feel like quitting. Why, because the joy of the Lord is your strength. The best, happiest, joyful, and most satisfying thing we can do is serve the Lord. No matter what kind of Christian service God has called you to do, it's an honor and a privilege to serve Jesus Christ. It is the most rewarding work in the world. It is full of joys, satisfying times, and triumphs. There is joy in pleasing the Lord because you are doing what He wants you to do, the way He wants you to do it. God delights in His people and it pleases His heart when His servants do His will from their hearts. There is joy in helping others come to know Jesus Christ and live for Him. No matter what task He called you to do, God will use the skills He has given you to help somebody if you direct them in the power of the Spirit and you do it for God's glory. You can trust your Father to see to it that nothing is ever wasted that is done in the will of God and for the love of God. As you serve the Lord nothing happens to you except what God ordains. 1 John 2:17 *"The world is passing away, and also its lusts, but the one who does the will of God lives forever"*. The Christian must not love the satanic world system because of its temporary nature. This world is in the continual process of disintegration headed for destruction. In contrast to the temporary world, God's will is permanent and unchangeable. Those who follow God's will abide as His people forever. While God offers eternal life to His children the present age is doomed. If our service for the Lord doesn't make us grow, two things may be true; either we are in the wrong place, or we have the wrong attitude toward the right place. Both are tragic, but being miserable in your place of Christian service does not necessarily indicate that you are in the wrong place; do not be too quick to quit; God may have put you there for your good as well as for the good of the work, and for the good of others. Maybe He has some unfinished work to accomplish in your life, maybe a little bit more growing, and a little bit more maturing; only God knows. The difficulty of the task God gives us is one of His loving gifts for our maturity. The more difficult the task the more patience and maturity we receive. Service is supposed to make us grow, and it will if we are in the right place with the right attitude. No matter how painful or disappointing service may seem to you, it is not being wasted. What ever you do in the service of Christ is never a waste. Matthew 25:21, "*His master said to him, "Well done, good and faithful slave. You were faithful with a few things, I will put you in charge of many things, enter into the joy of your Master.*" His master said to him, "*well done, you upright (honorable, admirable) and faithful servant, you have been faithful and trustworthy over a little. I will put you in charge of much. Enter into and share the joy (the delight, the blessedness) which your master enjoys*". Servants know nothing good can come from themselves, and when they have done all they can, they know they are but unprofitable servants. They acknowledge all they do is to the grace of God, and strength of Christ, and that no praise is due to them. This is said to show how acceptable a diligent servant is to Christ and to encourage the servant. Men can never be servants of Christ without the grace of God implanted in them. Servants seek not to please men, but their Lord and Master and not to their own honor and applause, but His glory. Enter into the joy of the Lord, not their own, but their Lord's, which Jehovah the Father has prepared for His people, and gives unto them. This happiness of theirs is expressed by joy, which will be full and perfect and without any interruption. Their joy will be unspeakable and glorious and continue forever. Everything a servant has they received from God. They have nothing they can call their own except sin. Our receiving from Christ is in order to our serving. It is a real Christian privilege to be a servant in promoting Christ's glory and the good of His people. The love of Christ constrains him to live no longer to himself, but for Christ who died for him, and rose again. Pleasing God ought to be your supreme motive for service. If it is you will hear well done good and faithful servant, when you stand before Him in glory.

Henry Crowell was only 19 years old when his father died of tuberculosis. When he was 17, Crowell discovered he had the same disease. To all appearance he was dieing. That may have moved Crowell to attend and evangelistic meeting in Cleveland Ohio, where the feature speaker was a man by the name of Dwight L. Moody. Moody told the crowd that the world had yet to see what could be done through a person whose life was fully consecrated to Jesus Christ. As Crowell reflected on this statement, he decided that he wanted to be that person. But how could God use him? He had no idea. He was convinced that he could never preach. He did believe, however, that he could be a businessman useful in the service of the King. He didn't know how long he would live, but he told God that in the time he had left he would support people like Dwight Moody, who could proclaim the gospel. He also asked for healing as he consecrated the remainder of his life to God. Crowell applied himself and invested his funds intelligently as the days passed. His health began to improve and that encouraged him to buy a mill. It had been owned by Quakers and was designed to produce cereal products. The Quaker oats company had begun. As Crowell's health continued to improve he also enjoyed a great deal of business success. God prospered the business and Henry Crowell put the funds that came in to work, giving 70 percent of his income to Christian causes. He was especially glad to be able to assist Moody Bible Institute in the midst of a dark financial time. He also helped begin the ministries of Moody Press, Moody Magazine, and Moody Radio Ministries. The man who thought he was headed for an early grave instead left his mark on the Christian church through his liberal giving and the wisdom he used in applying God's resources.

Do you know God personally?
Do you know the marvelous resources that are available through Jesus Christ?
Are you concerned about the needs of others so that you see them and want to help?
Do you have compassion for those with needs?
Are you willing to be a channel for God's glory?

Chapter 3

What a servant does *not* look like!

What does this mean to you and I in our Christian service? When we go through trials and tribulations, when we are attacked, or when our service seems to be in vain this gives us confidence and courage to keep going. Christian workers must endure our share of hardships, or the battle may be lost. The Holy Scriptures speaks about battling hardships in 2 Timothy 2: 3, "*Suffer hardships with me as a good soldier of Christ Jesus* ". A Christian in service to their Almighty Powerful God fights against the evil, the sinister world system, and the believer's sinful human nature. This concept of battle is a familiar one in the New Testament. Paul is constantly dealing with the conflict against the hostile world, his own persecution, and the persecution of the church.

God's revelation brings to light the hidden things of darkness and reveal the counsels of the hearts. Then each one's praise will come from God. It is awesome that God will find in each one of our services to Him something to praise. God sees our hearts and motives, while others see our actions. When you consider the great things He has done for you, bestowing all good things, in nature, providence, and grace according to the truth of His word you cant help but be cordial, sincere, and affectionate in a manner worthy of Him, as it says in 1 Samuel 12:24, "*Only fear the Lord and serve Him in truth with all your heart and consider what great things He has done for you*". We are to consider what great things the Lord has done for us, especially in the great work of redemption; we shall worship and serve the true Jehovah, the one and only Lord God. He only is to be worshipped and served, as Father, Son, and Spirit. In Psalm 2:11 it talks about worshiping God, "*Worship the Lord with reverence and rejoice with trembling.*" God only is to be worshipped and served. Here it is understood to serve the Lord Christ, the Son of God, and the King of kings and Lord of lords, Jehovah by preaching the unaltered inerrant word of God. We are to have joy of public worship, and the singing of psalms and hymns and spiritual songs which is a time of joy and rejoicing. The gospel is good tiding and great joy. The kingdom of God is not external but internal. Men should rejoice in Christ and have no confidence in the flesh. When someone does take their eyes of off Christ and puts their confidence in the flesh, whether it be fleshly desires or anything that takes their eyes off of God, those believers who are walking in the Spirit, filled with the Spirit, and evidence the fruit of the Spirit should lovingly restore the person who slipped into sin. The restoration of such a person is discussed in Galatians 6:1, "*Brethren, even if anyone is caught in any trespass you who are spiritual restore such a one in a spirit of gentleness each one looking to yourself so that you too will not be tempted*". Restore literally means to mend. The Greek word for looking strongly emphasizes to continually, and diligently look. Any person who is a child of God, lives and walks in the Spirit and stand by the power and grace of the Spirit of God, who would see another person falls into sin, is to reprove and rebuke, recover and restore the backslider. They should do in gentleness and meekness by gently telling them of their faults, and mildly reproving, which is a gift and fruit of the Spirit of God. A spiritual man should help the weak and rise up the fallen. We are to bear one another's burdens. So we shall fulfill the law of Christ. Restore such a one in the Spirit of gentleness, considering (ourselves) lest (we) also be tempted. The process of restoring may take years but we can't gift up, don't give up! It takes discipline in the restoration process. The servant during this process can be able and should be able to go back to service, but may not be able to go back to their original service; God can use them elsewhere in the harvest field where laborers are few.

Some people act like servants but they have a different agenda, they use people to get what they want instead of helping people to get what the other person needs. If we are not careful we can serve in such a way that we exploit the needs of others. We will serve others but deep down in our hearts and subconscious we will want to get recognition, position, titles, honors, and privileges. If your only motive for service is to be recognized and thanked, you had better get prepared for a lot of disappointments. If your motive is to please God and accomplish His will, what people say and do – or don't say and do – will not make a great deal of difference to you. Gods concern is for the worker as well as for the work. You need to ask yourself, where am I in my spiritual growth? Does God still have some work to do in me? When your service is the most difficult, God maybe doing His deepest work in your life, don't run away. God uses you to build His work, but He also uses the work to build you as He prepares you for the next assignment as well as for the eternal service in glory. You don't leave a ministry because it doesn't do anything for you any longer, you have to do some self evaluations and be honest with yourself to see if you are still growing, if you stopped growing and are going stagnant your work will suffer. Work by faith and leave the results with the Lord. To be a servant, a sensitive spirit and a tender heart are absolutely essential, but can easily become calloused. True servants of God help others whether they get anything out of it or not, their only concern is that God will be glorified and that people will trust Christ. Luke 10: 25-37 talks about this attitude, *"And the lawyer stood up and put Him to the test saying, "Teacher, what shall I do to inherit eternal life?" and He said to him, "what is written in the law? How does it read to you?" and he answered, "you shall love the Lord your God with all your heart, and with all your soul, and with all your strength, and with your entire mind, and your neighbor as yourself". And He said to him, "you have answered correctly, do this and you will live." But wishing to justify himself, he said to Jesus. "And who is my neighbor?" Jesus replied and said, "a man was going down from Jerusalem to Jericho and fell among robbers, and they stripped him and beat him and went away half dead. And by chance a priest was going down on that road and when he saw him, he passed by on the other side. Likewise a Levite also, when he came to the place and saw him, passed by on the other side. But a Samaritan, who was on a journey, came upon him, and when he saw him, he felt compassion and came to him and bandaged up his wounds pouring oil and wine on them, and he put him on his own beast, and brought him to an inn and took care of him. On the next day he took out two denarii and gave them to the innkeeper and said, "take care of him, and whatever more you spend, when I return I will repay you." Which of these three do you think proved to be a neighbor to the man who fell into the robbers hands? And he said". The one that showed mercy toward him." Then Jesus said to him, "go and do the same."* The lawyer, who supposedly knew the law of God, summed up the requirements of the law exactly as Christ did on another occasion. "Do and live" is the promise of the law, but since no sinner can obey perfectly, the impossible demands of the law are meant to drive us to seek divine mercy. This man should have responded with a confession of guilt rather than self-justification. This reveals the man's self righteous character. The prevailing opinion among scribes and Pharisees was that one's neighbors were the righteous ones only. According to them the wicked, as in sinners, Gentiles and especially Samaritans were to be hated because they were the enemies of God. The true righteous person has a righteous loathsome of all that is corrupt. It is not spiteful personal loathing of individuals. Godly hatred is marked by a broken-hearted servant, full of genuine love, grieving over the condition of the sinner. Jesus makes it clear that each has a responsibility to be a neighbor, especially to those who are in need. We shall not let our prideful heart work hard against these convictions. Christ gave an instance of a poor Jew in distress, relieved by a Good Samaritan. The servant helped the man who was robbed by thieves. This poor man fell among thieves who left him about to die in his wounds, he was ignored by those who should have been his friends and was cared for by a stranger, a Samaritan of the nation which the Jews most despised and detested and would have no dealings with. Granted it is impossible for us as Gods servants to do something about every need that we see or hear about, but we must never be thankful for a reason or an excuse to escape responsibility. We must guard against the hardening of the heart. It is interesting to observe how selfishness governs all, and how many excuses men will make to avoid trouble. The true Christian has the law of love written in his heart, the Spirit of Christ dwells in him, and Christ's image is renewed in his soul. We shall love our neighbor as ourselves. We must show the kindness and love of God our Savior toward sinful miserable men. We must neither have a blind eye, nor should we think only of ourselves when we see the needs of others. We can't do everything but we can do something and we must do it as Jesus Christ would so that He will be glorified. The people we serve have all kinds of needs, physical, emotional, relational, financial, but their greatest need is to come to the saving knowledge of Jesus Christ and to know His will. Servants do what they can to put food on the table, but unless we help people grow into a right relationship with God, whatever help we give will be only a quick fix until the next time they have a need. Then the cycle is repeated. The best thing we can do for them is not to solve their problems for them, but to show and tell about Gods grace so that they will be enabled to solve their own problems and not repeat them. Our attitude must be; sacrifice, and service to the glory of God.

You will meet problem people and problem situations wherever you go, so make up your mind to expect them, accept them, and let God use them to shape your life and your service. The devil wants to use problem people as weapons to tear you down, but the Spirit can use them as tools to build you up. If you stay on the job and trust God to work, you will experience Gods grace in a wonderful way and you will be a better servant for it. 2 Corinthians 1:3-4"*Blessed be the God and Father of our Lord Jesus Christ, the Father of mercies and God of all comfort who comforts us in all our affliction so that we will be able to comfort those who are in any affliction with the comfort with which we ourselves are comforted by God*". Paul praised the true God who revealed Himself in His Son Jesus Christ. Although the Son enjoyed the lofty position in heaven, He was willing to become a servant and submit Himself in His incarnation. Paul requested God to treat the sinful individual with kindness, love, and tenderness. God is the ultimate source of every true act of love and comfort. The Greek word for comfort is related to the word paraclete, one who comes alongside to help, another name for the Holy Spirit. Comfort often indicates softness and ease but that is not its meaning here. Paul was saying that God came to him in the middle of his suffering and troubles to strengthen him and give him courage and boldness. Affliction is a term used to refer to crushing pressure, because in Paul's life and ministry there was always something attempting to weaken, restrict, or confine his ministry, or even crush out his life. No matter what confronted him, Paul knew God would sustain and strengthen him. The purpose for the comfort from God is that believers might be comforted. Blessed be to God, is an ascription of praise and glory to God. He only can be blessed by men, by their praising and glorifying Him, and by giving honor and blessing to Him. Mercy and comfort are administered to the men only through the Lord Jesus Christ, the Son of God, and the Savior of sinners. He is described by His characteristic of mercy, and by His merciful disposition of His children. God is exceedingly merciful; He delights in showing mercy to His children, and to express the multitudes of His tender mercies. God is also described by His work of comforting the saints. The God of all comfort is His characteristic. There is no solid comfort but what comes from Him. Whatever compassion the saints enjoy they receive it from God, The Father of Christ. The compassion that they have from God through Christ in a covenant way is not small. They have great reason to bless the Lord. The apostle confirms the character of God, by His own experience. Paul had been in great tribulation and affliction for the sake of Christ and His gospel and was not left destitute of divine help and support. They had much compassion administered to them by the presence of God. God was pleased to comfort them in such a manner for the good of others and it showed that they were loved of God. It is the will of God that many who are in trouble and afflicted should be comforted. The persons He uses to comfort the afflicted are his ministering servants. We are encouraged to come boldly to the throne of grace, that we may obtain mercy and find grace to help in time of need. It is our Savior who says; let not your heart be troubled. All comfort comes from God, He comforts us by the Holy Spirit, by the rich mercies of His grace and our sweetest comforts are in Him. He is able to bind up the broken hearted, to heal the most painful wounds, and to give hope and joy under the heaviest sorrows. The favor God bestows on us is not only to make us cheerful, but also that we may be useful to others. Those who trust in the Lord shall not be ashamed. We shall trust in God for the future. It is our duty, not only to help one another with prayer, but in praise and thanksgiving. The trials and mercies will have a favorable ending to us and others. God wants to use our talents, He gave them to us, but along with the developing of our talents and spiritual gifts is the perfecting of our character. God needs servants' surrendered body to get His job done. There is no substitute for Godly character. No matter what talents or abilities you may have. If you don't have a Godly character or a servant's heart you don't have anything. The more you are like Christ, the more God can trust you with His blessing. The person who cultivates integrity realizes that there can be no division between secular and sacred in the Christian life, everything must be done to the glory of God. We are often tempted in our service to get rid of the very people God wants us to be a servant to. It is need that drives us to Christ, no matter what opposition we come across we shall not be driven from Him. Christ alone is able to heal. As in the story of the Canaanite woman who kept pleading with Jesus to heal her daughter who was possessed by a demon, the disciples wanted to chase her away but

Jesus tested her faith then healed her daughter in Matthew 15:21-28 *"Jesus went away from there, and withdrew into the district of Tyre and Sidon. And a Canaanite woman from that region came out and began to cry out saying, "have mercy on me, Lord, Son of David; my daughter is cruelly demon possessed". But He did not answer her a word, and His disciples came and implored Him saying, "send her away, because she keeps shouting at us." But He answered and said, "I was sent only to the lost sheep of the house of Israel." But she came and began to bow down before Him saying, "Lord, help me!" and He answered and said, "It is not good to take the children's bread and throw it to the dogs." But she said, "Yes, Lord, but even the dogs feed on the crumbs which fall from their masters table." Then Jesus said to her, "Oh woman, your faith is great, it shall be done for you as you wish." And her daughter was healed at once"*. Jesus' words with this woman are not to be understood as harsh or unfeeling. In fact, He was tenderly drawing from her and expression of her faith. The woman was a Greek, in other words she was a Gentile. With a loud voice, and being in great distress, she said have mercy on me. She was pleading to Jesus to cure her daughter. She was so much affected by her daughter being possessed that she made it her own problem. She expressed her faith in Jesus' power, and dominion, that all disease were at His command and control and that being Lord of all, He could remove them at His pleasure. She also showed her knowledge and belief of Him as the Messiah. A demon took possession to this woman's daughter and most grievously afflicted her, and her request to Him was, that He would cast the demon out of her, believing He had power to do so, without seeing or touching her, only by word speaking. Jesus did not answer her not because He did not hear her, or that He despised her petition or that He was not moved with it, but to try her faith and make her faith manifest itself. The Lord does not always and immediately answer the request of His people. The disciples came to Jesus, to the house where He was, and asked, saying, send her away. They desired that Jesus would grant her request and she might be dismissed. The reason they gave this request is because she cried after them, and because she was troublesome to them. She followed them wherever they went; there was no getting rid of her. Her cries were piercing that they could not bear to hear her cries any longer so the disciples asked Jesus that He would answer her request and dismiss her. She followed the disciples into the house; and fearing Christ's rejection to the request, she still pushed on, she still persevered, through all of her discouragement, her faith grew stronger. She had called Christ, Lord and the Son of David before, but now she worships Him as God. She said *"Lord help me"*, a short petition, but it fully expressed her case. She prays unto the Lord, by which she expresses His sovereignty, dominion and power. The request she makes is for *"help"* signifying that her case required it, it was such, that she could not help herself. Only God could help her, which she firmly believed. She had such sympathy, love and affliction to her daughter and the circumstances that she makes the case her own, and calls helping her daughter, helping herself. When Jesus said to the woman it is not right to take the children's bread and cast it to dogs, He said it to try her faith and make it more prominent. The "dogs" are meant to be the Gentiles. Christ here uses the common dialect of the people, and which this woman living upon the boarders of the Israelites nation, was acquainted with so that it was not so shocking and surprising, or quite so discouraging, as it would otherwise have been. She realizes that all He had said to her are true, that He was sent only to the lost sheep of the house of Israel, that she was indeed but a dog, a poor sinful creature, unworthy of any favor and that it was not right and fitting that all children's bread should be taken from them and given to the dogs. She suggests that even though the Gentiles were but dogs, and she one of them, yet she did not desire the affluence of the Jews, only that a crumb of mercy might be given her, so that her poor daughter might be healed, which was but a small favor. He seems surprised that she a woman and a poor Gentile should express such strong faith in Him, calling Him Lord, owning Him to be the Messiah, worshiping Him as God, believing Him able to do what could not be done by human ability. She believed she could succeed. Jesus said to the woman, what ever she wanted she shall get, or let the daughter be healed as you desire and in the way and at the very time you would have it. The power went forth from Christ and dispossessed the devil so that when she came home she found her daughter lying on the bed, quiet and perfectly well. A proud heart would not have done this but she turned it into an argument to support her request. The state of this woman is an emblem of a state of a sinner, deeply conscience of the misery of his soul. In all of the qualities of Christ, faith honors Christ most. Christ cured her daughter. He spoke and it was done. Let us who seek help from the Lord and receive no gracious answer, learn to turn even the unworthiness and discouragement into pleas for mercy. The disciples saw this woman as bothersome and pleaded with Jesus to send her on her way. Jesus used this woman and this situation as a tool to build her faith and build the faith of the disciples. My food is to do the will of Him who sent me and to finish His work. Serving God means working with people, and people not only have problems but they can be a problem. Because of the way they deal with their needs. Unless you really love these people you can never help them. When the people we serve irritate us or disappoint us the first thing we usually do is pray for them and tell the Lord to change them, what we ought to do first is pray for ourselves and ask God to increase our love. God often allows problem people to come into your life so that you will learn to depend more on His power and not on your own resources. God uses problem people to encourage us to pray, trust the word, and depend on the Spirit for love and grace. Difficult people and difficult circumstances can be used by the Spirit to help us grow and become more like Christ. Sometimes you feel like quitting and running away, that is the worst thing you can do. It will never solve your problems or meet the needs in your heart. God won't let His servant run away.

It is possible to be in Christian service for reasons other than the glory of the Lord. Some people are involved in ministry only for their own personal gain. If our motives for serving are anything other than to glorify God, then what we do will only be religious activity. God is glorified when people see the Lord and not the servant. The spiritual knowledge of the mysteries of grace were to be openly declared and made manifest before men. The light of God's word was not given merely for the disciples own private use but for the public good of mankind. Our light must shine, by doing such good works that men may see our good works and praise our Father in heaven. The disciples were to be the light of God's word so that God's light may be seen in their good works. Good works is meant by the disciple's sincerity, faithfulness, integrity, courage, and diligence in preaching the gospel. Their strict regard for the truth, the honor of Christ, and the well being of souls were utmost important to them. In their lives and conversations, they had very great care and concern to recommend by their example the doctrine of grace. Their ultimate goal was to glorify their Father which is in heaven. God is glorified when people see the Master and not the servant. Our aim must be to glorify God. When you find yourself more concerned about your image than your character and your work you have stopped glorifying God. Whatever God calls us to do, we can do with His help, or otherwise, He would never have called us. God is faithful to His word, His covenant, and His promise. He has promised to sanctify, cleanse, and make blameless His people from all their sins, and to preserve them until they are safe in His kingdom and glory. The saints are faithful to God and His calling. God faithfully calls you into the fellowship of His Son and to His kingdom and glory. He does so not only externally by His word, but internally by His Spirit and grace. He will execute His promises. When God calls He justifies, glorifies, gives grace, make perfect, establish a right relationship, and strengthens you. In 1 Thessalonians 5:24, Paul talks about God's faithfulness, "*Faithful is He who calls you, and He also will bring it to pass*". The Lord who has called us will also bring us to His glory and no one will be lost. We should pray, and press onward to complete holiness. We should pray to God for His perfect work until we are presented faultless before the throne of His glory. In Paul's life he determined to answer the call God put on his life, how does the call of God look on your life?

If you serve only to earn a salary, you will never do your best as long as you think you are underpaid. If you serve to get recognition, you will start doing less when people do not show their appreciation. The only attitude and outlook you must have is "*I am serving the Lord Jesus Christ*". In John 21:22 Jesus tells Simon Peter to follow Him and don't worry about anyone else and not to serve to get recognition, "*Jesus said to him, if I wanted him to remain until I come, what is that to you? You follow me.*" Jesus' statement was that if John lived until Jesus' second coming it was none of Peter's concern. He needed to live his own life in faithfulness, not compare it with any other. When Jesus said "*if it is My will that he stay till I come back what is that to you*", He meant that if it was Jesus' will that John should live until His second coming what was that to Peter? It was no concern of his. The saints were to mind their own business in following Christ and not concern themselves in things that do not have anything to do with them. Christ is to be followed by His people as their leader and commander, as the shepherd of the flock, and as a guide in the way they shall walk. He is the light of the world and a pattern and example of the saints. He is their Lord and Master in the exercise of grace in humility, meekness, love, zeal, and patience. They are to give up their will to the will of God. They are to have respect to moral life and Godly conversation. Saints know to follow Christ it is honorable, safe, comfortable, pleasant, and ends in happiness here and in the hereafter. It is the will of Christ that His disciples should mind their own business and not be concerned about their future, or anybody else's future. There are many things we are to concern ourselves with; other people's affairs are not one of them. We must quietly work and mind our own business. If we concern ourselves to following Christ we shall not find time to meddle with that which does not concern us. If you are working for Christ alone, you won't be bothered by what other workers do or what God does for them. If you worry and concern yourself with what is happening in the other persons life you will be the looser. God still gives His best to those who serve Him. Serving isn't easy, but you make it more difficult for yourself if you worry about what the other person is doing instead of what the Lord Jesus Christ is doing in your walk and your service to Him. You can't please everybody so don't even try. Just live and work in such a way that your Master will be able to say, "*you are my beloved servant, in whom I am well pleased*". Do an assessment of the level of your personal giving to the Lord. I would much rather have Jesus Christ as my Master than anyone else. He loves me, He knows all about me, He made me, He knows the future, and He gives me the power I need to serve Him acceptably and fruitfully. The thousands of times a day when I fail He forgives me and helps me start over again. He never leaves me nor forsakes me, and He rewards me graciously, though I do not deserve it. Could you want a better Master than that?

 A few years ago, my husband and I went to an outdoor concert. There were so many people around the stage area and the concert area that we were not able to see the performers. I was only able to see a small corner of the stage. I looked up at my husband and asked him if we can go somewhere else and sit and listen to the music. So we left and sat in an open field in our chairs. We sat there listening to the music and enjoyed our favorite past time of people watching. I had a nice time with my husband that day. People watching are a popular past time among Christian workers, but it's a dangerous one. When you serve you should stop watching other Christians and passing judgment on what they do or what God does with them. If you keep your eyes of faith on Christ and seek to please Him alone, you won't have either the time or the desire to watch others. God is working on them just as He is working on you. Have you ever complained because God gave others a better deal than He gave you? Perhaps, the people don't seem to work as hard as you do, or maybe they haven't been in Christian service as long as you have. Yet, God bypassed you and rewarded them abundantly. Satan can use a thing like that to get a foothold in your life, make you bitter and create problems in your ministry and service. God created us to do His work the way He wants us to do it as in Ephesians 2:10 says, *"For we are His workmanship, created in Christ Jesus for good works, which God prepared beforehand, so that we would walk in."* Good works can not produce salvation, but are the result of God-empowered fruits and evidence of it. A believer's sanctification and good works are ordained before time began. For we are His workmanship, a new creature, the author of it is God, it is not man's work, nor of angels, but it is God's work. We are a new creature and a work of Almighty power and created in Christ Jesus. As soon as a man becomes a new creature, he is openly and visibly in Christ and he is fit and ready and in a capacity to perform good works, a new man formed in him is formed for righteousness. God has appointed good works to be done by His people and in His word He has declared what they are. It is His will not only that they should do them but continue to do them. Their entire life should be one continued series of good works. For we are His workmanship created in Christ Jesus for good works, which God prepared beforehand that we should walk in them. For good works is not a narrow phrase referring merely to specific acts of so called Christian service. It refers to the whole life. He has foreordained the works of the man He is making. He has been ahead of me preparing the place to which I am coming, manipulating all the resources of the universe in order that the work I do may be a part of His whole great and gracious work. God must have a purpose for us all. Obedience to the will of God gives you wings not chains, you are never freer than when you fulfill the plan God has for your life. Failures in you do not stop God from accomplishing His will in your life.

We are to be people of our word. What we say we should do. We shall do everything in our power to accomplish what we promised. We shall not be people who change our minds, and break our words. God never changes His mind and therefore never recalls His promise. In the scriptures when Jesus is said to repent, it does not mean He changed His mind; but only changed His way. If the Lord sees that we trust in His mercy, and accept His salvation, that we indulge no secret lust, and continue not in rebellion, but strive to serve and glorify Him, we can be sure that He looks upon us as that we are accepted in Christ, and that our sins are all pardoned. How wonderful is the grace of God! How wonderful is His redeeming love! How wonderful is His forgiving mercy, and of the new creating spirit! Even though God's counsel still stands, let us continue earnest in prayer that we shall be examples of God's rock solid, unchanging ways. In Numbers 23:19, the scriptures say that, "*God is not a man that He should lie, nor a son of man, that He should repent, has He said, and will He not do it? Or has He spoken and will He not make it good*"? In comparison to the unreliability of man, God is reliable, solid, sure and unchanging. HE does not change therefore His words always come to pass. Man is a creature consisting of a body of flesh and blood, of a soul, and a created and finite spirit. God, though He has a body of flesh and blood, ascribed to Him, He is eternal, immense, and infinite. God is not like a man, who goes astray from the womb speaking lies. God is true, and every man is a liar. He is God and He can not lie. His promises and counsels are faithful and true. The scriptures are inspired by Him and are so very true. The prophecies of God are accomplished in awesome ways. He prophesied and promised, that we shall be happy, that He would be true and faithful to us. There is no way, by any means whatsoever, to make Him false and unfaithful to His word. Repentance is found in men, who repent of what they have done, or change their minds as to what they intended to do. Nothing of this kind is attributed to God. He never changes His mind, alters His counsels, changes His purposes, and modifies His decrees. He never varies in His affections to His people, or makes void His choice or covenant with them. His calling of us by His grace and His gifts of grace bestowed upon us, are without repentance. There was no reason to hope or believe that God would change His purpose or promise in respect to our outward happiness and enjoyment. Has He said, and shall He not do it, or has He spoken and shall He not make it good, whether it be with regard to things temporal, spiritual, or eternal, for there is no variableness nor shadow of turning in His mind. He never forgets His word, He foresees all events, He is able to perform, and is true and faithful and therefore whatever is gone out of His lips will never be altered, but will be most certainly fulfilled. We should use this description of Jesus Christ as an example as to how we shall live, and walk.

Those of us, who know God, know Gods ways, know Gods word, and recognize His voice shall not be fearful. We shall have strength and courage to rely on the almighty powerful God. We should be strong in the Lord and in the power of His might trusting and relying on Him. We should take heart and be of good courage. The Lord God goes with us, He will not fail us or forsake us, and He will not fail to fulfill His promises to us. He will not leave us until He had given us complete victory over our fears. Moses encourages the people of Israel, and also encourages us about overcoming our fears in Deuteronomy 31:6-8, "*Be strong and courageous do not be afraid and tremble at them for the Lord your God is the one who goes with you He will not fail you or forsake you. Then Moses called to Joshua and said to him in the sight of all Israel, be strong and courageous for you shall go with this people into the land which the Lord has sworn to their fathers to give them and you shall give it to them as an inheritance. The Lord is the one who goes ahead of you; He will be with you. He will not fail you or forsake you, do not fear or be dismayed*". Moses addressed Joshua in this exhortation in front of all Israel to encourage all of them and also all of us that God will be with us at all times. The foolishness and stupidity of Israel would be seen in the fact that they would rebel against God who as a Father had brought them forth and formed them into a nation. This idea of God as Father of the nation is emphasized in the Old Testament, while the idea of God as Father of individual believers is developed in the New Testament. When God said through Moses remember the days of old, He was reminding them to reflect on their past history and to inquire about the lessons that they had already learned and are to be learned in time. It is the same with us, we are to reflect on our past and how God rescued us from our past, and that should encourage us to believe that He will be faithful in the future. The Most High is a title for God emphasized His sovereignty and authority over our past, present and future. Fear not nor be afraid, is a promise to every true believer in the Lord. Be strong and of good courage, is said to the people of God. The word of the Lord goes before us, to guide and direct us, to assist and strengthen us, to protect and defend us, to give success and victory over fear. He will not fail or forsake us. He will not fail to give us faithful and true counsel and direction. He will give us strength and fill us with courage and deliver us from fear. Fear not neither be dismayed, at any difficulties that might lie in the way of finishing so great an undertaking since the Lord will be with us. We are encouraged by faith and hope of Gods constant presence with us. He will never fail us, nor forsake us. Those shall do well, who have God with them, ought to be of good courage. We shall do victoriously if we resist the devil he will flee from us.

Most Christian workers are prone to think either more highly of themselves than they should or less highly than they ought. If we think too highly of ourselves we will get proud and start pushing our way into what we think is a more important place. Pride is a natural element of our being, even though it is still sin. We need to be cautious of it and we need to arm against it. In Proverbs 29:23 it talks about pride, "*A man's pride will bring him low, but a humble spirit will obtain honor*". If we think less highly, we will too easily get discouraged and want to quit. When we get discouraged and want to quit, the same attitudes and feelings we had in previous ministries that we helped in of not being appreciated, will creep up, and you will want to quit that ministry also. Then pretty soon you will go from one ministry to another to another until you run out of ministries. Then you will start to look for a new church. Both attitudes of not thinking highly enough of you and thinking too highly of yourself are wrong. There has to be an equal balance. When we have the equal balance it helps when we receive our assignment from God. Each assignment from God prepares us for the next assignment. God's servants must never use their assignments as temporary stepping stones for something greater. In the spiritual body, some assignments are fitted for one type of person and that person fits well into that assignment from God and others for another sort of assignment that they fit well into. When it comes to moving His servants, God's plan is never wrong, and His timing is never off. Sometimes He moves us to a bigger place, but He may move us to a smaller place that we are suppose to make bigger. He may put us in a situation for which we feel totally unprepared and in which we are not at all comfortable. So much the better, He is giving us room to grow. We are to do all the good we can, to one another, and for the common good. There is no place in the Lord's work for people who are so anxious to climb the ladder of success and get to the top that they forget that exaltation comes neither from the east nor from the west nor from the south, but God is the judge. He puts down one, and exalts another. But as we must not be so proud of our talents and abilities, that we are not humble any longer and we become lazy in being available to others. We must not think of ourselves so low as to say I am nothing, therefore I will sit still and do nothing that does not bring glory to Christ. We shall think that we are nothing in me and therefore I will be available to the utmost God in the strength of the grace of Christ. Whatever our gifts or situations may be let us try to make ourselves available in a humble, diligent, cheerful way and in simplicity not seeking our own credit but the good of many for this world and that which is to come. Psalms 75: 6-7 talks about this promotion from God, "*For not from the east, nor from the west, nor from the desert comes exaltation, but God is the judge; He puts down one and exalts another*". All the saints make up one body in Christ, who is the head of the body, and is the center of their unity. God is the one that raises men to high places and sets them there. Only through God, kings reign, they have their crowns, scepters, thrones and kingdoms, there is no power but what is of God. God distributes riches and honor at His will, and He can take them away when He pleases. There is a day coming when the Lord alone shall be exalted! God is omniscient He knows all persons and things; He searches and knows the hearts of all people. He will bring every secret thing into judgment. He will bring to light the hidden things of darkness and makes manifest the secret things of the heart. God is omnipotent, able to do all things, raise the dead, call to judgment, bring all before Him, pass the sentence, and execute the judgment. God is omnipresent; there is no fleeing from Him, no escaping his righteous judgment. God's judgments are holy, just, and true. God will render to every man according to his works. He will puts one down and sets up another, He humbles or brings low, the ones who are proud, haughty and arrogant, and He exalts the one who is lowly and humble. He removes kings and sets up kings, puts down the mighty from their seats, and exalts the other who is humble. Those He makes humble by His grace He raises unto high positions, to be kings and priests, and to sit among princes and to inherit a throne of glory. Serving the Lord Jesus Christ is the greatest work in the world. No matter how difficult the work or how many times we feel like quitting we can keep going and growing in the way we serve, the way God tells us to in His word.

A Christian should not seek their own honor, applause, or to have their own way. They should honor Christ, the good of others, and the peace of the church. Servant of God is not prideful, contentious, or haughty. When confronted with a difficult situation, a servant of God with an outstanding attitude makes the best of it, while he gets the worst of it. The future not only looks bright when the attitude is right but also the present is much more enjoyable also. Servants of God do not have the 7deadly sins – pride, covetousness, lust, envy, anger, gluttony, and sloth. These are all the matters of attitude, inner spirit, and motives. A poor attitude will take us places we do not want to go. A good attitude puts you in the place of greatest potential. People don't care how much you know, until they know how much you care. Belief is inward conviction, faith is outward action. When you know your purpose in life and are growing to reach your maximum potential, you're well on your way to being a success. But there is one more essential part of the success journey, helping others. With out that aspect, the journey can be a lonely and shallow experience. If you are like most people, helping others is something you can do right where you are at. Success in life has nothing to do with what you gain in life or accomplish for yourself, it is what you do for others. It is when we regard one another as more important than ourselves. Christ's servant lives by what Philippians 2:3-7 says, "*Do nothing from selfishness or empty conceit but with humility in mind, regard one another as more important than yourselves. Do not merely look out for your own personal interests, but also for the interest of others. Have this attitude in yourselves which was also in Christ Jesus who although He existed in the form of God did not regard equality with God a thing to be grasped but emptied Himself taking the form of a bond servant and being made in the likeness of men*". This speaks of the pride that prompts people to push for their own way. Empty conceit or empty glory refers to the pursuit of personal glory which is the motivation for selfish ambition. Nothing can be more contrary to the Spirit of the Gospel than the conduct of contentious persons not having any regard to reason or truth, or yielding to the infirmities of the weak. An example of this is when Paul talks about Diotrephes in 3 John 1:9, "*I wrote to the church, but Diotrephes, who loves to be first, will have nothing to do with us*". Such persons and conduct are very injurious to the comfort and harmony of the saints. Humility of mind is a term which means to be humble. Regard one another as more important than yourselves is a basic definition of true humility. Christ is the ultimate example of selfless humility. Christ has always encompassed this crucial characteristic. When Paul says in lowliness of mind, let each one of us esteem the other better than ourselves, he is talking about the things of grace, spiritual enlightenment, knowledge and judgment. This is in regard to spiritual things and spiritual gifts. He should consider his own gifts as a gift of God, and make use of it for God's glory. He should not be prideful or boastful in his gifts. He should not admire them or lift them up above other person's gifts.

Christ followers do not judge or criticize one another. A fellow believer in Christ is your brother or sister. Romans speak of this in, Romans 14:10-12 from the Message Bible, "*So where does that leave you when you criticize a brother? And where does that leave you when you condescend to a sister? I'd say it leaves you looking pretty silly – or worse. Eventually we are all going to end up kneeling side by side in the place of judgment facing God. Your critical and condescending ways aren't going to improve your position there one bit. Read it for yourselves in scripture, "as I live and breath, God says, every knee will bow before me, every tongue will tell the honest truth, that I and only I am God". So tend to your knitting, you've got your hands full just taking care of your own life before God*" I like that, "tend to your knitting", in other words keep doing what you are doing for Christ! Every believer will give an account of himself and the Lord will judge the decisions made, including those concerning issues of conscience. As in 2 Corinthians 5:10, "*for we must all appear before the judgment seat of Christ, that each one may receive what is due him for the things done while in the body, whether good or bad*". Followers of Christ should not judge or despise one another they have one Master and all are brethren, we will all stand before the judgment seat of God. In Matthew 16:27, the Amplified bible reads the judgment as, "*For the Son of man is going to come in the glory (majesty, splendor) of His Father with His angels and then He will render account and reward every man in accordance with what he has done*". God being omniscient, and omnipotent, shall appear in His glory. Jesus Christ is the Messiah, and a just God and Savior and encourages all His children to look to Him for salvation. Jesus is sitting on His throne of glory, He is Lord of all, and He is the true and just judge who sits on His judgment seat. All the saints shall stand before God, bow unto Him, own Him as their Lord and is judged by Him. The Lord is the final judge of our service. He set us free from the fear of people and the desire to please them at the expense of pleasing God. We can't please everybody, nor should we try. God is easier to please than some people. He knows us intimately, He loves us perfectly, and therefore He can evaluate our work accurately. Anyone who tries to serve the Lord will be criticized by both friends and enemies, and lets admit it we probably do our own share of criticizing others. The bible warns us against criticizing and judging in 1 Corinthians 4:5,"*Therefore do not go on passing judgment before the time but wait until the Lord comes who both will bring to light the things hidden in the darkness and disclose the motives of men's hearts and then each man's praise will come to him from God.*" Therefore judge nothing. This is said to prevent ill-considered and impulsive judgment. Be slow in judgment, not hasty to pass sentence, it is best to leave things to the great day when we give an account so that we will not condemn one another. Judge nothing until the Lord comes, who at the fixed time will certainly come to judge and that suddenly, in an hour no man knows of, will bring to light the hidden things of darkness, those hidden things of dishonesty, corruption, depravity, perversion, and the unhealthy vile things. These are not for the glory of God and the good of men. These are nothing but filth. Forget yourselves long enough to lend a helping hand. Think of you the way Christ thought of Himself. He had equal status with God but didn't think so much of Himself that He had to cling to advantages of that status no matter what. When the time came, He set aside the privileges of deity and took on the status of a slave, became human! Having become human He stayed human! Every man shall praise of God by their words and actions, to which it will be said, "well done good and faithful servant, enter into the joy of the Lord". He who aims to please men would not prove himself a faithful servant of Christ. It should be our comfort that men are not our final judge. There is a day coming that will bring men's secret sins into open and discover the secrets of the hearts. Then every slanderer believer will be justified and every faithful servant approved and rewarded. The word of God is the best rule by which to judge men. Pride commonly is at the bottom of quarrels, self – conceit contributes to the pride to produce undue self-esteem. All are instruments, employed by God with various talents and abilities. Every Christian strong or weak whatever may be his gifts, talents and abilities shall give an account of himself to God, for He will be the judge. All shall stand before God and give an account of himself and no one else, to God of all his thoughts, words, and deeds, of his time and talents, of all his gifts of nature, providence and grace, and how they have been exercised for the glory of God.

As servants we should not be rude, arrogant, or disobedient. The duty of a servant is summed up in one word, obedience. The servant of old ancient times was generally slaves. Slaves in both Greek and Roman culture had no rights legally and were treated as commodities. There was much abuse and seldom good treatment of slaves. The apostles taught the servants and masters how a servant should act, and how a master should act, and what the difference is in their duties till slavery was taken out of Christianity. As Paul explains in Ephesians 6:5-8,"*Slaves be obedient to those who are your masters according to the flesh, with fear and trembling in the sincerity of your hearts as to Christ, not by way of eye service as man pleasers but as slaves of Christ, doing the will of God from the heart. With good will rendered service as to the Lord and not to men knowing that whatever good thing each one does this he will receive back from the Lord whether slave or free."* Paul's admonishment applies equally well to all employees. The term, obedient refers to continued, uninterrupted, submission to ones earthly master or employer. Fear and trembling does not refer to freight but respect for their authority. Even if an employer does not deserve respect in his own right, it should still be given to him with genuine sincerity as if one was serving Christ, Himself. To serve ones employer well is to serve Christ well. Eye service is working well only when being watched by the boss. Man pleasers is working only to promote ones welfare rather than to honor the employer and the Lord whose servants we really are. Someone who is a man pleaser does pretend to do great work when the master is watching; when the master is not watching he slacks off. He does this in order to get his masters affections, and then neglect his masters business when his master is absent. They ought to attend to his service in his absence as well as in his presence and so seek to please him. Depending on our attitude and actions God will give us credit and will reward us according to our work. No good thing done for His glory will go unrewarded. A Christian who is being a diligent, trustworthy, honest servant to their worldly master is doing the will of God from their heart meaning not in a religious way. They are yielding cheerfully and heartily to the obedience of their own masters, with good will, not grudgingly, or with an ill will. They do not look at is as if they are forced to do it, but they have a ready mind and a cheerful spirit, taking delight in their work and looking at it as a pleasure to serve their master. They do it because it is the will of the Lord and is well pleasing in His sight. Knowing that whatsoever good thing any man does, according to the will of God, from right principles in his heart and with a view of Gods glory he shall receive a reward from the Lord, whether he is bond or free, a bondman or a free man, a master or a servant. God will reward even the filthiest work done from the sense of duty and with a view to glorify Him. Masters should act in the same manner, being just to servants, as you expect they should be to you. Show them good-will and concern and be careful to approve yourselves to God. Do not be cruel, brutal, domineering, or overbearing. You have a Master to obey and the both of you are but fellow servants to Jesus Christ. If masters and servants would consider their duties to God, and the account they must shortly give to Him, they would be more mindful of their duty to each other, and thus families would be more orderly and happy.

If Christianity is truth it should make a difference in the church and in the home that flows out into the marketplace. Part of walking worthily of our calling therefore is learning to view our jobs not merely as an economic necessity or an avenue of advancement, but a service to Christ. The apostle Paul analyzes our labor in those terms. If we are to conceive of our jobs as service to Christ, Paul teaches us the meaning of service. The first thing to notice is that this passage is addressed to slaves. We must not get distracted by the issue of slavery for that is not the main point of this passage but we should pause on it. People wonder why a New Testament church in which there was neither bond nor free in Christ did not attack such a cruel institution. Rather, Paul simply accepts it and tells people how to live in it. The fact is that that New Testament method of dealing with such social issues was not to attack them directly but to deal with them indirectly through its moral influence on individuals. Post-modern people tend to assume that we are defined by our social position, and that therefore the way to improve our lots is by changing the social structure that defines us. Our motive for service should be to please God and that Christ will reward you. In the last days Christ will say "well done good and faithful servant" and we will know that we have pleased Him. Christ does receive our service (or lack thereof) as if done personally for Him. We must train ourselves to look past ourselves and see instead the One who humbled Himself as a servant, who girded Himself with a towel and washed the disciples feet, who said, "forgive them for they know not what they do", even as He was being tortured to death for us. If God asked you to be a servant how would you approach it? I would hope with sincere respect, diligence, real enthusiasm, and even love, no doubt?

Chapter 4

What is a bond servant?

Contrary to popular belief a bond servant is not one of the ladies in any of the James Bond movies. It is not a person who chases after someone who jumped bail, someone who did not show up for court, you will not find a television show called "*dog the bond servant*". Bond Servant is a servant who does work of any kind for his master. In the New Testament a servant could be released from service after six years, they would be able to go their own way, but a bond servant is someone who decided they didn't want to go on their own after six years, that they actually liked being with their master and so they stayed indefinitely. In the New Testament the word Doulos is frequently used to designate a master's slave or a servant bound to a master. The term points to a relationship of absolute dependence in which a servant is dependent on the master. The servant can exercise no will or initiative on his or her own.

Doulos is applied to several Old Testament persons, such as Moses, and the prophets. Paul and James both refer to themselves as servants of God. Paul also calls himself a servant of Christ.

Bond slave, which is also another name for a bond servant, was the lowest of the low. It was the lowest form of animal life. You had no will of your own. You were owned by your master and he could do with you whatever he or she pleased. You were cattle in his ownership, a piece of property, a human tool.

Bond servant appears only once in the King James Version of the Holy Bible in Leviticus 25:39 where it is translates EBHEDH – a slave," *thou shall not cause him to render the service of a bond servant*" or slave. The Revised Version frequently uses bondservant (doulos) instead of the word servant that is used in the King James Version

The law of the servant guaranteed freedom after a specific period of six years unless the servant himself elected permanent servitude but this would be service not in a context of abuse but of love. Any permanent involuntary servitude of a Hebrew servant to a Hebrew master was obviously undesirable for Israelite society and was unknown in Israel. This is explained in Deuteronomy 15:12-17, "*If your kinsman, a Hebrew man or woman, is sold to you, then he shall serve you six years, but in the seventh year you shall set him free. When you set him free you shall not sent him away empty handed. You shall furnish him liberally from your flock and from your threshing floor and from your wine vat, you shall give him as the Lord your God has blessed you. You shall remember that you were a slave in the land of Egypt, and the Lord your God redeemed you; therefore I command you this day, it shall come about if he says to you, "I will not go out from you", because he loves you and your household, since he fares well with you, then you shall take an awl, and pierce it through his ear into the door, and he shall be your servant forever. Also you shall do likewise to your maidservant".* Provision was also made to ensure the proper treatment of female servants who could not deliberately be left destitute. The reason for the sale would be default, an alternative repayment of a debt, and a period of servitude would substitute for the repayment. If the Hebrew fell on hard times or owed a debt to someone and couldn't pay, the Hebrew would go to a property owner and offer himself to the property owner for a time. A Hebrew might decide to sell himself to someone more prosperous in exchange for funds or goods to pay off a debt or solve a financial hardship. This self imposed slavery from a Hebrew would serve his master six years, with freedom being declared in the seventh year. When a slave has completed his time of service his former owner was to make ample provision for him so that he would not begin his state of new freedom destitute. The master was to put some small stock into their servant's hands when sent out, when they had not received any wages in the six years he was serving his master. The Israelites, who were formerly enslaved in Egypt, were to treat their own slaves as God treated them while they were in slavery. In certain circumstances, a slave might prefer to remain with the family after the required six years of servitude. The treatment that the slave received might make him want to live with his master permanently. The love he received might encourage him to come to the master and say I don't want to leave. When a slave decides he does not want to leave. He has to be marked for life. If the servant should not want to go out of the masters house, nor quit his service, his master or his family, but chooses rather to stay with them than to have his liberty. If the servant saw that he is well used by the master, and the servants wants for nothing, and enjoys peace and quietness, and has everything to make him happy and he is well content and highly pleased. He would then be marked with a hole in his ear, by using a spike tool called an awl then he would become a servant forever. The master was to take an awl and push it through the ear lobe to signify a life long commitment. The slave must be bored by the master not his son or his messenger. An awl is a pointed instrument for piercing small holes in leather, and wood. The awl is not to be put through the ear of the servant at the master's house, but at a judicial court, of which he is to declare his desire to continue with his master. Boring through the ear into the doorpost represents a strict and close obedience of a servant to his master and how he is and ought to be fully sold out to the service of his master as long as he shall live. They did this because without blood there is no blood covenant. After the six years if the servant wanted to leave and he was single or unmarried when he entered his master's service he should go out the way he came in, If he had a wife before he started his servitude, she shall leave with him. If his master gave him a wife, she is not to go out with him. She being the master's slave and bought with his money he had the right onto her, and to the children belonging to her. This is an emblem of the cheerful obedience of the people of Christ to him their master. They have a love that flow from them to Him. Their love for God is deeper and stronger than all persons and things. They love God with all their heart and soul. They pay special attention to His ordinance, and His truth. They fare well, having plenty of spiritual blessings and provisions. They are well clothed with the righteousness of Christ, in who is all their delight. Their presence is in their Lord and Master. We are to remember that we are debtors to Divine Justice and have nothing to pay with; we are slaves, poor, and perishing. The Lord Jesus Christ, became poor, shed His blood has made a full and free provision for the payment of our debts, the ransom for our souls, and supplies all of our wants and needs. When the gospel is clearly preached they will triumph over the selfishness of the heart and over the unkindness of the world, doing away the excuses that rise from unbelief, distrust, and covetousness. Our obedience to God springs from our love to Him and to His cause and interest.

Whoever gives themselves up to sin, sells themselves to work wickedness, makes sin their trade, business, and employment, who take delight and pleasure in it, and these are the servants of corruption. Sin has dominion over them, and they obey it they are a bond servant, a slave of it; they are in bondage to that sin, if grace does not step in and prevent this from happening. This is discussed in Romans 6:16, *"Do you not know that when you present yourselves to someone as slaves for obedience you are slaves of the one whom you obey, either of sin resulting in death or of obedience resulting in righteousness."*, also in 2 Peter 2:19,*"promising them freedom while they themselves are slaves of corruption for by what a man is over come by this he is enslaved"*, and in John 8:34-35,*"Jesus answered them, truly; truly I say to you everyone who commits a sin is a slave of sin. The slave does not remain in the house forever."* The kind of slavery that Jesus had in mind was not physical slavery but slavery to sin. The idea of "commits sin" means to practice sin habitually. The ultimate bondage is not political or economical enslavement but spiritual bondage to sin and rebellion against God. Jesus is not talking about someone that commits one single act of sin, as Noah, Lot, David, Peter, and others did. They were not servants of sin or ones who do not sin through ignorance, weakness of the flesh and the power of temptation. They do not commit sin in the spirit of lusting, though they are not without sin, they live without it in thought, word, or deed. They fall into it but they do not continue or live in it. They rise up out of it, through the grace of God, and by true repentance. They are not to be regarded as servants of sin. Through our Lords words many are convinced, and encouraged to believe in His teaching, rely on His promises, and obey His commands. They are to flee all temptation of evil. If they do this, they would be His disciples, and by the teaching of His word and spirit they would learn where their hope and strength lay. Jesus plainly reminded them, that the man, who practiced any sin, was, in fact, a slave to that sin. Christ in the gospel offers us freedom, and those whom Christ makes free are free indeed. But often we see persons disputing about liberty of every kind, while they are slaves to some sinful lust. No bondage is as terrible as that of sin, from which Christ frees the believer. Those who are not slaves, but free in the social sense, are in the spiritual sense made slaves of Christ in salvation. Do not be troubled at all of this, or uneasy with it, do not be anxious. Bear the yoke patiently. Teach people how to behave. Show people how to have an internal, special, powerful, saving call of the grace of GOD. Bring people out of darkness into the Light, out of bondage into liberty, from their sinful companions to the company and society of Christ. Bring people from their own self-righteousness, to the grace and righteousness of Christ and out of the world into the kingdom and glory of Christ. We are united in Christ, and called into fellowship and communion with Him. The Lords servants are free from sin, not from falling into sin, but free from the bondage of living in sin. They are free from sins guilt and damning power. He is free from Satan, not from his temptations and insults but from his dominion and captivity. He is ransomed from sin by the redemption of Christ. Sin has no power in Christ's servant after conversion. It has no influence over him, like it had before. He is so safe and secure in Christ, that he can never be destroyed by sin. In a short time Satan will be bruised under his feet. He is free to all the privileges and immunities of the house of God. He is a very happy man, he has peace with God, the presence of Christ, joy in the Holy Spirit, fellowship with the saints, and a well grounded hope of glory, he is not only called to the liberty of grace, which he enjoys, but will be delivered into his glorious liberty of the children of God; and therefore has no reason to be uneasy with his civil servitude.

How does the call of God look on our lives? Are we a bond servant of Jesus Christ? Are we living a changed life? Don't take the grace of God for granted! There must be a change! That change has to come from the Holy Spirit! Are you willing to say whatever, wherever, whenever, however, anytime, anyplace, anything, use me Lord, I am here?!! What is it you want me to do?

The apostles went forth from Jerusalem, and preached everywhere, not only in Judea, and in the neighboring countries, but all over the world. The Lord worked with them, making their ministry useful for the conviction and the conversion of large multitudes of soon to be followers of Jesus Christ. They formed and settled an abundance of Gospel churches. All of this was done by the power and grace of Christ without whom they could do nothing, and confirming the word with signs, as it says in Mark 16:20, "*And they went out and preached everywhere, while the Lord worked with them and confirmed the word by the signs that followed.*" Though the doctrine they preached was spiritual and heavenly and directly in opposition to the spirit and temper of the world, it met with much opposition, and was devoid of all worldly supports. After a few years Gods message went forth unto the ends of the earth. Christ's ministers now do not need to work miracles to prove their message; the scriptures are proved to be Divine origin. Those who reject or neglect the gospel of Christ have no excuse. The effects of the gospel when faithfully preached and truly believed change the characters of mankind is proof, a miraculous proof, that the gospel is the power of God unto salvation, to all who believe. As in Acts 4:4, "*but many of those who had heard the message believed and the number of the men came to be about five thousand.*" The doctrine of the gospel, preached by Peter and John, though they had the opposition of the priest, the captain of the temple, and the Sadducees, they could not stop the gospel of our Lord and Savior Jesus Christ spreading around the world and was glorified. There were so many people converted at this time. This number does not include the three thousand that were converted under the first sermon but regards those who now became true believers and were added to the church so that there where now eight thousands persons, a great increase indeed! They are now willing people. As described in Acts 2:41, "*so then those who had received His word were baptized and that day there were added about three thousand souls.*" That promise and prophecy had a remarkable accomplishment on these converts. Not all that heard the sermon of Peters received his doctrine in this manner only some. The ones that did readily received it which shows the distinguishing grace of God in this instance, as soon as they received the word they were comforted by it.

Chapter 5

Jesus Christ, the ultimate example of bond servant!

Jesus Christ, the ultimate example of bond servant! He came to seek and to save that which was lost. He came to reconcile man back to God. Even as a great teacher with many followers, He was still prepared to take off His outer garment and to wash His closest disciples' feet, which was a shock to them all. Jesus of course was giving them a lesson in humility. The lesson for us from his example, of course, is that we, like Jesus Christ, are to be humble as He was humble, and He was God in the flesh. How much more so should we be humble? What God wants from us is humility, not so much our qualifications, not so much what we've done. God does not want our resume, God can't work with a resume; what He wants is our humility. God is telling us, "I want you; I don't want your resume". When you compare your or anyone else resume with God's resume, then you realize you've got plenty of cause for humility. Jesus was patient with His disciples when He washed the feet. We all run out of patience sometimes. Parents run out of patience with their children; probably children run out of patience with their parents; teachers run out of patience with their students. What's interesting in the gospels is that Jesus Christ never seemed to run out of patience. He was constantly teaching and trying to enlighten His group of people who didn't yet even have the ability to learn patience and receive the Spirit of God yet. In Matthew 17:14-19 is a story of Jesus' patience and healing," *When they came to the crowd, a man came up to Jesus, falling on his knees before Him saying, "Lord have mercy on my son, for he is a lunatic and is very ill, for he often falls into the fire and often into the water. I brought him to your disciples and they could not cure him", and Jesus answered and said, "You unbelieving and perverted generation how long shall I be with you? How long shall I put up with you? Bring him here to Me." And Jesus rebuked him and the demon came out of him, and the boy was cured at once. Then the disciples came to Jesus privately and said, "Why could we not drive it out?"* Now the time's running out; Jesus is going to be crucified, He is going to die, and He is going to be resurrected. Apparently He has already taught His disciples these truths, and He's dismayed; He's down; He's discouraged about it, but He doesn't run out of patience. He then, of course says, *"Bring him to Me,"* and He casts out the demon. The disciples turn to God and they say," *Why couldn't we cast it out?"* And Jesus takes that as an opportunity to teach them. It's amazing how patient He was with them. They should have understood; He hoped they would understand, but often they didn't. He was patient right up until the end. Patience is part of Jesus' interaction with them. Another example that He gives us is that Jesus corrected His disciples. The relationship between Christ and His disciples was not all candy bars and sweetness. He loved them; He served them; He cared for them, but there were times when He corrected them. He drew their attention to the areas where they needed to change. He admonished them. The relationship between Christ and His disciples is an interesting study. It was a strong enough relationship that He could encourage them; He could express disappointment with them; He could reprimand and correct them. An example of this is in Mark 10:13-16,"*And they were bringing children to Him so that He might touch them, but the disciples rebuked them. But when Jesus saw this, He was indignant and said to them, "Permit the children to come to Me; do not hinder them; for the kingdom of God belongs to such as these. Truly I say to you, whoever does not receive the kingdom of God like a child will not enter it at all." And He took them in His arms and began blessing them, laying His hands on them.*" So Jesus gives us an example in this area as well. When we serve people, we have to be patient as well. When we serve people, there are times to be direct. There are times when it's not appropriate to give a candy bar; sometimes we have to admonish and correct as Jesus Christ did, because they didn't understand. Something else to keep in mind in regards to the practical aspects of service, is that service sometimes goes unrecognized. There are times when people do things in the church, and nobody knows anything about it. People will serve; people will help in certain ways and not receive any recognition for their service. Service can sometimes be covert; service can sometimes be completely anonymous, as Matthew speaks about in Matthew 6:1-4,"*Beware of practicing your righteousness before men to be noticed by them; otherwise you have no reward with your Father who is in heaven. So when you give to the poor, do not sound a trumpet before you, as the hypocrites do in the synagogues and in the streets, so that they may be honored by men. Truly I say to you, they have their reward in full. But when you give to the poor, do not let your left hand know what your right hand is doing, so that your giving will be in secret and your Father who sees what is done in secret will reward you.*" Sometimes God will hold back recognition. There are times in our lives as Christians, when, if we desire recognition, God may deliberately withhold it, we have to serve anyway. Sometimes God realizes that what some people want more than anything else is for people to notice them, or what they do. You know, you go around doing something and you feel, well, nobody's noticing. Nobody knows, the important people don't know what I'm doing. Don't they notice? Be careful with that kind of attitude. If it seems like no one is noticing someone is, God! Sometimes God withholds the recognition and gives a little bit of publicity at the appropriate time. Another point in Jesus Christ's work as a servant is that he never deviated from His mission. Jesus Christ was very goal oriented. Let's take notice of Christ's example and teaching. On the night of the final Passover, the disciples were arguing over who was the greatest. Notice Luke's account of the incident in Luke 22:24-27, "*Also a dispute arose among them as to which of them was considered to be greatest. Jesus said to them, 'The kings of the Gentiles lord it over them; and those who exercise authority over them call themselves Benefactors. But you are not to be like that. Instead, the greatest among you should be like the youngest, and the one who rules like the one who serves. For who is greater, the one who is at the table or the one who serves? Is it not the one who is at the table? But I am among you as one who serves'*". Not only did Jesus teach the principle of how to be great, but also He lived it. This may be one reason why Christ instituted the foot washing service, to model and to teach His disciples the proper approach to leadership. He acknowledged that He was their Lord and teacher. Yet He was willing to wash their feet, the job of a lowly servant. In John 13:15 Christ said, "*I have given you an example, that you should do as I have done to you.*" Christ expects us to follow His example in our relationships with one another. We are to be servants and to serve one another with humility. Jesus Christ daily lived a charitable servant way of life. His whole life was dedicated to serving others. He was a true servant. He constantly taught, encouraged, healed and visited during His ministry. He truly was the greatest example of a loving servant in the history of mankind. Christ had to teach them all a valuable lesson as Scriptures say in Matthew 20:25-28, "*But Jesus called them to Himself and said, 'You know that the rulers of the Gentiles lord it over them, and those who are great exercise authority over them. Yet it shall not be so among you; but whoever desires to become* great *among you, let him be your* servant. *And whoever desires to be first among you, let him be your slave-just as the Son of Man did not come to be served, but to serve, and to give His life a ransom for many*". Now what Jesus Christ does in this passage, of course, He takes the concept of greatness that the ancient Jewish people had , and He turns it. They had certain concepts about what greatness was; it was to become prestigious; it was to throw your weight around; it was to be in authority; and that included mistreating people at times. And Jesus said, "*No, in the Christian community in the church, if you want to be great, you accomplish that through service.*" He turns it on its head and He does the same for us today. If you think about the concepts of greatness in our society sometimes, you know, people think greatness is prestige, greatness is having lots of money; greatness is being on TV and being regarded as being one of the best looking people in the whole country. So Jesus makes this point that greatness in the Church of God is quite, quite different. Greatness in the Church of God is in contrast to greatness in the society back then and in our society. It's not prestige, it's sometimes not visible; greatness is quite different. Christ explained that there are two different approaches to leadership-the world's approach and the servant approach. The natural approach in this world is to use authority to lord it over others. Christ did not say that there are no positions of authority, but that authority and power is to be used to serve. We have been called to be kings and priests in the Kingdom of God. That means that we will serve humanity in the future. The greater the responsibility in the Kingdom, the greater will be the opportunity to serve. However, we won't be in the Kingdom unless we are learning to apply the mind of Christ in all of our relationships today. We will not automatically become servants in the Kingdom if we do not learn to be servants today. What about the future; what about Jesus Christ as a servant in the future? We see some amazing things in the scriptures that Jesus Christ will continue to serve when He comes back. He will be Lord of lords. He will be King of kings. He will be crowned and given power over the entire world, in charge of the entire earth, and we might think well, when he comes back as King of Kings, he'll be the King, he won't be the servant any longer. He won't be serving people because after all, he will have been glorified. There's a remarkable little detail here in Luke 12:37,"*Blessed are those slaves whom the Master will find on the alert when He comes; truly I say to you that He will gird Himself to serve and have them recline at the table and will come up and wait on them.*" Jesus Christ once again talking about servants. Now I don't know exactly how that's going to play out. I imagine Christ is referring to the wedding supper, but it says it very clearly that Jesus Christ will come and serve those who've been good servants. Hopefully, that's you and me if we're faithful, if we serve without that desire for recognition, if we continue to serve right up to the second coming of Jesus Christ or the end of our lives. But He's going to serve us. He's going to serve us probably at the table and at the wedding supper, I think that's what's referred to. Jesus Christ, you see was, is, and will be the eternal servant. The paradox is that when we try to become great God doesn't give greatness, when we serve, that's the way to greatness. It's the exact opposite of the world's system. Though Jesus Christ is worthy of all rights, privileges, and honors and could never be disqualified from the rights, privileges, and honors of His deity, His attitude were not to cling to those things or His heavenly position. Jesus humbled Himself and gave up His power as the Son of God and came to earth in human form; He was conceived by the Holy Spirit in the Virgin Mary's womb. He left His familiar surroundings of heaven, to come and identify with fallen man. He was willing to give them up for a season as Jesus explains in John 5:41,"I *did not receive glory from men*", also in John 6:15,"*So Jesus, perceiving that they were intending to come and take Him by force to make Him king, withdrew again to the mountain by Himself alone*". He emptied Himself of all the rights and privileges of his Kingship, as it explains in Philippians 2:3-11, "*do nothing from selfish or empty conceit but with humility of mind regard one another as more important than yourselves, do not merely look out for your own personal interests but also for the interest of others. Have this attitude in yourselves which was also in Christ Jesus, who although He existed in the form of God, did not regard equality with God a thing to be grasped, but emptied Himself taking the form of a bond-servant and being made in the likeness of men. Being found in appearance of a man, He humbled Himself by becoming obedient to the point of death, even death on a cross. For this reason also, God highly exalted Him and bestowed on Him the name which is above every name, so that at the name of Jesus, every knee will bow of those who are in heaven and on earth and under the earth, and that every tongue will confess that Jesus Christ is Lord to the glory of God the Father.*" The word "emptied" comes from the theological word kenosis. Which is the doctrine of Christ's self emptying of Himself in His incarnation. This was the self renunciation, not of emptying Himself of deity nor an exchange of deity for humanity. The *New International Version* of the Holy Scriptures explains verse 6 rather well,*" Who, being in very nature God, did not consider equality with God something to be grasp"*, also verse 7 says,*" but made Himself nothing",* the sense of this is that Jesus Christ, who was God, who was there with the Father, didn't hold on to it. He let it go, because that was part of the plan that God the Father and Jesus Christ had. The New English Bible says of the same scripture, "*For the divine nature was His from the first, yet He did not think to snatch at equality with God*", finally, The New Jerusalem Bible says, "*Who being in the form of God did not count equality with God something to be grasped.*" He didn't hold on to it; He let it go. He was God! He had it made, in a sense. He was there in heaven; He had the power of a spirit being and He gave it up, because He knew there was work to be done. Jesus did however, renounce or set aside his privileges in several areas:

1.) Heavenly glory
   a. While on earth He gave up the glory of the face-to-face relationship with God and the continuous outward display and personal enjoyment of that glory,
2.) Independent authority
   a. During His incarnation Christ completely submitted Himself to the will of the Father,
3.) Divine prerogative
   a. He set aside the voluntary display of His divine attributes and submitted Himself to the Spirit's direction,

4.) Eternal riches
    a. while on earth Christ was poor and owned very little,
5.) Favorable relationship with God
    a. He felt the Fathers wrath for human sin while on the cross.

When Paul says that Jesus took the form of a bond servant, Paul uses the Greek word "Form" which indicates exact essence as a true servant. When Jesus took on the form of a bond servant this was voluntary, it was not forced. He appeared as a bond servant in human nature, and was a servant to His Father, who chose, called, sent, upheld, and regarded Him as a prudent, diligent, and faithful servant. Man often looks at power and prestige but is unable to relate to the idea of servant hood. If we love Jesus then naturally we will want to obey Him as Jesus says in John 14:15,"*If you love Me you will keep My commandments*", also in John 14:24,"*He who does not love Me does not keep My words, and the word which you hear is not Mine, but the Father's who sent Me*". We know and realize that without Him, we can do nothing of eternal value, and our desire needs to be, to do the will of our heavenly Father, as Jesus speaks about in John 5:19,"*Therefore Jesus answered and was saying to them, truly, truly, I say to you the Son can do nothing of Himself, unless it is something He sees the Father doing, for whatever the Father does these things the Son also does in like manner*", also Jesus speaks about this in John 5:30,"*I can do nothing on My own Initiative. As I hear, I judge, and My judgment is just, because I do not seek My own will but the will of Him who sent Me*". Jesus was claiming that the judgment He exercised was because everything He did was dependent upon the Father's word and will. The common perception among people is to get to the top and to step on those who are beneath you. It's a dog eat dog world mentality; but this is not God's way. 'The first will be last and the last will be first.' Jesus, behaving in His most meek and humble manner, was also a servant to His people, and ministered to men, partly by preaching the gospel to them. As it speaks about in the Old Testament Scriptures in Isaiah 53:7,"*He was oppressed and He was afflicted, Yet He did not open His mouth; Like a lamb that is lead to slaughter, and like a sheep that is silent before it shearers, So He did not open His mouth.*" In the Old Testament Scripture book of Zachariah 9:9 it says," *Rejoice greatly O daughter of Zion! Shout in triumph, O daughter of Jerusalem, Behold, your king is coming to you, He is just and endowed with salvation, humble and mounted on a donkey, even on a colt, the foal of a donkey.*" The theme of Isaiah is servant hood as it applies to God's people. Isaiah has trouble answering this question, 'How can a sinful people become God's servants?' Israel was supposed to be a 'Light to the gentiles' as the Scriptures says in Genesis 12:1-3,"*Now the Lord said to Abram, "Go forth from your country, and from your relatives, and from your fathers house, to the land which I will show you; and I will make you a great nation, and I will bless you and make your name great; and so you shall be a blessing, and I will bless those who bless you and the one who curses you I will curse, and in you all the families of the earth will be blessed*". Often God's way does not appear logical; but being as He is God then He must know the best way and our goal must be to follow. Jesus trod the path of humility and servant hood and achieved the greatest act the world has ever seen. He lived for God's 'will to be done…here on earth as it is in heaven.' Jesus lived, and then died for sinful mankind upon the cruel agonizing cross of Calvary and after three days rose again, gloriously and triumphantly. In prophesying the coming of Jesus Christ, Isaiah reveals what will happen to Him and His servant life in Isaiah 42:1-4,"*Behold, My Servant, whom I uphold; My chosen one in whom My soul delights. I have put My Spirit upon Him; He will bring forth justice to the nations. He will not cry out or raise His voice, nor make His voice heard in the street. "A bruised reed He will not break and a dimly burning wick He will not extinguish; He will faithfully bring forth justice. "He will not be disheartened or crushed until He has established justice in the earth; and the coastlands will wait expectantly for His law*", also in Isaiah 49:1-6,"*Listen to me, O islands, and pay attention, you people from afar. The Lord called Me from the womb; from the body of my mother He named Me. He has made My mouth like a sharp sword and in the shadow of His hand He has concealed Me; and He has also made Me a select arrow, He has hidden Me in His quiver. He has said to Me, "You are My Servant, Israel, in whom I will show My glory." But I said, "I have toiled in vain, I have spend My strength for nothing and vanity; yet surely the justice due to Me is with the Lord, and My reward with My God." And now says the Lord, who formed Me from the womb to be His Servant, to bring Jacob back to Him, so that Israel might be gathered to Him (for I am honored in the sight of the Lord, and My God is My strength), He says, "It is too small a thing that you should be My Servant to raise up the tribes of Jacob and to restore the preserved ones of Israel; I will also make You a light of the nations so that My salvation may reach to the end of the earth*", also in Isaiah 50:4-9,"*The Lord God has given Me the tongue of disciples, that I may know how to sustain the weary one with a word. He awakens Me morning by morning, He awakens My ear to listen as a disciple. The Lord God has opened My ear; and I was not disobedient nor did I turn back. I gave My back to those who strike Me, and my cheeks to those who pluck out the beard; I did not cover My face from humiliation and spitting for the Lord God helps Me, therefore, I am not disgraced; therefore, I have set My face like flint, and I know that I will not be ashamed. He who vindicates Me is near; who will contend with Me? Let us stand up to each other; who has a case against Me? Let him draw near to Me. Behold, the Lord God helps Me; who is he who condemns Me? Behold, they will all wear out like a garment; the moth will eat them*". This is prophetic of Jesus Christ once again. He made up His mind; He was going to go through with the crucifixion. He knew how painful it was going to be; he knew how difficult it would be humanly speaking. Jesus Christ was determined to do what he had to go through with it, As Luke explains in Luke 9:51-52,"*When the days were approaching for His ascension, He was determined to go to Jerusalem; and He sent messengers on ahead of Him, and they went and entered a village of he Samaritans to make arrangements for Him.*" This is all part of God's plan, this was what Jesus had to do. Sometimes you wonder; how could He have gone through with it? How could He have hung on that tree, or the cross, or the stake, or whatever it was, and gone through with that terrible death? Part of what sustained Him was that He knew this was part of God's plan that He had to go through with it. He knew there was a group of people that would come after that in the Spirit that would be given to Him by God after his death and resurrection. It was all decided beforehand. The Lord Jesus Christ and God the Father decided that He was to be the one who would come. He was determined, and so the lesson for us as well is that we are to be determined. Now I know He arrived at the garden of Gethsemane, and He prayed that if it would be possible for the cup to pass from Him, but He understood, and it had been made clear throughout eternity that there was a plan, and he never deviated from His mission. This is an example for us as well. Jesus, the promised Messiah, arrived and He bridged the gap between fallen man and God, so that 'whoever calls upon the name of the Lord shall be saved. It was the early believers who were responsible to tell the world that we are 'Justified by faith' and the early servant disciples went forth in obedience to the great commission. They followed the example of Jesus, the first great servant. No one should be born into the life of servant hood - it is something that has to be agreed to, and worked toward - and the preparation is often done in obscurity. The best leaders are those who have learnt to serve others before they have come to prominence. Jesus had thirty years of training and preparation; Moses spent the best part of forty years on the backside of the desert before he was able to lead Israel into freedom. David the shepherd boy spent years with the flock before becoming King and even when Samuel had anointed him as a young man, he still looked after the sheep before being promoted to serve at the court of King Saul. Elisha served the prophet Elijah for twelve years before he was released with power and an intense anointing. Let's take a look at this application principle in our everyday life and in our family, marriage, church and job. As parents, we are in charge of our families. Are we also their servants? The most powerful way we influence and teach our children is by our example. From the time a child is born, parents generally spend the next 18 years, and sometimes more, feeding, clothing, providing shelter, educating, teaching and especially loving their children. Our approach must be one that is established upon love and dedicated to the growth and to the development of our families. In marriage, are we dedicated to serving one another? Many marriages fail because of selfishness, a lack of concern and neglect. Marriage gives us a wonderful opportunity to apply the principles of humility and love on a daily basis. Jesus Christ is the head of the Church. He is in charge. The Church is the bride of Christ. The bride submits to her husband and serves Him. Yet, we know that Jesus Christ also serves the Church. He is the head and constantly guides and gives direction to us. Through the Spirit of God He guides, inspires, teaches, helps, encourages, intervenes and leads us. We respond to Him because we know that He gave His life for us. Even though He is the head of the Church, both He and the Father serve the Church and always have our best interest at heart. We have all been placed in the Body as God sees fit, just like the Scriptures says in 1 Corinthians 12:18,"*But now God has placed the members, each one of them, in the body, just as He desired*". God has given each of us responsibilities, gifts, talents and abilities. Why? Not for selfish purposes, but for the overall good of the Body. Each part of our physical body serves the rest of the body. We are not placed in the Body for privilege, but for service. We have all been called to be servants. We use our gifts and talents as an opportunity to make a difference in the lives of others. We use whatever position God gives us, whether it would be a member, a minister or an administrator, to serve others out of deep concern and humility. This is an approach and attitude that God wants all of us to develop. We should not have the attitude that any kind of service is below us. Service is humble and service can also be lowly. A lot of opportunities, I think, in the church have been missed, because people have taken the wrong approach and said, "Oh that's below me. I don't want to do that because …it's below me, it's not for me to do." We shouldn't take the attitude - it's below me. Jesus Christ never took that attitude. He didn't say this is work that is below me. Let this mind or attitude be in us that was in Christ Jesus. Excellence can be attained only by the labor of a lifetime. Servant hood like many Christian principles such as sacrifice, self-control, commitment to God and full surrender may at first appear unappealing, and perhaps that is only natural at first sight. But if Jesus is not Lord of all, then He is not Lord at all! He has the power to work miracles, and heal diseases. Jesus had compassion on His chosen ones, and went around healing their sick. As Matthew talks about in Matthew 14:14,"*When He went ashore He saw a large crowd and felt compassion for them and healed their sick.*" Mark also talks about Jesus healing in Mark 1:41,"*Moved with compassion Jesus stretched out His hand and touched him and said to him "I am willing, be cleaned.*" Jesus cheerfully and diligently attended to His redemptive work. He was often prophesied of a servant in which several places He is called "my servant the Messiah". Put these two together "the form of God" and "the form of a servant" and admire the amazing God Jesus Christ. Jesus submissively did the will of the Father by taking on all the essential attributes of humanity even to the extent that He identified with basic human needs and weaknesses as Hebrews 4:15 explains, "*For we do not have a high priest who can not sympathize with our weaknesses, but one who has been tempted in all things as we are yet without sin.*" If we desire to become real disciples and servants of God, then we have to abide and play by His rules and not our own. A true servant is not self imposing or self promoting, but is called and commended by God and approved of Him to do certain works in areas which have been planned by God as Scriptures explains in 2 Corinthians 10:18,"*for it is not he who commends himself that is approved but he whom the Lord commends*", and in Ephesians 2:10,"*for we are His workmanship created in Christ Jesus for good works, which God prepared beforehand so that we would walk in them*". True servants will want to do the will of His Father to get a better foothold on the Rock of Christ. When criticism comes, they will be able to stand strong, because they delight to do His will. Jesus never lost sight of where He came from and where He was heading and neither must we. Jesus is the only perfect Servant and He was not forced into that role- it was one He freely chose. We too like Abraham, have that choice. Abraham was a servant of God due to his obedience, sacrifice and loyal service to the Master and later he was called a 'friend of God' as it says in Isaiah 41:8,"*But you Israel," My servant, Jacob whom I have chosen, Descendant of Abraham My friend*". Likewise the twelve disciples of Jesus, who had been enrolled in Jesus' college of everyday life, graduated from being servants to friends due to their obedience, as told about in John 15:14-15,"*You are my friends if you do what I command you, no longer do I call you slaves for the slave does not know what his master is doing, but I have called you friends, for all things that I have heard from my Father I have made known to you.*" Paul affirms that Jesus eternally has been God. Although He outwardly looked like a man there was much more to Him (His deity, His Kingship, His Lordship) that many people recognized naturally. Look at the life and influence of Jesus of Nazareth throughout history and you will see that Jesus Christ is, in fact, the living Son of God. He and His message always produce great changes in the lives of men and of nations. Wherever His teachings and influence have gone, the holiness of marriage has been emphasized, women's rights and voice in society acknowledged; schools and universities of higher learning established; laws to protect children made; slavery abolished; and a multitude of other changes accomplished for the good of mankind. Personally I have seen tremendous change in my own life after becoming a follower of Jesus. Jesus humbled Himself further in that He did not demand normal human rights but subjected Himself to persecution and suffering at the hands of unbelievers. Jesus went beyond persecution to the furthest extent in His humiliation in dying as a criminal following Gods plan for Him. Even further humiliation was Jesus' death in the fact that it was not an ordinary means but was accomplished by crucifixion – the cruelest, most excruciating, most degrading form of death ever devised. The Jews hated this manner of execution. Christ humiliation and exaltation by God are inseparably linked. Notice the two natures of Christ, His divine nature and human nature. Jesus, being in form of God, the divine nature, as the eternal and only begotten Son of God, did not consider it a robbery to be equal with God and to receive divine worship from men. In His human nature, He became like us in all things except sin as the Scriptures explains in 1 Peter 4:21-22,"*For you have been called for this purpose since Christ also suffered for you, leaving you an example for you to follow in His steps, who committed no sin nor was any deceit found in His mouth.*" Christ not only took upon Him the likeness and fashion, and form of a man but of one not appearing in splendor and majesty. His whole life was a life of poverty and suffering. But the lowest and final step was His dying the death of the cross, exposed to public hatred and scorn. The exaltation was of Christ's human nature in union with the divine. At the name of Jesus, not the mere sound of the word, but the authority of Jesus all should pay solemn homage. It is to the glory of God the Father, to confess that Jesus Christ is Lord. It is God's will that all men should honor the Son as they honor the Father. Here we see such motives to self-denying love as nothing else can compare as the Holy Scriptures talks about in 2 Corinthians 8:9,"*for you know the grace of our Lord Jesus Christ, that though He was rich, yet for your sake He became poor, so that you through His poverty might become rich.*' Do we love and obey the Son of God? There is no accident in God, whatever is in God, is God. He is the Jehovah, I am what I am, and so is His Son. Christ in His glorious form, having all the infinite and unspeakable glories and divine nature with the Father, was in the same form, nature, and essence of the Father. So He must be equal to the Father, for He has the same perfections as eternity, omniscience, omnipotence, omnipresence, immutability, and self existence. He has the same glorious names as God, the mighty God, the true God, the living God, and God over all, Jehovah, the Lord of glory. Isaiah 9:6 talks about the names of Christ,"*for a child would be born to us, a son will be given to us and the government will rest on His shoulders, and His name will be called, Wonderful Counselor, Mighty God, Eternal Father, Prince of Peace.*" The term "Counselor" means more than one who gives advice: it is like an attorney, one who represents a client before the bar of justice. Jesus will act in this capacity when he serves as Mediator between God and men. He will deal with the people and reconcile them to God, and thereby provide them everlasting life. Jesus will indeed be a "Wonderful Counselor" and a righteous Judge. He has the same works of creation and providence is ascribed to God, and the same worship, and honor given to Him. Christ enjoyed this equality. He is the Son of God, and in terms easy to be understood declares His proper deity, His unity and equality with the Father and signify that anyone that saw the One, saw the other. He did not act in a pretentious way to show forth the glory of His divine nature, but rather hid it. It is true that Christ did not seek vain glory and popular applause but shunned it. Usually after having performed a miracle Christ would charge the person to whom He performed the miracle on, or His disciples not to speak of the miracle as in the story of the man who was a leper in Matthew 8:2-4."*And a leper came to Him and bowed down before Him and said, "Lord if You are willing You can make me clean". Jesus stretched out His hand and touched Him saying, "I am willing be cleaned", and immediately his leprosy was cleaned, and Jesus said to him, " see that you tell no one but go show yourself to the priest and present the offering that Moses commanded, as a testimony to them.*" He performed miracles at another time to manifest His glory, as proof of His deity and Messiahship as in the story of the synagogue leader's daughter being risen from the dead and the women who had been suffering from a hemorrhage that by one touch to Jesus' garment she was healed, in Matthew 9:18-26,"*while He was saying these things to them a synagogue official came and bowed down before Him and said, "my daughter has just died but come and lay your hands on her and she will live", Jesus got up and began to follow him and so did His disciples. And a woman who had been suffering from a hemorrhage for twelve years came up behind Him and touched the fringe of His cloak for she was saying to herself," if I only touch His garment I will get well" but Jesus turning and seeing her said," Daughter take courage your faith has made you well" at once the women was made well. When Jesus came into the official's house and saw the flute-players and the crowd in noisy disorder, He said, "Leave, for the girl has not died but is asleep", and they began laughing at Him, but when the crowd had been sent out, He entered and took her by the hand and the girl got up. This news spread throughout all that land*'. Jesus was often criticized by the religious rulers of the day for the methods that he used and even for the day of the week (Sabbath) in which he performed life changing miracles. The rulers wanted to know what right he had to do these works. They scoffed at his humble upbringing and deemed him uneducated, but as always, the common people heard Him and were glad and joyful. Jesus did not come to those who thought that they were ok, but He came to those who knew that they were not. Jesus said "The healthy do not need a doctor, but only those who are sick; I have not come to call the righteous, but sinners to repentance.**" Jesus Christ s the second person in the Holy Trinity possesses all the divine Excellencies. He is co-equal, with the Father as He says in John 10:30," *I and the Father are One*", also in John 14:9, "*Jesus said to him," have I been so long with you and yet you have not come to know Me, Phillip? He who has seen Me has seen the Father; how can you say show us the Father*". God the Father created the heavens and the earth and all that is in them according to His own will, through His Son Jesus Christ, by whom all things continued in existence as it talks about in John 1:3,"*All things came into being through Him, and apart from Him nothing came into being that has come into being,*" and in Colossians 1:15-17,"*He is the image of the invisible God the firstborn of all creation. For by Him all things were created both in the heavens and on earth, visible and invisible, whether thrones or dominions or rulers or authorities, all things have been created through Him and for Him. He is before all things and in Him all things hold together,*" Jesus Christ had always existed as the second member of the God family. Through Him the Father created all things that are "in heaven and that are on earth, visible and invisible…. All things were created through Him and for Him. And He is before all things, and in Him all things consist". This Great Being was willing to humble Himself and be made as a man. The attitude or mind that Christ had was one of love in the fact that when He gave His life, He showed ultimate humility and service. Jesus accepted all the essential characteristics of humanity and so became the God-man, as the Scriptures explains in Colossians 2:9,"*for in Him all the fullness of Deity dwells in bodily form*". Jesus Christ represents humanity and deity in indivisible oneness as the New Testament book, John 5:23 explains," So *that all will honor the Son even as they honor the Father. He who does not honor the Son does not honor the Father who sent Him*'. The purpose of Jesus Christ incarnation was to reveal God, redeem men, and rule over God's kingdom as the scriptures speaks of in, John 1:29,"*The next day he saw Jesus coming to him and said behold the Lamb of God who takes away the sins of the world!*", also in Hebrews 7:25-26,"*Therefore He is able also to save forever those who draw near to God through Him, since He always lives to make intercession for them. For it is fitting for us to have such a high priest, holy, innocent, undefiled, separated from sinners, and exalted above the heavens*". Jesus laid aside His right to the full privilege of co-existence with God, assumed the place of a Son, and took on an existence appropriate to a servant. When Jesus Christ walked around Jerusalem and Judea, He had to be identified. He looked pretty well like any other Jewish man of His age. He wasn't unusual in appearance, as Isaiah describes in Isaiah 53:2,"*For He grew up before Him like a tender shoot, and like a root out of parched ground; He has no stately form or majesty that we should look upon Him, nor appearance that we should be attracted to Him.*" Though unrecognized by the world Jesus was observed carefully by God who ordered every circumstance of his life. Jesus did not wear any of the usual emblems of royalty, making His true identity visible only to the discerning eye of faith. Jesus as a Servant could easily mingle with the educated or the uneducated, the able bodied and the disabled, the rich and the poor, and impart His wisdom to them. Jesus did not judge the dysfunctional outcasts of His day like the lepers, the woman caught in adultery or the Samaritan lady at the well, but showed them the true way to go; the true way to God and in doing so restored their dignity and self worth. It has been said that Jesus was interested in three classes of people: the least, the last and the lost. In the eyes of man many individuals may not appear to be worth much, but in the eyes of God we are all special: God has no favorites and does not show partiality. Jesus saw the possibilities in the weakest and potential goodness in the worst. While Jesus was denounced for inviting Himself to eat at Zaccheus house, He knew that the dishonest tax collector would get converted, make restitution and follow Him and in doing so become a true son of Abraham as the story goes in Luke 19:1-10, **"*He entered Jericho and was passing through. And there was a man called by the name of Zaccheus, he was a chief tax collector and he was rich. Zaccheus was trying to see who Jesus was and was unable because of the crowd for he was small in stature. So he ran on ahead and climbed up into a sycamore tree in order to see Him, for He was about to pass through that way. When Jesus came to the place, He looked up and said to him,"Zaccheus hurry and come down for today I must stay at your house.* And he hurried and came down and received Him gladly. When they saw it they all began to grumble, saying, "He has gone to be the guest of a man who is a sinner." Zaccheus stopped and said to the Lord, "Behold, Lord, half of my possessions I will give to the poor and if I have defrauded anyone of anything I will give back four times as much," and Jesus said to him," today salvation has come to this house because he too, is a son of Abraham. For the Son of Man has come to seek and to save that which was lost.*" Jesus Christ accomplished our redemption through the shedding of His blood and sacrificial death on the cross, and that His death was voluntary, sympathetic, substitutionary, and redemptive as Jesus explains in John 10:11-15,"*I am the good shepherd: the good shepherd lays down His life for the sheep. He who is a hired hand and not a shepherd who is not the owner of the sheep sees a wolf coming and leaves the sheep and flees and the wolf snatches them and scatters them. He flees because he is a hired hand and is not concerned about the sheep. I am the good shepherd and I know my own and my own know me. Even as the Father knows Me and I know the*

Father and I lay down My life for the sheep", also in Romans 5:8,*"but God demonstrates His own love toward us, in that while we were yet sinners Christ died for us"*, also in 1 Peter 2:24,*"and He Himself bore our sins in His body and on the cross so that we might die to sin and live to righteousness for by His wounds we were healed"*. A true servant like Jesus will be loving but firm, gentle, kind, tactful and speak the truth in love using wisdom. Jesus was sensitive to people's needs, but also ready to challenge them "Do you want to be made well?" "What do you want me to do?" You cannot help those who refuse to be helped, but in saying this, we should not be deterred by the fragility and faltering faith of those who we seek to reach out to. Often a servant will be taken advantage of and this can be a hard thing to swallow, we may have to 'go the extra mile.' When dealing with broken and dejected people, we need to tread carefully, lest we damage the freshly fallen, pure and unique snowflake that is on their path. Sometimes time is paramount, as with the snowflake, it can only stay around for a certain amount of time before it melts and then evaporates. Based on the effectiveness of the death of our Lord Jesus Christ, the believing sinner is freed from the punishment, the penalty, the power and one day the very presence of sin, and that he is declared righteous, given eternal life, and adopted into the family of God, as it is explained in 1 Peter 3:18,*"for Christ also died for sins, once for all, the just for the unjust so that He might bring us to God having been put to death in the flesh but made alive in the spirit"*. Our justification is made sure by Christ's physical resurrection from the dead and that He is now ascended to the right hand of the Father, where now He is our intercessor, our advocate and High Priest. In Hebrews 7:25 the Scriptures speaks of Jesus being our intercessor," *therefore He is able also to save forever those who draw near to God through Him since He always lives to make intercession for them"*, also in 1 John 2:1*"My little children I am writing these things to you so that you may not sin, we have an advocate with the Father, Jesus Christ the righteous"*. In the resurrection of Jesus Christ from the grave, God confirmed the deity of His Son, and gave proof that God has accepted the atoning work of Christ on the cross. Jesus' bodily resurrection is also the guarantee of a future resurrection life for all believers, as John explains in John 5:26-29,*"For just as the Father has life in Himself even so He gave to the Son also to have life in Himself and He gave Him authority to execute judgment because His is the Son of Man. Do not marvel at this for an hour is coming in which all who are in the tombs will hear His voice and will come forth those who did the good deeds to the resurrection of life, those who committed the evil deeds to a resurrection judgment"*, also in John 14:19,*"after a little while the world will no longer see Me but you will see Me because I live you will live also"*. Jesus Christ will return to receive the church, which is His body, unto Himself at the rapture and returning with His church in glory, will establish His millennial kingdom on earth. Acts 1:9-11,*"and after He had said these things He was lifted up while they were looking on and a cloud received Him out of their sight and they were gazing intently into the sky while He was going behold two men in white clothing stood beside them, they also said, "Men of Galilee why do you stand looking into the sky? This Jesus who have been taken up from you into heaven will come in just the same way as you have watched Him go into heaven"*, also it talks about this in 1 Thessalonians 4:13-18,*"But we do not want you to be uninformed, brethren, about those who are asleep so that you will not grieve as do the rest who have no hope for if we believe that Jesus died and rose again even so God will bring with Him those who have fallen asleep in Jesus. For this we say to you by the word* *of the Lord that we who are alive and remain until the coming of the Lord will not precede those who have fallen asleep. For the Lord Himself will descend from heaven with a shout with the voice of the archangel and with the trumpet of God and the dead in Christ will rise first. Then we who are alive and remain will be caught up together with them in the clouds to meet the Lord in the air and so we shall always be with the Lord. Therefore comfort one another with these words"*. Jesus Christ is the One through whom God will judge all mankind as it is explained in John 5:22-23,*"for not even the Father judges anyone, but He has given all judgment to the Son, so that all will honor the Son even as they honor the Father, he who does not honor the Son does not honor the Father who sent Him"*. In the Holy Scriptures we are told that Jesus will judge the living inhabitants of the earth at His glorious return because Jesus is the mediator between God and man, as it speaks of in Colossians 1:18,*"He is also the head of the body, the church and He is the beginning, the firstborn from the dead, so that He Himself will come to have first place in everything". Jesus is the coming King who will reign on the throne of David"*. He is the final judge, anyone who fails to place their trust in Him as Lord and Savior will be judged as it speaks of in Acts 17:30-31,*"therefore having overlooked the times of ignorance God is now declaring to men that all people everywhere should repent because He has fixed a day in which He will judge the world in righteousness through a man in which He has appointed having furnished proof to all men by raising Him from the dead"*. As a judge he will bless the people as the psalmist wrote concerning Jesus in Psalms 72:4, *"May He vindicate the afflicted of the people, save the children of the needy and crush the oppressor."* The Lord Jesus Christ the Messiah as the personal servant was chosen because the Lord delights in Him and put His Spirit on Him and we are warned to listen to Him and obey Him in Luke 9:35,*"Then a voice came out of the clouds saying ,"this is my Son, the chosen one, Listen to Him,"* and in Revelation 13:8,*"All who dwell on the earth will worship Him, everyone whose name has not been written from the foundation of the world in the book of life of the Lamb who has been slain"*, and in Matthew 17:5, *"While he was still speaking a bright cloud overshadowing them and behold a voice out of the cloud said "this is my beloved Son with whom I am well pleased; listen to Him"*. At His second coming Christ will rule over a kingdom in which justice prevails throughout the world. The millennial kingdom is not for Israel alone though the Messiah will reign on the throne of David in Jerusalem and Israel will be the glorious people, in fact all the nations of the world will experience the righteousness and justice of the Messiah King as it speaks about in Isaiah 42:1-4 *"Behold My Servant whom I uphold, My chosen one in whom My soul delights. I have put my Spirit upon Him. He will bring forth justice to the nation. He will not cry out or raise His voice, nor make His voice heard in the street. A bruised reed He will not break and a dimly burning wick He will not extinguish; He will faithfully bring forth justice. He will not be disheartened or crushed until He has established justice in the earth; and the coastlands will wait expectantly for His law. Thus says God the Lord, who created the heavens and stretched them out, who spread out the earth and its offspring, who gives breath to the people on it and the spirit of those who walk in it. I am the Lord I have called You in righteousness, I will also hold You by the hand and watch over You, and I will appoint You as a covenant to the people, as a light to the nations, to open blind eyes to bring out prisoners from the dungeon and those who dwell in darkness from the prison."* This is God speaking. Christ was to be God's servant. Now of course Christ Himself was God. We understand that from other scriptures. He wasn't a street preacher, He preached in the synagogues as it says in the above Scripture, *"He will not cry out, nor raise His voice, nor cause His voice to be heard in the street."* He took the message of the gospel first of all to His own people in the synagogues. Later, of course, it was taken elsewhere; this is part of the work that He was given to do. Remember the story of the woman caught in adultery in John 8? In John 8:3-11 the Scriptures tells the story of the women caught in adultery, *"The scribes and the Pharisees brought a woman caught in adultery and having set her in the center of the court, they said to Him, "Teacher this woman has been caught in adultery, in the very act. Now in the Law Moses commanded us to stone such a woman; what then do you say?" They were saying this, testing Him so they might have grounds for accusing Him. But Jesus stooped down and with His finger wrote on the ground. But when they persisted in asking Him, He straightened up and said to them, "He who is without sin among you, let him be the first to throw a stone at her." Again He stooped down and wrote on the ground. When they heard it, they began to go out one by one, beginning with the older ones, and He was left alone and the woman, where she was, in the center of the court. Straightening up, Jesus said to her, "woman where are they? Did no one condemn you?" She said, "No one, Lord." And Jesus said, "I do not condemn you, either. Go. From now on sin no more."* Well this is telling us that Jesus Christ at His coming didn't lean hard on somebody already bruised, somebody who is already hurting. He told her to go and sin no more. He knew she was already hurting, she already felt remorse. As it says in the above Isaiah's passage," *A bruised reed He will not break, and smoking flax He will not quench; He will bring forth justice for truth"* Part of Jesus' commission as a servant was that He was not going to fail as it says," *He will not fail nor be discouraged"*. He was going to do the work that He was given to do as the passages continues, *"Till He has established justice in the earth; and the coastlands shall wait for His law."* It's very interesting, these prophesies of Isaiah mingle together what Christ was to do at His First Coming, and what He will yet do at His Second Coming. Isaiah was inspired to picture Christ as the servant at His First Coming and Second Coming, and often the prophecies of the First Coming and the Second Coming are kind of fused together. You need a little hindsight, discernment, and guidance of the Spirit of God to figure out exactly what is being referred to. God didn't inspire the prophets to write like historians. Sometimes the prophets didn't know how far in the future they were seeing. Jesus Christ was that "covenant of the people", not to the exclusion of the law of God, but He was the center of the covenant as Isaiah's passage speaks about, *"I, the Lord, have called You in righteousness, and will hold Your hand, I will keep You and give You as a covenant to the people"*. There are some remarkable things said here about Jesus Christ and about the way in which He's to serve. He is the Servant. Ultimately when Jesus rules over His Kingdom, He will receive international recognition for the effectiveness of His reign, as it speaks about in Isaiah 52:13-15,"*Behold My Servant will prosper, He will be high and lifted up and greatly exalted. Just as many were astonished at you, My people, So His appearance was marred more than any man and His form more than the sons of men. Thus He will sprinkle many nations; Kings will shut their mouths on account of Him; for what had not been told them they will see, and what they had not heard they will understand."* Once again this is prophetic of Jesus Christ; He's God's servant. Jesus knew how to deal with people, how to work with people. Jesus Christ was exalted, but first of all He had to serve, He had to bring service and go through a great deal of suffering. He

went through a terrible beating, an enormous scourging, as Isaiah puts it, *"Just as many were astonished at you, so His appearance was marred more than any man"*. They pushed a crown of thorns down on His head, you know, you've probably seen in the movies and some of the artwork the way they picture it. The crown of thorns pressed down on His head so heavily that the blood was streaming down His face. He went through a terrible beating. When Isaiah said, *" So He shall sprinkle,"* probably a better translation of this word is "startle" many nations. Once again we're reading about the return of Jesus Christ, what He is to do in serving when He comes back at the Second Coming. He shall "startle" many nations, because if you look at the context sprinkle doesn't exactly fit. When Isaiah says, *" Kings shall shut their mouths at Him"* this is Christ at His return; this is the kings of the earth seeing Jesus Christ coming back as Lord of lords and clapping their hand over their mouth in astonishment. *"For what had not been told them they shall see, and what they hadn't heard they shall consider.*
Through Christ's crucifixion and resurrection He conquered satan and death and in triumph returned to God those who were once sinners and prisoners of satan as it is explained in Ephesians 4:8,*"Therefore it says, " When He ascended on high, He led captive a host of captives, and He gave gifts to men."* After a triumph a king would bring home spoils and prisoners from the war he was in, here is a depiction of Christ returning from His battle on earth back to the glory of the heavenly city with the trophies of His great victory at Calvary. Jesus had absolute authority in His actions as well as His words as described in Luke 4:32,*"and they were amazed at His teaching for His message was with authority."* Jesus tenderly leads and feeds His flock as it describes in Isaiah 40:11,*"Like a shepherd He will tend His flock, in His arms He will gather the lambs and carry them in His bosom, He will gently lead the nursing ewes"*. Never before has there been such a desperate need for a competent ruler. We need one who is able to lead the hate infected nations of earth out of despair and into trust and goodwill. Without this the individual or the nation can have no lasting peace, or security. Jesus said in Matthew 11:28-30, *"Come to Me, all you who labor and are heavy laden and I will give you rest. Take My yoke upon you and learn from Me, for I am gentle and lowly in heart and you will find rest for your souls, for My yoke is easy and my burden light"*. Things around us can be really bad, but when we are next to the Lord, then He will give us the grace and the strength to go on. When we are weak, then we are strong - because we draw from His resources knowing that as it says in Philippians 4:13, *"I can do all things through Christ who strengthens me"*. As the apostle Paul affirmed in Colossians 1:29, *"I also labor, striving according to His working which works in me mightily"*. We are reminded that Jesus will rule over His people and bless them as the prophet wrote about in, Psalms 72:11-14,*"And let all the kings bow down before Him, all nations serve Him, for He will deliver the needy when he cries for help. The afflicted also and him who has no helper. He will have compassion on the poor and needy, and the lives of the needy he will save. He will rescue their life from oppression and violence and their blood will be precious in His sight."* He will do more than establish peace between nations. Jesus will establish universal peace, which will mean peace among and within nations, community peace, family peace, and most important of all, peace of heart. This peace of heart will result from being at peace with God. The world of mankind today is alienated from God through wicked works, as it says in Ephesians 4:18-19,*"being darkened in their understanding, excluded from the life of God because of the ignorance that is in them,*

because of the hardness of their hearts", also in Colossians 1:21,*"and although you were formerly alienated and hostile in mind, engaged in evil deeds"*. The Prince of Peace, while serving as Mediator, Counselor, and Judge, will reconcile men to God. No longer will the human race be in rebellion against the Creator. As they are in harmony with Him and enjoy the sunshine of his favor, they will have life everlasting as it says in Psalms 30:5," *For His anger is but for a moment, His favor is for a lifetime, weeping may last for the night, but a shout of joy comes in the morning"*. Among the many titles applied to Jesus, Servant stands out as one of His favorites. Jesus was considered a servant because:

a) the prophets predicted that a servant would come and suffer.

b) He offered us a powerful model of servant hood.

c) The blessing that accompanied His meekness.

d) The obligation of servant hood.

e) Jesus was humble.

f) Jesus died at Calvary as the "suffering servant.

Paul in Philippians 2:5 states the following: "*Let this mind be in you which was also in Christ Jesus.*" The New American Standard Bible states it this way, "*Have* this attitude *in yourselves which was also in Christ Jesus.*" What attitude or frame of mind was Paul referring to? The Verses 6 and 7 of Philippians 2, help to explain the attitude that Christ had. "*Who, being in very nature God, did not consider equality with God something to be grasped, but made himself nothing, taking the very nature of a servant, being made in human likeness*" Jesus is undoubtedly our example of a servant, and with Jesus as our example, we are called to be servants. Jesus' mission was to despondent and broken people by creating a new way of thinking about ministry. He clearly associated himself with the restorative ministry of the Suffering Servant, who served through great sacrifice. What then is the outcome of serving as Jesus Christ served? What's the end product of it? In Philippians 2:8-10, Jesus Christ teaches us that service is the way to greatness; service is the way to please God, "*Being found in appearance as a man, He humbled Himself by becoming obedient to the point of death even death on a cross. For this reason also, God highly exalted Him and bestowed on Him the name which is above every name, so that at the name of Jesus every knee will bow of those who are in heaven and on earth and under the earth"*. That's the ultimate greatness. That's what God will give to Jesus Christ. That's the destiny that we will have as well as servants of God, servants of Jesus Christ. In His kingdom, Jesus Christ will be the eternal servant, and we will serve with Him. Jesus' concept of a servant reveals a pattern that embraces deep humility, disregards personal agendas, and puts others first. The New Testament clearly indicates that Jesus' servant teaching caught fire with His disciples as revealed in Acts 2:42,"*They were continually devoting themselves to the apostles teaching and to fellowship, to the breaking of bread and to prayer, also Acts 4:32,"and the congregation of those who believed were of one heart and soul and not one of them claimed that anything belonged to him was his own but all things were common property to them*". This is an example of a caring church in which leaders and followers expressed a mutual and active servanthood toward one another. The leadership in the early church chose to follow Jesus' example of Christ's self-imposed humiliation and servanthood by deep humility, a sense of sacrificial service to others, and a willingness to suffer hardship. A real servant will never ask his master "What can you do for me?" but "What can I do for you?" In the army there is a common saying that when the superior officer says to his subordinate "When I say jump, you jump. And when you are half way up you say, "How high?"" The higher rank calls the shots and not the other way round. Those of us who have enlisted into God's army need to remember this; God is in charge and we must obey His call even if we have to go over the top and into battle with no guarantee of a safe return. Jesus Christ was prophesied to be the servant; this was all planned ahead of time. He was to come and give the ultimate act of service laying down his life, opening the doors of salvation, so that you and I could look forward to the kingdom and to eternal life, living forever as sons and daughters of God.

Chapter 6

Paul, a bond servant of Jesus Christ

Though physically unimpressive Paul possessed an inner strength granted him through the Holy Spirit's power. The grace of God proved sufficient for his every need, enabling this noble servant of Christ to successfully finish his spiritual race. In Philippians 3:5-6 Paul said about himself that he was *"Circumcised on the eighth day; of the nation of Israel of the tribe of Benjamin, a Hebrew of Hebrews; as to the law, a Pharisee as to zeal, a persecutor to the church; as to the righteousness which is in the law found blameless"*. Paul was circumcised on the prescribed day, the eighth day. All the Jews were direct descendants of Abraham, Isaac, and Jacob. Saul was Paul's Hebrew name, Paul was his Greek name. Paul was from the tribe of Benjamin and his Jewish heritage was unquestionably pure. Benjamin was the second son of Rachel and one of the elite tribes of Israel who along with Judah, remained loyal to the Davidic dynasty and formed the southern kingdom. Paul's beginnings are very interesting; they highlight the cosmopolitan world that was the Roman Empire. He was born in an Asian city located on the southern coast of Turkey called Tarsus in about the time of Christ's birth. Paul was born to Hebrew parents, who were also Roman citizens, who maintained the Hebrew tradition and language even while living in a pagan city. It is important to note that even though Judea was within the Roman Empire most Jews were not Roman citizens. Citizenship outside of Italy was an honor reserved for people who made great contributions to the Empire. Thus, we may presume that Paul's parents were people of influence and perhaps even moderate wealth. Tarsus was an important city in the Roman province of Cilicia, located on the banks of the Cydnus River near the border of Asia Minor and Syria (modern Turkey). It served as both a commercial and educational center; it was crowded with commerce while its university ranked with those of Athens and Alexandria as the finest in the Roman world. To the Jew, "zeal" was the highest single virtue of religion. It combines love and hate, because Paul loved Judaism, he hated whatever might threaten it. Paul outwardly kept the standard of righteous living advocated by God's law, so that no one could accuse him of violation. Acts 22:3 Paul says," *I am a Jew, born in Tarsus of Cilicia, but brought up in the city, educated, under Gamaliel, strictly according to the law of our fathers, being zealous for God just as you all are today"*. Paul was educated by his mother until the age of five. From age five to ten he studied with his father in the Hebrew Scriptures and traditional writings. At the same time, being a Roman citizen and living in a Greek and Roman environment, he received a thorough education in the Greek language, history, and culture. At the age of fourteen Paul was sent to Jerusalem to train to be a Rabbi. His teacher was a prominent man named Gamaliel. Rabbis, at the time, were also taught another trade. The idea was to keep teachers from becoming a burden on society. They also wanted to have something to fall back on during hard times. Paul was trained to be a tent-maker, though he spent much of his early life in Jerusalem as a student of Gamaliel. Paul was born among the Hellenistic Jews of the Diaspora. As a student of Gamaliel, Paul received extensive training both in the Old Testament laws and in the rabbinic traditions which taught him how to be a Pharisee. There were two great rabbinical schools, those of Hillel and Schammai. Hillel, the grandfather of Gamaliel, held that tradition was superior to the Law. The school of Schammai despised traditionalists, especially when there teachings clashed with the writings of Moses. The religious school of Gamaliel (Hillel) was chiefly oral and usually had a prejudice against any book but Scripture. They used a system of Scriptural exegesis, and Josephus in his writings expressed the wish to have such a power of exegesis. When school was in session, learned men met and discussed scriptures, gave various interpretations, suggested illustrations, and quoted precedents. The students were encouraged to question, doubt, and even contradict. Just as his father before him, Paul was a Pharisee, a member of the strictest Jewish sect. Paul grew to be a man of firm convictions and fiery temperament. He always acted on his beliefs. Thus, when he was confronted with what he took to be a heresy to Judaism, he worked with all his might to silence it. This heresy would one day come to be known as Christianity and Paul was among the foremost of its persecutors. Paul was present at the stoning of Stephen, and though he did not participate, he encouraged the violent act that destroyed the first of the martyrs. He then participated in a general persecution including, "going from house to house, he dragged out the believers, both men and women and threw them into jail." He then undertook a mission to Damascus. There he intended to continue attacking Christians. However, on the way, he had a vision. This vision is described several times in the Holy Bible, three times in the book of Acts. Paul saw Jesus who asked why Paul persisted in persecuting Him. Paul was miraculously converted to Christianity while on his way to Damascus to arrest Christians in that city. This meeting with Jesus made Paul a Christian. When Paul became a Christian, his very thorough education was enormously helpful. He was able to assimilate Christian doctrines rapidly and relate them accurately to the Scripture teaching he had received. From his education, both from Gamaliel and in the desert from the Lord Jesus Christ, Paul developed a divine viewpoint attitude toward human history. He succeeded in making Christianity a universal religion, not just in the spiritual sense but also in the physical sense. Paul's influence on Christian thinking arguably has been more significant than any other New Testament author. Paul declared that the Christian church is the body of Christ, and depicted the world outside the Church as under judgment. Spreading the Gospel far and wide across the Roman Empire was Paul's mission. The intensity of the apostle Paul for the gospel soon became well known, because of what Paul said we are to be doing in Ephesians 6:18,"*With all prayer and petition, pray at all times in the Spirit and with this in view be on the alert with all perseverance and petition for all the saints*". Paul was always praying for everyone as Paul said in Ephesians 3:14-19,"*For this reason I bow my knee before the Father from whom every family in heaven and on earth derives its name, that He would grant you according to the riches of His glory to be strengthened with power through His Spirit in the inner man,*" also in Philippians 1:8-11,"*For God is my witness, how I long for you all with the affection of Christ Jesus, and this I pray that your love may abound still more and more in real knowledge and all discernment so that you may approve the things that are excellent in order to be sincere and blameless until the day of Christ, having been filled with the fruit of righteousness which comes through Jesus Christ, to the glory and praise of God*". Paul was consumed with praying for the saints. He endeavored to line up with God's will on their behalf as Paul talks about in Colossians 1:9,"*For this reason also, since the day we heard of it, we have not ceased to pray for you and to ask that you may be filled with the knowledge of His will in all spiritual wisdom and understanding*", also in 2 Thessalonians 1:11,"*to this end also we pray for you always that our God will count you worthy of your calling and fulfill every desire for goodness and the work of faith with power.*" Paul's prayers were characteristic of a true servant's heart. Thirteen epistles in the New Testament are traditionally attributed to Paul. He apparently dictated all his epistles through a secretary, who would usually paraphrase the core of his message, as was the practice among first-century scribes. These epistles were circulated within the Christian community, where they were read aloud by members of the church along with other works. Paul's epistles were accepted early as scripture and later established as part of the Scriptures. Critical scholars regard Paul's epistle to be the earliest written books of the New Testament. Paul's letters are largely written to churches which he had visited; he was a great traveler, visiting Cyprus, Asia Minor (modern Turkey), mainland Greece, Crete, and Rome. His letters are full of expositions of what Christians should believe and how they should live. He provides the first written account of what it is to be a Christian and thus of Christian spirituality. Paul actually wrote Romans, First Corinthians, Second Corinthians, Galatians, Philippians, First Thessalonians, and Philemon. Paul wrote down much of the theology of atonement. Paul taught that Christians are redeemed from the Law and from sin by Jesus' death and resurrection. His death was a restoration; as well as propitiation, and by Christ's blood, peace is made between God and man. By baptism, a Christian shares in Jesus' death and in his victory over death, gaining, as a free gift, a new, justified status of Sonship. Paul's theology of the gospel accelerated the separation of the messianic sect of Christians from Judaism, a development contrary to Paul's own intent. He wrote that the faith of Christ was absolute in salvation for Jews and Gentiles alike, making the difference between the followers of Christ and mainstream Jews inevitable and permanent. He successfully argued that Gentile converts did not need to become Jews, get circumcised, follow Jewish dietary restrictions, or otherwise observe *Mosaic Law as* described in Acts 15: 1-2,"*Some men came down from Judea and began teaching the brethren, unless you are circumcised according to the custom of Moses, you can not be saved. And when Paul and Barnabas had great dissension and debate with them, the brethren determined that Paul and Barnabas and some others of them should go up to Jerusalem to the apostles and elders concerning this issue*". The key question raised was whether Gentile converts needed to be circumcised. Paul's writings give some insight into his thinking regarding his former place in Judaism. He is theologically critical of claims of moral superiority of Jews while strongly approving of the notion of a special place for the Children of Israel. His aggressive and authoritative writing style suggests that Paul's prominence in Judaism and the Temple leadership must have been quite high. In his writings Paul persistently relied on the persecutions he endured from Jews and Gentiles as his claim to closeness to Jesus. In Romans 1: 1-7 Paul provides a list of his own apostolic claim and his post-conversion convictions about the risen Christ," *Paul, a bond-servant of Christ Jesus, called as an apostle, set apart for the gospel of God, which He promised beforehand through His prophets in the Holy Scriptures, concerning His Son, who was born of a descendant of David according to the flesh, who was declared the Son of God with power by the resurrection of holiness, Jesus Christ our Lord, through whom we have received grace and apostleship to bring about the obedience of faith among all the Gentiles for His name's sake, among whom you also are the called of Jesus Christ; to all who are beloved of God in Rome, called as saints: Grace to you and peace from God our Father and the Lord Jesus Christ."*

1. Paul describes himself as
   A. a servant of Christ Jesus
   B. called to be an apostle
   C. set apart for the gospel of God
2. Paul describes Jesus as
   A. having been promised by God "beforehand" through his prophets in the holy Scriptures
   B. being the Son of God
   C. having biological lineage from David ("according to the flesh")
   D. having been declared to be the Son of God in power according to the Spirit of holiness by his resurrection from the dead
   E. being Jesus Christ our Lord
   F. The One through whom we have received grace and apostleship to bring about the obedience of faith for the sake of his name among all the nations, "including you who are called to belong to Jesus Christ."

The first journey Paul took was led initially by Barnabas but was inspired by the Holy Spirit, as described in Acts 13: 1-5,"*Now there were at Antioch in the church that was there, prophets and teachers: Barnabas and Simeon who was called Niger and Lucius of Cyrene and Manean who had been brought up with Herod the tetrarch, and Saul. While they were ministering to the Lord and fasting, The Holy Spirit said, "Set apart for Me, Barnabas and Saul for the work to which I have called them." Then when they had fasted and prayed and laid their hands on them, they sent them away. So being sent out by the Holy Spirit they went down to Seleucia and from there they sailed to Cyprus. When they reached Salamis, they began to proclaim the word of God in the synagogues of the Jews, and they also had John as their helper.*" This initial journey takes Paul from Antioch to Cyprus then southern Asia Minor (Anatolia), and back to Antioch. On Cyprus, Paul rebukes and blinds Elymas the magician who was criticizing their teachings as the story is told in Acts 13:6-12,"*When they had gone through the whole island as far as Paphos, they found a magician, a Jewish false prophet whose name was Bar-Jesus, who was with the proconsul, Sergius Paulus, a man of intelligence. This man summoned Barnabas and Saul and sought to hear the word of God. But Elymas the magician (for so his name is translated) was opposing them, seeking to turn the proconsul away from the faith. But Saul, who was also known as Paul, filled with the Holy Spirit, fixed his gaze on him, and said, "You who are full of deceit and fraud, you son of the devil, you enemy of all righteousness, will you not cease to make crooked the straight ways of the Lord? Now, behold," the hand of the Lord is upon you, and you will be blind and not see the sun for a time." And immediately a mist and darkness fell upon him and he went about seeking those who would lead him by the hand. Then the proconsul believed when he saw what had happened, being amazed at the teaching of the Lord.*" From this point on, Paul is described as the leader of the group. Antioch served as a major Christian center for Paul's evangelizing. His missionary journeys brought him to Asia Minor, Greece, Macedonia and eventually Rome. There is no question that his Roman citizenship and his intense training as a Pharisee helped him immensely in this mission. He was arrested several times because of his preaching and several times was saved because of his elevated status within the Roman Empire. Jesus commissioned Paul to preach His message to the Gentiles. Right afterward Paul immediately began proclaiming the gospel message. Gentiles are the name given to people who are not Jewish. Despite the agreement achieved at the Council of Jerusalem as understood by Paul, Paul recounts how he later publicly confronted Peter, also called the "Incident at Antioch" over Peter's reluctance to share a meal with Gentile Christians in Antioch. Writing later of the incident, Paul recounts: "I opposed [Peter] to his face, because he was clearly in the wrong". Paul reports that he told Peter: "You are a Jew, yet you live like a Gentile and not like a Jew. How is it, then, that you force Gentiles to follow Jewish customs?" This incident is told about in Galatians 2:11-14,"*But when Cephas came to Antioch, I opposed him to his face, because he stood condemned. For prior to the coming of certain men from James, he used to eat with the Gentiles; but when they came, he began to withdraw and hold himself aloof, fearing the party of the circumcision. The rest of the Jews joined him in hypocrisy, with the result that even Barnabas was carried away by their hypocrisy. But when I saw that they were not straightforward about the truth of the gospel, I said to Cephas in the presence of all," If you, being a Jew, live like a Gentile, and not like the Jews, how is it that you compel the Gentiles to live like Jews?*" Paul recognized that the message of Jesus was for all men. He noted that Jesus died on the Cross not only for our sins, but to take on the burden of Mosaic Law. Thus, a Christian need not first become a Jew in order to follow Jesus. Paul said that Christians are saved by their faith alone. The Spirit was active in Paul's life, convicting him of sin, convincing him of the Lordship of Jesus Christ, transforming him, and indwelling him permanently, he was then filled with the Spirit and empowered for service. Paul identifies himself in the lowly term as bond slave. Paul was no self serving preacher. He was no conceited prophet. He was not a man out for himself trying to make a name or draw a crowd, though every generation you will find preachers like that. What stands out was that Paul was not a self appointed preacher, but a humble servant that the Lord has sent. The inclusion of Jews in the church had already been established at Pentecost, so Saul, because he was a Jew and because he was an apostle in his own right received the Spirit without any apostles present because Christ personally chose him and commissioned him for service as the Scriptures says in Acts 9:20, "*And immediately he began to proclaim Jesus in the synagogues saying "He is the Son of God.*" The content of Paul's message was that Jesus Christ is God. Paul traveled for years spreading the gospel and being instructed and taught by the Lord Jesus Christ but rather than immediately travel, Paul instead went to Nabatean Arabia, a wilderness desert that stretched east of Damascus, down to the Sinai Peninsula south and east of the Dead Sea where Paul spent 3 years. During that time, he received much of his doctrine as direct revelation from the Lord. Paul asserted that he received the Gospel not from any person, but by a personal revelation of Jesus Christ as Paul explains in Galatians 1:11-16,"*For I would have you know, brethren that the Gospel which was preached by me is not according to man. For I neither received it from man nor was I taught it, but I received it through a revelation of Jesus Christ. For you have heard of my former manner of life in*

Judaism, how I use to persecute the church of God beyond measure and tried to destroy it and I was advancing in Judaism beyond many of my contemporaries among my countrymen being more extremely zealous for my ancestral traditions. But when God, who had set me apart even from my mother's womb and called me through His grace, was pleased to reveal His Son in me so that I might preach Him among the Gentiles. I did not immediately consult with flesh and blood nor did I go up to Jerusalem to those who were apostles before me, but I went away to Arabia and returned once more to Damascus." After his conversion, Paul went to Damascus, where Acts states he was healed of his blindness and baptized by Ananias of Damascus as it is explained in Acts 9:10-19, "*Now there was a disciple at Damascus named Ananias and the Lord said to him in a vision, "Ananias," and he said "here I am Lord" and the Lord said to him, "Get up and go to the street called Straight, and inquire at the house of Judas, for a man from Tarsus named Saul, for he is praying, and he has seen in a vision a man named Ananias come in and lay his hands on him, so that he might regain his sight". But Ananias answered "Lord I have heard from many about this man, how much harm he did to "Your" saints, at Jerusalem, and here he has authority from the chief priests to bind all who call on Your name." But the Lord said to him "Go for he is a chosen instrument of Mine, to bear My name before the Gentiles and kings and the sons of Israel for I will show him how much he must suffer for My name's sake." So Ananias departed and entered the house and after laying his hands on him said, "brother Saul, the Lord Jesus, who appeared to you on the road by which you were coming, has sent me so that you may regain your sight and be filled with the Holy Spirit." And immediately there fell from his eyes something like scales and he regained his sight, and he got up and was baptized, and he took food and was strengthened*". Ananias was one of the leaders of the Damascus church and so therefore one of Saul's targets. Paul went to Jerusalem and there gained official sanction from the elders of the Church, including Peter and James, to bring the message of Jesus to the Gentiles. Along with Barnabas, he then went on his first Missionary Journey to Cyprus, Antioch in Pisidia, Iconium, Lystra and Derbe. During this journey they met many hardships. Paul was even stoned, though not killed, in Lystra. It was an ironic twist that Paul underwent the same gruesome punishment he had sanctioned for Stephen and for the very cause Stephen had suffered. After being prepared for ministry by the Lord, he returned to minister in nearby Damascus, as it says in Galatians 1:17-18," *Nor did I go up to Jerusalem to those who were apostles before me but I went away to Arabia, and returned once more to Damascus. Then three years later I went up to Jerusalem to become acquainted with Cephas and stayed with him fifteen days*". Paul says that he then went first to Arabia, and then came back to Damascus. Three years after his conversion he went to Jerusalem and there he met James and stayed with Simon Peter for 15 days as he described in Galatians 1:18-24,"*Then three years later I went up to Jerusalem to become acquainted with Cephas and stayed with him fifteen days, but I did not see any of the other apostles except James the Lords brother. (Now in what I am writing to you I assure you before God that I am not lying). Then I went into the region of Syria and Cilicia. I was still unknown by sight to the churches of Judea which were in Christ, but only they kept hearing "He who once persecuted us is now preaching the faith which he once tried to destroy". And they were glorifying God because of me.*" After three years of being taught and instructed by the Lord Jesus Christ, He went around spreading the gospel, encouraging believers and being encouraged by believers. Paul determined to answer the call that God put on his life to the utmost of his ability. The intimacy Paul had with God was not something the other religions of his day could relate to. The Pagans thought their gods were distant and so did the Jewish people. To Paul, God was not a theological abstraction, but an intimate friend. Paul knew that the existence of God can easily be perceived by anyone, that man can become aware of God, but that many men's deliberate sin halted this good beginning by immoral activities which accompanied their idolatry. Therefore, Paul had an intense hatred of idolatry of any kind. Paul's teaching shows that the only reality is God. Idolatry distorts man's conception of the world and external nature. Idolatry is the enemy of mankind.. Paul's description in Galatians states that 14 years after his conversion he went again to Jerusalem as he talks about in Galatians 2:1-10,"*then after an interval of fourteen years I went up again to Jerusalem with Barnabas taking Titus along also. It was because of a revelation that I went up and I submitted to them the Gospel which I preach among the Gentiles, but I did so in private to those who were of reputation for fear that I might be running or had run in vain. But not even Titus who was with me, though he was Greek was compelled to be circumcised. But it was because of the false brethren secretly brought in who had sneaked in to spy out our liberty which we have in Christ Jesus, in order to bring us into bondage. But we did not yield in subjection to them for even an hour, so that the truth of the Gospel would remain with you. But from those who were of high reputation (what they were makes no difference to me God shows no partiality), well those who were of reputation contributed nothing to me. But on the contrary seeing that I had been entrusted with the Gospel to the uncircumcised just as Peter had been to the circumcised. (For he who effectually worked for Peter in his apostleship to the circumcised effectually worked for me also to the Gentiles), and recognizing the grace that had been given to me, James and Cephas and John who were reputed to be pillars, gave to me and Barnabas the right hand of fellowship, so that we might go to the Gentiles and they to the circumcised. They only asked us to remember the poor, the very thing I also was eager to do.*"   It is not completely known what happened during these so-called "unknown years," but both Acts and Galatians provide some partial details, as it talks about in Acts 11:19-26,"*So then those who were scattered because of the persecution that occurred in connection with Stephen made their way to Phoenicia and Cyprus and Antioch speaking the word to no once except to Jews alone. But there were some of them, men of Cyprus and Cyrene who came to Antioch and began speaking to the Greeks, also preaching the Lord Jesus and the hand of the Lord was with them, and a large number who believed turned to the Lord. The news about them reached the ears of the church at Jerusalem and they sent Barnabas off to Antioch. Then when he arrived and witnessed the grace of God he rejoiced and began to encourage them all with resolute heart to remain true to the Lord for he was a good man and full of the Holy Spirit and of faith and considerable numbers were brought to the Lord. And he left for Tarsus to look for Saul, and when he had found him, he brought him to Antioch. And for an entire year they met with the church and taught considerable numbers and the disciples were first called Christians in Antioch.*" When a famine occurred in Judea, Paul and Barnabas journeyed to Jerusalem to deliver financial support from the Antioch community. According to Acts, Antioch had become an alternative center for Christians following the dispersion of the believers after the death of Stephen. Now Paul was a bond servant so that means he was more than a servant. He gave his life to Christ through thick and thin. Bond servants of Jesus Christ are not a servant of sin, nor of satan, nor of man, nor of tradition, but of Jesus Christ as explain in Romans 1:7-15,"*To all who are beloved of God in Rome, called as saints, grace to you and peace from God our Father and the Lord Jesus Christ. First I thank my God through Jesus Christ for you all, because your faith is being proclaimed throughout the whole world. For God whom I serve in my spirit in the preaching of the gospel of His Son is my witness as to how unceasingly I make mention of you, always in my prayers making requests, if perhaps now at last by the will of God I may succeed in coming to you. For I long to see you so that I may impart some spiritual gifts to you, that you maybe established: that is, that I may be encouraged together with you while among you, each of us by the others faith, both yours and mine. I do not want you to be unaware; brethren that often I have planned to come to you (and have been prevented so far) so that I may obtain some fruit among you also, even as among the rest of the Gentiles. I am under obligation both to Greeks and to barbarians, both to the wise and to the foolish. So for my part, I am eager to preach the gospel to you also who are in Rome.*" The apostle Paul epitomizes what it really means to have the right perspective on true spiritual service. Although many years have past since this passage was written, it is still relevant and alive with Paul's affection. As you study this passage, you can see Paul's great love for the church in Rome, a group he had never met. Paul not only prayed for the believers in Rome, but also asked God if he might be part of the answer to his prayer. That is a refreshing statement because so many people today want someone else to do the work of the ministry rather than themselves. I have heard people praying, "Lord, raise up someone to reach my neighbor." The real answer to that prayer ought to be the one who prayed it! Superficial servers, unlike Paul, are never satisfied with their situations, and are therefore thankless. They focus on their own insatiable appetites for glory. Show me a thankless heart and I'll show you a proud, self-centered individual. Even when you can't find things in your own life to be thankful for, you can always find many things that God is doing in someone else's life. If there's one thing we know about the apostle Paul, it's that he had a thankful heart. In almost every one of his epistles, Paul expressed thanks for the ones to whom he wrote. The only exception is the epistle to the Galatians. The Galatians had defected from the gospel and were functioning in the flesh. All the churches Paul wrote to needed to be corrected, but even though he saw the need for instruction, he also could find something to be thankful for. He was always able to see God's purposes being accomplished. Paul expressed what is in the heart of all true servants of God-- an attitude of gratitude. Some people go through life dwelling on the negative. English novelist and poet Thomas Hardy said he had a friend who would be the first to spot the manure pile in a beautiful meadow! Some people refuse to be grateful for the good that God is doing in someone else's life. If it isn't happening to them, they think it's bad. The apostle Paul didn't express his thanks by saying, "I'm so thankful for what God has done for me"; rather he said, "I thank God for you." He received as much joy from someone else's success as he did from his own. Paul said this to Timothy, who was wavering in his faith in 2 Timothy 2:21-22, "*Therefore if anyone cleanses himself from these things he will be a vessel for honor, sanctified, useful to the Master prepared for every good work, Now flee from youthful lusts and pursue righteousness, faith, love and peace, with those who call on the Lord from a pure heart.*" A willing spirit is a mark of true spiritual service. It is the service that renders not only prayer but also the willingness to be part of the answer. If you pray, "Lord, I want this to be done and if need be, I'll do it," then you're showing a willing heart. Do you desire to be part of the solution in your prayers for others? Do you regularly pray for your neighbors, yet are unwilling to be used by God to reach them? If so, ask God to begin to make you the solution to your prayers for others. Seek to be "a vessel unto honor, sanctified, and fit for the master's use, and prepared unto every good work". You should be just as thankful for them as you would be for yourself as Philippians 2:3 says," *Do nothing from selfishness or empty conceit but with humility of mind regard one another as more important than yourselves.*" Paul was so in tune with God's purposes that they became the source of his thanksgiving as he says in Philippians 1:1-3," *Paul and Timothy bond-servants of Christ Jesus, to all the saints in Christ Jesus who are in Philippi, including the overseers and the deacons. Grace to you and peace from God our Father and the Lord Jesus Christ. I thank my God in all my remembrance of you*", also Paul expresses his thankfulness in Philemon 4,"*I thank my God always making mention of you in my prayers*". Regardless of his condition, Paul remained thankful to God. He was consistently filled with joy because his joy had nothing to do with his present circumstances. He was concerned only about proclaiming the cause of Christ as Paul says in 1 Corinthians 2:1-5,"*And when I came to you, brethren, I did not come with superiority of speech or of wisdom, proclaiming to you the testimony of God. For I determined to know nothing among you except Jesus Christ, and Him crucified. I was with you in weakness and in fear and in much trembling, and my message and my preaching were not in persuasive words of wisdom, but in demonstration of the Spirit and the power so that your faith would not rest on the wisdom of men, but on the power of God.*" Paul came to Corinth after being beaten and imprisoned in Philippi, run out in Thessalonica and Berea, and scoffed at in Athens so he may have been physically weak, but in that weakness he was most powerful. There were no theatrics or techniques to manipulate people's response. His fear and shaking were because of the seriousness of his mission. Though Paul expounded the whole counsel of God to the church and taught in Corinthians the Word of God the focus of his preaching and teaching to unbelievers was Jesus Christ who paid the penalty for sin on the cross. Until someone understands and believes the gospel, there is nothing more to say to them. The scope of Paul's thanksgiving was all-encompassing. By this statement, Paul showed his heart was toward all the Roman believers. He was not biased nor did he choose favorites. He didn't look for what was wrong with people. He was simply thankful. Many people are not thankful because they don't think they have what they deserve. But if you really received what you deserved, you would be in hell forever. Paul was thankful that the faith of the believers in Rome had been spoken of throughout the world. In saying he was thankful for their faith; he was referring to the genuineness of their salvation, and the clear testimony of their lives. He was thankful that they were a redeemed fellowship manifesting the life and the power of the Lord Jesus Christ, even in the midst of severe Roman persecution. Their faith added credibility and integrity to the message of Christianity. Wouldn't it be honoring to God to be famous throughout the entire world for your faith? Some churches are famous for their pastor; others for their architecture. Some are famous for their art: others for their organ. Some are even famous for their choirs, or the different celebrities that attend. But wouldn't it be great to be famous around the world for your faith? People want to attend a church where the pastor and the congregation believe God and take Him at His Word. A thankful heart is essential for true spiritual service. One who is thankful realizes that God has a reason for everything that happens. One who serves externally, legalistically, or ritualistically will not find very many things to be thankful for in his life because he is not grateful for the things God has already done for him. Do you have a thankful heart? Are you overwhelmed with thanksgiving for what God has done? If you are, that will take out any bitterness or resentment you may be feeling toward God or anyone else. There is so much to be thankful for. The devil often tempts us by saying, "You deserve better than that. You don't have to be thankful." He attempts to play a game with our minds, but when he does, step back and say, "No! There is too much to be thankful for!" The apostle Paul was thankful in the midst of his distresses because his joy came not from his own success, but from the advance of God's Kingdom. Paul was an initiator who is most often seen as a strong, determined, bold, and dynamic individual. Paul was an intellectual whose logic was brilliant even though he did not flaunt it. He was a genius--the greatest theologian the church has ever known. Paul was intimate, very sensitive, loving, warm, and gentle man of God. He had the zeal of a prophet, the mind of a teacher, the determination of an apostle, but also the heart of a shepherd. Paul was no paid preacher with a fee in the place of his heart. He wasn't a preacher with a bag of old-hat sermons in the place of passion. He had a true shepherd's heart whose focus is on right motives. Before Paul moved into the full explanation of the good news, he wanted to open his heart to the believers in Rome. It was most important for him to do so because the Christians in Rome don't really know him at all. They might have questions as to why he is writing to them and why if he is the great apostle to the Gentiles, why he has never come to their city before? Paul wanted to explain the question of why he was writing and why he had not come. Because of his heart for people, Paul cared deeply about their spiritual maturity, yet had been unable to come because God has not allowed him to come. Since the Romans had never met him, the only way they could have had insight into his heart was if he wrote and then came to them. In Romans 1:8-16, the apostle opened his heart to reveal the character of his service for Christ. Paul was responsible for the spread of Christianity throughout the Roman Empire, more than any other individual. He made 3 missionary journeys, through much of the Mediterranean world, tirelessly preaching the gospel he had once sought to destroy. In preaching the gospel the apostle sought to bring people to the obedience of God and not to the obedience of men. Paul would not attempt to alter the doctrine of Christ, either to gain their favor, or to avoid their wrath. In an important a matter as this we must not fear men, nor seek their favor. Paul received the gospel by revelation from heaven. He was not lead into Christianity, as some are, merely by education. Paul's salvation and his service continued perfectly. God chose him to communicate His grace to all people. Paul began his ministry preaching to the Jews but his primary calling was the Gentiles. The gospel Paul preached was not human in origin or it would have been like all other human religions, permeated with works, righteousness born of man's pride and satans deception. Paul had been raised in Judaism and knew that the Romans might not be able to differentiate between real service to Christ and ritualism. He knew the external, religious activity of the Pharisees, Sadducees, scribes, chief priests, and elders. He knew that much of their service was merely routine, ritualistic, physical, superficial, and temporal. Paul also grew up in a Gentile world and knew how the priests of the pagan gods served. They served out of the fear that if they didn't perform certain functions, the gods would crush them, or bring calamity on their cities and towns. As a result, their service to the gods was shallow and superficial. Paul had become a willing slave of Christ which cost him a great deal of suffering from others. Such personal sacrifice is exactly opposite the goal of pleasing men as Paul talks about in Galatians 1:10," *For am I now seeking the favor of men, or of God? Or am I striving to please men? If I were still trying to please men, I would not be a bond servant of Christ*". He did not preach himself or seek to set up his own power and authority over men. He did not seek recognition for his own eloquence, learning, or ability. He did not seek to gain either applause or riches to himself. He did not teach human wisdom, the vain philosophy of the Gentiles, the tradition of the elders, the commandment of men, the power and purity of human nature, or the righteousness of men, but delivered divine wisdom and intellect. Paul summed up his entire perspective for the Romans in the statement "God . . . whom I serve with my spirit". He was saying that his service came from within, not from without. He served with a pure and holy motivation. What motivated him was not what people thought, it wasn't peer pressure or some legal obligation, but a heart motivated to accomplish the will of God. He persuaded things concerning God, and the kingdom of God as the Scriptures speaks about in Acts 19:8,"*Paul entered the synagogue and spoke boldly there for three months, arguing persuasively about the kingdom of God*". To persuade is to teach as it says in Acts 18:4,"*Every Sabbath he reasoned in the synagogue, trying to persuade Jews and Greeks*", also in 2 Corinthians 5:11,"*since, then, we know what it is to fear the Lord, we try to persuade men. What we are is plain to God, and I hope it is also plain to your conscience*". The apostle did not teach them to listen to himself or any of the other apostles but they were to listen to God, who spoke by his Son, Christ, who is God as well as man. He is to be listened to in all matters of doctrine, worship, and duty. Paul did not teach them to regard the traditions of the elders or to obey the commandments of men, but on the contrary the ordinances of Christ who is the One and only Lord, the only Master whose orders are to be observed. Paul taught not to trust in men's wisdom, strength, riches, and righteousness, but in the living God, the grace of God and in the blood righteousness and sacrifice of Christ, not for the sake of gaining honor, glory, and applause from men as the Pharisee and false apostles did but for the glory of God. Paul and the apostle taught and persuaded men not to believe in things human but believe in things divine. He taught that without the grace of the Spirit of God, no man should see the kingdom of heaven and with out the justifying righteousness of Christ no man should enter into the kingdom of heaven. As the Lord has done before him, Paul preached the things concerning the grace and love of God. He never pleased or sought to please men in his ministry which was the grace of God. The only pleasing of men which is right and which the apostles recommends is mentioned in Romans 15:2,"*each of us should please his neighbor for his good, to build him up*", and also in 1 Corinthians 10:31-33,"*Whether then you eat or drink, or whatever you do, do all to the glory of God. Give no offense either to Jews or to Greek or to the church of God, just as I also please all men in all things, not seeking my own profit but the profit of the many, so that they may be saved*". This principle gives glory of God, and edification, and salvation to men. There is a pleasing of men that is wrong which is done by concealing, or corrupting the doctrines of the gospel to gain the affection and applause of men and amass wealth to themselves as the false apostles did. Paul was acting as a man pleaser when he held the clothes of those that stoned Stephen, made havoc of the church, having men and women sent to prison and persecuted the followers of Christ. Paul said to please men and to be servants of

Christ are inconsistent, and incompatible. No man pleaser can be a true faithful servant of Christ or deserve the name of one. Around 50 A.D. Paul returned to Jerusalem to report to the church elders. His visit provoked a dispute over whether Christians had to first become Jews. Paul said no. The controversy was temporarily resolved in his favor and he went on his second and third missionary journeys to Galatia, Phrygia, Macedonia and Greece. He even went to Athens where he argued with philosophers as well as pagans. It was during this period that he met Luke, a doctor who would become a close friend and would eventually write one of the gospels as well as the book of Acts. There arose a conspiracy among forty Jews to assassinate Paul, but Paul's nephew brought him a warning of the plot. The Romans decided to send him to Caesarea to Felix, the procurator (governor) of Judea. Five days later, the high priest Ananias (not the same Ananias who was sent by God to Paul after his conversion) and some of the Sanhedrin appeared, with Tertullus as their advocate. They made charges, which Paul denied. Felix delayed the proceeding further until Claudias Lysias, the captain of the Roman troops in Jerusalem, could come to give evidence. After a few days, Felix' wife, Drusilla, a Jewess, wanted to see and hear Paul. Paul appeared and gave the gospel to Felix and Drusilla. Felix trembled but was unrepentant. He wanted a bribe from Paul to not acquit him. Felix kept Paul a prisoner in Caesarea (under loose house arrest) for two years until the arrival of Festus, the new governor. Festus wanted Paul taken back to Jerusalem, but Paul was aware of the danger there and uttered the Latin word, Caesarem apello which means "I appeal to Caesar!" Festus was thus obliged to make arrangements for Paul to travel to Rome under escort. About this time, King Agrippa II, with his sister, Berenice, came to visit Festus, the new governor. Festus pleaded ignorance of Jewish law, so Paul made his testimony before Agrippa, with the greatest of pomp and ceremony. This episode was one of the greatest defenses of the gospel ever recorded. Festus decided then that Paul was innocent of anything wrong, and he would have let him go free if he had not appealed to Caesar. After his third missionary journey, Paul returned to Jerusalem where he ran into a dispute with the Sanhedrin. He was the object of a huge civil disturbance. For this, he was arrested and eventually brought to Caesarea. Paul was falsely accused by some of the Jews, savagely beaten by an angry mob, and arrested by the Romans. While there, he was questioned and tried several times, but his enemies could not seem to make their charges stick. Even so, he was held by the governor, Felix, who was afraid he might again create problems in Jerusalem. The next governor, Festus, seemed to not want to come to a decision on his case. Though two Roman governors, Felix and Festus, as well as Herod Agrippa, did not find him guilty of any crime, pressure from the Jewish leaders kept Paul in Roman custody. After two years the apostle exercised his right as a Roman citizen and appealed his case to Caesar. It was against the law to put a Roman citizen in jail so in Acts 16:37 it says, *"But Paul said to them, "they have beaten us in public without trial, men who are Romans, and have thrown us into prison and now are they sending us away secretly? NO indeed! But let them come themselves and bring us out."* To inflict corporal punishment on a Roman Citizen was a serious crime. It was even more serious because Paul and Silas did not receive a trial. As a result, the magistrates faced the possibility of being removed, from office and having Philippi's privileges as a Roman colony revoked as explained in Acts 22: 25-29,*"but when they stretched him out with thongs, Paul said to the centurion who was standing by, "Is it lawful for you to scourge a man who is a Roman and uncondemned?" When the centurion heard this he went to the commander and told him saying "what are you about to do? For this man is a Roman." The commander came and said to him "tell me are you a Roman" and he said "yes". The commander answered "I acquired this citizenship with a large sum of money" and Paul said "but I was actually born a citizen". Therefore those who were about to examine him immediately let go of him and the commander also was afraid when he found out that he was a Roman, and because he had put him in chains".* Roman citizens were exempted from such brutal methods of interrogation. Paul now exerted his right as a Roman citizen. His claim would not have been questioned, because the penalty for falsely claiming Roman citizenship was death. The Lord made Paul a missionary to the Gentiles, even revealing to him during the period of his arrest in Palestine, and during his subsequent trials before Jewish and Roman authorities, that he should "be of good cheer, for you must bear witness of Jesus at Rome." After a considerable stay at Antioch after his second missionary journey, Paul departed and went over all the country of Galatia and Phrygia in order to strengthen the disciples as it says in Acts 18:23,"*And having spent some time there he left and passed successively through the Galatian region and Phrygia, strengthening all the disciples*". He came to Ephesus where He found there twelve disciples of Apollos who had only received John's baptism and were not aware of the Holy Spirit and Church Age mysteries. He taught three months in the synagogue in Ephesus. In the face of opposition, he took his classes to the school of one, Tyrannus, where he taught daily for two years. Exorcists were converted and books of magic were burned by the new converts. He paid a visit to Corinth, then returned to Ephesus where he wrote 1 Corinthians. Paul left for Troas and Macedonia because of the danger in Ephesus from the silversmiths and craftsmen who made articles for the worship. He sailed to Macedonia to meet Titus, landed at Neapolis and went to Philippi where he was "comforted by Titus." He sent Titus to Corinth with the second Corinthian letter and instructions for completing the collection there for needy Christians. Paul traveled through Macedonia and finally arrived at Corinth himself, staying there about three months and writing Romans. He took ship for Miletus where he met for a few days with Ephesian elders. He then sailed (island hopping to Coos, Rhodes, and Patara) to Tyre. From Tyre he sailed to Ptolemais and reached Caesarea. Paul was warned not to visit Jerusalem. He went anyway and was warmly received by the brethren. He had an interview with James and the elders. A charge was brought against him by the Sanhedrin that "he taught all the Jews among the Gentiles to forsake Moses, saying that they ought not to circumcise their sons, neither to walk after their customs." The Sanhedrin asked Paul to do a public act of the Law in order to prove his faith. There were four men who were to undergo the ritual associated with the Nazarite vow, and Paul was requested to put himself under that vow and to pay the costs of the other four men. He did so. After this some Jews from Asia stirred up the people against him, charging him with bringing Greeks into the Temple. A Gentile man from Ephesus named Trophimus was with Paul, and the Jews supposed that Paul had brought him into the temple, which would have been a sacrilege. The mob took Paul to kill him, but soldiers of the Roman garrison appeared. Paul spoke to the mob in his own defense, telling of his mission to the Gentiles. They shouted "Away with such a fellow from the earth, for it is not fit that he should live".The Roman soldiers took Paul to the governor's castle for interrogation by scourging, at which time Paul claimed his Roman citizenship. The next morning he was taken before the Sanhedrin, but there was no conclusion because of the dissension between the Sadducees and Pharisees. Paul was taken back to the castle for protection, and it was that night that the Lord appeared to Paul telling him to be of good cheer as Paul explains in Acts 23:6-11,"*But perceiving that one group were Sadducees, and the other Pharisees, Paul began crying out in the Council,*" *Brethren I am a Pharisee, a son of Pharisees, I am on trial for the hope and resurrection of the dead!*" *as he said this there occurred a dissension between the Pharisees and Sadducees and the assembly was divided. For the Sadducees say that there is no resurrection, nor an angel, nor a spirit, but a Pharisee acknowledge them all. And there occurred a great uproar and some of the scribes of the Pharisaic party stood up and began to argue heatedly, saying, "We find nothing wrong with this man; suppose a spirit or an angel has spoken to him?" and as a great dissension was developing the commander was afraid Paul would be torn to pieces by them and ordered the troops to go down and take him away from them by force and bring him into the barracks. But on the night immediately following, the Lord stood at his side and said "take courage for as you have solemnly witnessed to My cause at Jerusalem so you must witness at Rome also.*" When the Lord said "take courage" He meant "be of good cheer". He was sent on the next ship to Rome. However, the ship met heavy seas and wrecked on the Island of Malta. Paul prayed and was visited by an Angel and the entire crew was saved. Paul eventually took another boat and reached Italy. He was met by supporters and eventually made it to Rome. Paul, being a bond servant of Christ went through many harrowing experiences as he talks about in 2 Corinthians 11:23-33,"*Are they servants of Christ? – I speak as if insane – I more so: in far more labors, in far more imprisonments, beaten times without number, often in danger of death. Five times I received from the Jews thirty-nine lashes. Three times I was beaten with rods, once I was stoned; three times I was shipwrecked, a night and a day I have spent in the deep. I have been on frequent journeys, in dangers from rivers, dangers from robbers, dangers from my countrymen, dangers from the Gentiles, dangers in the city, dangers in the wilderness, dangers in the sea, dangers among false brethren, I have been in labor and hardship through many sleepless nights, in hunger and thirst, often without food, in cold, and exposure. Apart from such external things there is the daily pressure on me of concern for all the churches. Who is led into sin without any intense concern? If I have to boast, I will boast of what pertains of my weakness. The God and Father of the Lord Jesus, He who is blessed forever, know that I am not lying. In Damascus the Ethnarch under Aretas the king was guarding the city of the Damascenes in order to seize me, and I was let down in a basket through a window in the wall, and so escaped his hands*", also the Scriptures talks about this in Acts 9:23-25, "*When many days had elapsed, the Jews plotted together to do away with him. But their plot became known to Saul. They were also watching the gates, day and night so that they might put him to death, but his disciples took him by night and let him down through and opening in the wall, lowering him in a large basket.*" Paul ministered a period of three years, in Nabatean Arabia, an area encompassing Damascus south to the Sinai Peninsula. Damascus was a walled city; the gates were the only conventional means to escape. Paul used an unconventional way to escape. He was lowered down in a large basket that was large enough to be a large hamper suitable for hay, straw, or bales of wool. When Paul asked, "*Are they servants of Christ*", Paul had already emphatically denied that they were however; some of the Corinthians still believed they were. Paul accepted that belief for the sake of argument then went on to show that his ministry was in every way superior to the false apostle's so-called ministry. Paul was often in danger of death. Paul received thirty-nine lashes, because forty was the maximum number that could legally be administered in Paul's day, the Jews reduced that number by one to avoid accidentally going over the maximum. Jesus warned that His followers would receive such beatings. Far worse than the occasional physical sufferings Paul endured was the constant, daily burden of concern that he felt for the churches. Those who were weak in faith, or were "led into sin" caused him intense emotional pain. The apostle gives an account of his labors and sufferings, not out of pride or vain-glory but to the honor of God, who enabled him to do and suffer so much for the cause of Christ and shows wherein he excelled the false apostles, who tried to lessen his character and usefulness. It amazes us to reflect of this account of his dangers, hardships, and sufferings and to observe his patience, perseverance, diligence, cheerfulness, and usefulness in the midst of all these trials. Paul never served the Lord without a wholehearted commitment. By doing that, he distinguished himself from the workers, those whose labor was external and insincere. He also separated himself from the heathen, cultic priests. The Holy Spirit was behind the scenes, energizing the service of the apostle Paul. It is interesting to observe that the phrase translated "to serve" comes from the Greek verb that is frequently translated "worship." It is always used in the New Testament to refer to religious service or worship. Many think of worship as stained-glass windows and pipe organs, but the Bible says the same word that means worship also means service. The greatest worship you ever render to God is to serve Him. For Paul, service was a total commitment as he explained in Romans 12:1-2,"*Therefore I urge you brethren by the mercies of God, to present your bodies a living and holy sacrifice, acceptable to God, which is your spiritual service of worship. And do not be conformed to this world but be transformed by the renewing of your mind, so that you may prove what the will of God is, that which is good and acceptable and perfect.*" With everything Paul had, physical, spiritual and emotional, he served to his fullest. In Philippians 3:3 Paul makes the same distinction between internal, spiritual worship, and external, fleshly worship," *For we are the true circumcision who worship in the Spirit of God and glory in Christ Jesus and put no confidence in the flesh.*" In 2 Timothy 1:3 Paul wrote, "*I thank God whom I serve with a clear conscience the way my forefathers did, as I constantly remember you in my prayers night and day.*" He was saying, "You can look deep inside me and see that I serve God with a whole heart. Paul's service was an act of deep, genuine, and honest worship. That is the real measure of true spirituality. The only way to serve God is with total commitment. At the time that the Jewish leaders were plotting to kill Paul, he never lost his perspective as it talks about in Acts 20:3,"*After the uproar had ceased, Paul sent for the disciples, and when he had exhorted them and taken his leave of them he left to go to Macedonia. When he had gone through those districts he had given them much exhortation, he came to Greece. And there he spent three months, and when a plot had formed against him by the Jews as he was about to set sail for Syria he decided to return through Macedonia.*" Even in that particular situation he was still filled with thanksgiving. When Paul was on his way to Jerusalem, he was constantly told he would be put in chains and his life would be in imminent danger. But it never bothered Paul in the least because he had a thankful heart. Our utmost diligence and service in our difficulties and trials appear unworthy of notice when compared with his. It may lead us to ask whether or not we really are followers of Christ. After a traumatic trip, including a violent, two week storm at sea that resulted in a ship wreck, Paul had finally reached

Rome. The Acts recounts that on the way to Rome he was shipwrecked on "Melite" (Malta), as described in Acts 28:1-2," *When they had been brought safely through, then we found out that the island was called Malta. The natives showed us extraordinary kindness, for because of the rain that had set in and because of the cold, they kindled a fire and received us all.*" While on the island he was met by Publius and the islanders, who showed him "unusual kindness" as described in Acts 28:7,"*Now in the neighborhood of that place were lands belonging to the leading man of the island, named Publius, who welcomed us and entertained us courteously three days.*" Eventually released for a brief period of ministry, he was arrested again and suffered martyrdom at Rome. According to Christian tradition, Paul was beheaded in Rome during the reign of Nero around the mid-60s at *Tre Fontane Abbey* (English: Three Fountains Abbey) By comparison, tradition has Peter being crucified upside-down. Eusebius of Caesarea, who wrote in the fourth century, states that Paul was beheaded in the reign of the Roman Emperor Nero. Whatever his end, it is certain that Paul was a great influence on modern Christianity, both through his missionary work and his writing. It has been said that if it were not for Paul and a few others such as Barnabas that Christianity would have remained a small unknown branch of Judaism. Paul was the leading missionary to the Gentiles. Besides being an enthusiastic speaker, Paul was also a capable writer. His letters make up the bulk of the epistles in the Bible. Because his writings were so treasured, they are among the most studied today. The words of Paul carry weight far greater than those of James or Peter. Paul's thoughtfulness, gentleness and steadfastness permeate his letters. Paul was a charismatic individual. He was a sure leader of men. Seldom did he doubt himself. He saw his mission as not only bringing the "Good News" to the Gentiles, but also to organize the Church so that it would grow, even when he was not present to urge it on. Thus, he created an organization and trained leaders. This organization would one day become modern Christianity as it came to succeed the original authority of the Church in Jerusalem. Today Christians see Christ through Paul's teaching. Paul was vitally shaped by a dramatic meeting with Christ on the Road to Demascus and it was this drama, linked with his intensity that would mold Christianity for the next two Millenia. The apostle Paul was one of the most famous citizens of the Roman Empire and without question one of the most influential individuals in history. He was used by the Lord in his missionary and evangelistic activities to set in motion a great deal of the organization known as the Christian Church, the Body of Christ on earth, to the extent that billions of human beings have been directly or indirectly affected by his ministry. Under the inspiration of the Holy Spirit, he wrote the foundation documents for the Christian way of life, the Word of God which has changed the lives of millions.

Chapter 7

James, a bond servant of Jesus Christ and a half brother of Jesus.

James was the oldest half brother of the Lord Jesus, as his lineage is explained in Mark 6:3, "*is not this the carpenter the son of Mary, and brother of James and Joses and Judas and Simon? Are not his sisters here with us? And they took offense at him*". These were actual half brothers and sisters of Jesus, though in the Holy Scriptures does not tell the names of Jesus' sisters we can tell from this passage that there was more than one. Since James' name always appears first in lists, this suggests he was the eldest among them. Throughout Jesus' ministry His half brother James, along with the other three brothers, didn't give Jesus the respect due Him as John 7:1-5 explains," *After these things Jesus was walking in Galilee for He was unwilling to walk in Judea because the Jews were seeking to kill Him. Now the feast of the Jews, the feast of booths, was near. Therefore His brothers said to Him "leave here and go to Judea so that your disciples also may see your works, which you are doing for no one does anything in secret, when He Himself seeks to be known publicly. If you do these things show Yourself to the world. For not even His brothers were believing Him.*" It appears they thought He was not thinking clearly, and perhaps they wanted Him gone from their home. James and Jesus' other brothers showed Him no honor, which saddened Jesus, who spoke from personal experience when He said in Mark 6:4,"*Jesus said to them, "A prophet is not without honor except in his hometown and among his own relatives and in his own household.*" The People of Nazareth still thought of Jesus as one who carried on His fathers trade, as a craftsman who worked in wood and other hard materials. The common earthly position of Jesus and His family caused the townspeople to stumble, they refused to see Him as higher than themselves and found it impossible to accept Him as the Son of God and Messiah. The normal Jewish practice was to identify a son by his father's name. Perhaps, the reason this was not done here was because Joseph was already dead, or because Christ's audience was recalling the rumors concerning Jesus' illegitimate birth. A man was called the son of his mother if his father was unknown. They were purposely insulting Him with this title as a reference to His illegitimacy. There is nothing else known about James other brothers and sisters, except Jude, whose Hebrew name is Judah, who wrote the epistle of Jude. We surely know who Jesus Christ was, but who was Jude's brother James, who was obviously well-known to the early church, since Jude merely had to mention his name, with no other explanation, for everyone to know who he was? There were three such well-known men named James during the time of the New Testament record. The first was the apostle James, who along with his brother the apostle John, were among the twelve apostles. Even in the passage in Josephus' Jewish Antiquities the Jewish historian describes James as "the brother of Jesus who is called Christ". He was literally born and raised in the same family of Jesus Christ. While most Christians believe that Jesus was, as the Son of God, born of a virgin, defining the relationship of James the Just to Jesus requires some further discussion. The Bible refers to Jesus as the "first-born son" of Mary, which seems to imply later sons. The Jews living in Jerusalem in Christ's time still adhered to the Mosaic Law, which advised married couples to be fruitful and have many children and that this would indicate, assuming Mary and Joseph were average Jews, that they would have had more children after Mary gave birth to Jesus, thus making James a brother of Jesus. James was not like Jesus as a boy. While James grew up in the same house with Jesus in Nazareth, he was miles apart from Jesus' thinking for the early part of his life. He was the first born after Jesus. Jesus was his older brother. James says he is a bond servant of Christ but he doesn't say he is Jesus' brother. Why James didn't say he was the brother of Jesus was because his real relationship to Jesus wasn't physical it was spiritual. His relationship wasn't made possible by Mary their mother, it was made possible by the grace of God. The consequences of living in a household with an older brother are predictable. Throughout his childhood and young adult life, he was an unbeliever; he had seen life in the raw. He had watched Jesus grow, and his anger and hostility that he had intensified, so that at the point of Jesus declaring Himself as the Messiah, James thought He was mad, At first James thought Jesus lost His senses, when Jesus claimed to be the Messiah. James held onto that opinion, right onto young manhood until he had to make a decision. At the time of the cross it is possible he was still an unbeliever. The Scriptures do not sugarcoat this. The lack of belief by James and the other brothers is confirmed by the absolute silence about them in the gospels. None of the accounts of Jesus' ministry mentions them in any role. Though Jesus and James had the same mother, Jesus was the son not of Joseph, as James was, but of God the Father Himself—a fact that wouldn't fully sink into James' mind for years. It wasn't until Jesus' resurrection and His appearance to James and the disciples that James finally really understood who his half brother was. All in all, it is a well founded conclusion that James, the brother of Jesus – like Paul – made a remarkable conversion from a non-believer during the lifetime of Jesus to a leader in the earliest years of the Christian movement. Although the personal appearance of the risen Jesus to His brother James is reported only once in the New Testament, one can wonder, what could have ever happened to James that could have converted him to a believer apart from the appearance of the resurrected Christ? James knew Jesus while He was alive and certainly knew about His teachings and even Jesus' miracles. None of this, however, convinced him, so what could the apostles have said to convince this man? Logically, only a personal encounter with Jesus, as mentioned by Paul, would explain his 180 degree change in beliefs and actions. According to Paul, an inspired apostle, Jesus appeared to James following his resurrection. As already noted, before the crucifixion, his brothers were unbelievers. It was the resurrection of Jesus which brought them to faith. Immediately after the cross Jesus paid a visit to James. Around that time James received Jesus as his Lord and Savior. Four years after the resurrection James not only converted to Christianity; he had become a recognized leader in the early church. Later on Paul also gives an important clue as to why James became a Christian, in the early resurrection creed in 1 Corinthians 15:3-8, Paul writes,"*For I delivered to you as the first importance what I also received that Christ died for our sins according to the scriptures, and that He was buried and that He was raised on the third day according to the scriptures and that*

He appeared to Cephas then to the twelve. After that He appeared to more than five hundred brethren at one time most of whom remained until now but some have fallen asleep, then He appeared to James then to all the apostles and last of all as to one untimely born, He appeared to me also." The testimony of eyewitnesses was added to support the reality of the resurrection. These included John and Peter together, and also separately, the five hundred who have seen the risen Christ, and James the brother of Jesus. One can argue which James this is because the lack of a surname in Bible times can occasionally be quite confusing. However, the context makes it clear, that this is not James the son of Zebedee (the brother of John) or the other apostle James: James the son of Alphaeus. Therefore this must be James, the Lord's brother. God moved and molded James to be one of the significant leaders of the early church. God's grace rescued James from a life of skepticism and transformed him into a radical follower of Jesus Christ. James never was a skeptic after that. He came around through Gods work of grace. God grabbed his heart and for the first time he looked at Christianity in a whole new light. He saw hypocrisy not in Jesus, but in those who followed his brother. He was also known as, Saint James the Just, James the Righteous, James of Jerusalem, James Adelphotheos ("the brother of God" Adelphotheos), or James, the Brother of the Lord. James was called "the Just" because of his righteousness and devotion. The name also helps distinguish him from other important figures in early Christianity of the same name, such as James, son of Zebedee. There were more than one person named James, and different titles are used to distinguish between them. In the list of the disciples found in the Gospels, two disciples named James are mentioned in the list of twelve disciples that is found in Matthew 10:2-4," *And he called to him his twelve disciples and gave them authority over unclean spirits, to cast them out, and to heal every disease and every affliction. The names of the twelve apostles are these: first, Simon, who is called Peter, and Andrew his brother; James the son of Zebedee, and John his brother; Philip and Bartholomew; Thomas and Matthew the tax collector; James, son of Alphaeus, and Thaddaeus; Simon the Cananaean, and Judas Iscariot, who betrayed him.*" These brothers who are also all fisherman, represent and inner circle of disciples often seen closest to Jesus. James, the son of Zebedee, is also known as James the Great, who is not the same James as James the Just. James, son of Alphaeus, however, is usually identified with James the Less. James the Just was the leader of the Christian movement in Jerusalem in the decades after Jesus' death. He was an important figure in early Christianity and a pillar in the church, emphasizing the role in establishing and supporting the church. James, Cephas (Simon Peter) and John, were all esteemed as pillars. Paul lists James with Cephas (better known as Peter) and John as the three "pillars" of the Church in Galatians 2:9," *and recognizing the grace that had been given to me, James and Cephas and John, who were reputed to be pillars, gave to me and Barnabas the right hand of fellowship, so that we might go to the Gentiles and they to the circumcised.*" The only conclusion these leaders could make was that God's grace was responsible for the powerful preaching of the gospel and the building of the church through Paul's efforts. In the near east the right hand of fellowship is represented a solemn vow of friendship and a mark of partnership. This act signified the apostle's recognition of Paul as a teacher of the true gospel and a partner in ministry. James later was raised to be the leader in the Jerusalem church. James became a leading figure in the church at Jerusalem. . In many ways James' epistle resembles Jesus' Sermon on the Mount, loaded as it is with encouragement and filled with gems to help build

Christian character. The second-century writer and historian Hegesippus referred to Jesus' brother as James the Just and characterized him as zealous for the law of God. Many statements from James' letter prove Hegesippus was right; it represents a book of Christian proverbs that cover subjects that touch many aspects of Christian life. James apparently became the overseeing pastor of the Jerusalem church. The epistle of James presents many problems to those who hold to the view that Jesus taught we no longer need to keep God's laws, or that those laws were somehow abolished at Christ's death and resurrection. But, if anyone knew how Jesus lived and what He taught and believed, it was James, a member of Christ's own household. When Peter was released from prison he came to the house of Mary where many in the church had come together to pray for him. According to Peter's account of that evening, the Lord had instructed him to tell James and the brethren of his prison escape, which Peter then did the whole account is recorded in Acts 12:3-17,"*When he (Herod) saw that it pleased the Jews, he proceeded to arrest Peter, also. Now, it was during the days of Unleavened Bread. When he had seized him, he put him in prison, delivering him to four squads of soldiers to guard him, intending after the Passover to bring him out before the people. So Peter was kept in the prison, but prayer for him was being made fervently by the church to God. On the very night when Herod was about to bring him forward, Peter was sleeping between two soldiers bound with two chains, and guards in front of the door were watching over the prison. And behold an angle of the Lord suddenly appeared as a light shone in the cell; and he struck Peters side and woke him up, saying "get up quickly", and his chains fell off his hands, and the angel said to him, "Gird yourself and put on your sandals," and he did so. And he said to him, "Wrap your cloak around you and follow me." And he went out and continued to follow, and he did not know that what was being done by the angel was real but thought he was seeing a vision. When they had passed the first and second guard they came to the Iron Gate that leads to into the city, which opened for them by itself, and they went out and went along one street and immediately the angel departed from him. When Peter came to himself he said, "Now I know for sure that the Lord has sent forth His angel and rescued me from the hand of Herod and from all that the Jewish people were expecting." And when he realized this, he went to the house of Mary, the mother of John, who was also called Mark, where many were gathered together and were praying. When he knocked at the door of the gate, a servant-girl named Rhoda came to answer. When she recognized Peter's voice, because of her joy she did not open the gate but ran in and announced that Peter was standing in front of the gate. They said to her, "You are out of your mind", but she kept on insisting that it was so. They kept saying," It is his angel". But Peter continued knocking and when they had opened the door they saw him and were amazed. But motioning to them with his hand to be silent, he described to them how the Lord had led him out of the prison. And He said report these things to James and the brethren". Then he left and went to another place.*" James, the Lords brother, at this time is now head of the Jerusalem church. According to Jewish superstition, each person had his own guardian angel who could assume that persons form. Some readers will recall that in the early days of the Church, about 44 C.E., King Herod Agrippa killed the apostle James, the son of Zebedee and one of the original 12. Thus it must be another James where Luke records that Peter sent news of his release from prison to someone named James. Though as many as seven different people by the same name have been identified in the New Testament, it is James the brother of Jesus who is the most likely in this case. Jesus' brothers were present with the apostles in Jerusalem as the Church began after Jesus' departure. This same James appears later in Acts as the leader of the church at Jerusalem. The writings of the New Testament, as well as other written sources from the Early Church, provide some insights into James' life and his role in the Early Church. The short book of James is a moral, doctrinal and literary masterpiece. Of the four men named James in the New Testament, only two may have possibly written this epistle. No one has seriously considered James the Less, the son of Alphaeus, or James the father of Judas, not Iscariot. Some have suggested James the son of Zebedee, and the brother of John, but he was martyred too early to have written it. That leaves only James the brother of Christ and brother of Jude, who also wrote the epistle that bears his name. While some have thought its content at odds with the writings of Paul, its emphasis on living according to, the perfect law, the law of liberty, and the royal law. This concept is explained in James 1:25,"*But one who looks intently at the perfect law, the law of liberty, and abides by it, not having become a forgetful hearer but an effectual doer, this man will be blessed in what he does*", also James 2:8,"*If however you are fulfilling the royal law according to the Scripture," You shall love your neighbor as yourself," you are doing well*". James repeatedly upholds the need to keep God's laws, emphasizing the Ten Commandments. He refers to God's law not as something unnecessary or optional, but as "the *royal* law" as it says in James 2:8,"*If, however you are fulfilling the royal law according to the Scripture, 'You shall love your neighbor as yourself, you are doing well.*" He specifically mentions several of the Ten Commandments, then calls them "*the law of liberty*" as described in James 2:11-12,"For He who said, "Do not commit adultery," also said, "Do not commit murder," Now if you do not commit adultery but do commit murder you have become a transgressor of the law. So speak and so act as those who are to be judged by the law of liberty". Why that designation? Because James understood that only by obeying God's laws can mankind experience *true freedom*—freedom from want, sorrow and suffering, from the degrading and painful consequences of sin. He encourages each of us to be a "doer of the law" as it is described in James 4:11,"*Do not speak against one another, brethren. He, who speaks against a brother or judges his brother, speaks against the law and judges the law; but if you judge the law you are not a doer of the law but a judge of it.*" James drew an analogy of looking into a mirror to make his point about the importance of God's Ten Commandments as it says in James 1:23-25, "*For if anyone is a hearer of the word and not a doer, he is like a man observing his natural face in a mirror; for he observes himself, goes away, and immediately forgets what kind of man he was. But he who looks into the perfect law of liberty and continues in it, and is not a forgetful hearer but a doer of the work, this one will be blessed in what he does*". In other words, said James, we should look into the perfect law of liberty and evaluate where we stand in relation to God's holy, spiritual laws, which help us understand what sin is as described in Romans 7:7-12,"*What shall we say then? Is the law sin? May it never be! On the contrary, I would not have come to know sin except through the law, for I would not have known about coveting if the law had not said," You shall not covet." But sin, taking opportunity, through the commandment, produces in me coveting of every kind, for apart from the Law sin is dead. I was once alive apart from the Law, but when the commandment came sin became alive and I died, and this commandment which was to result in life proved to result in death for me. For sin taking an opportunity through the commandment deceived me and through it killed me. So then, the Law is holy, and the commandment is holy and righteous and good.*" When we look into a mirror and scrutinize our physical appearance, we may see a smudge on our face or a hair out of place. Yet, if we put the mirror away, we tend to forget our imperfections rather quickly because they are no longer visible to us. James shows how this physical analogy reflects an empty Christianity that requires nothing of us beyond mere belief as explained in James 1:26-27,"*If anyone thinks himself to be religious, and yet does not bridle his tongue but deceives his own heart, this mans religion is worthless. Pure and undefiled religion in the sight of our God and Father is this; to visit orphans and widows in their distress, and to keep oneself unstained by the world.*" James tells us that God's law shows our *internal* imperfections—those of the heart and mind. God's perfect law of liberty, including the Ten Commandments, is like a spiritual mirror we can look into and see ourselves for what we are. We must never put this mirror away; we must keep it ever in mind to motivate us to deal with our imperfections. James was saying, in effect, that we can't simply *talk* Christianity; we must live it. Mere talk accomplishes nothing. In both the Old and New Testament, God's revealed inerrant sufficient and comprehensive Word is called "Law". The presence of His grace does not mean there is no moral law or code of conduct for believers to obey. Believers are enabled by the Sprit to keep genuine freedom from sin. As the Holy Spirit applies the principal of Scriptures to believer's hearts they are freed from sins bondage and enabled to obey God. Sovereign law is the idea that law is supreme and binding. James is not advocating some kind of emotional affection for oneself; self love is clearly a sin. The command is to pursue meeting the physical health and spiritual wellbeing of ones neighbor with the same intensity and concern as one does naturally for ones self. James's emphasis on the practice of right living is found early in the letter. At the close of the first chapter he sets the tone for what will follow. He draws the contrast between natural human ways of behaving and God's ways of behaving. We should not be slow to hear, quick to speak and quickly angered. Human anger cannot produce godly righteousness. It is the Word of God that instructs us in right ways. But knowing is not enough, he writes; we must act on what we know to be right. Otherwise it is like looking at our image in the mirror, seeing what is wrong, and doing nothing to fix what we find. Thus, defining meaningful religion, James expresses its core in terms of both self-control and positive, outgoing action. The theme of acting on belief will recur throughout the letter. There is mention of him in the Gospel of John and the early portions of the Acts of the Apostles; however, the later chapters of the Acts of the Apostles provide evidence that James was an important figure in the Christian community of Jerusalem. James the brother of the Lord surnamed the Just was made head of the Church at Jerusalem. The Apostle James' self-disciplined life strengthened his significance even more. He did not drink either wine or other spirituous beverages, abstained from meat meaning he was a vegetarian and wore only linen clothing. He bathed daily at dawn in cold water, and was a life-long Nazirite. This one was holy from his mother's womb. He had the custom of going off by himself in the temple for prayer, and there he would pray for his people on bended knee. He was so often stretched out on the ground in prayer that the skin on his knees became calloused. He alone had the privilege of entering the Holy of Holies, since indeed he did not use woolen garments but linen and went alone into the temple and prayed on behalf of the people. He was on bended knee in front of God for his people so much that it is reported that his knees had acquired the hardness of camels' knees. James used at least thirty references to nature. For example he talked about the surf of the sea in James 1:6,"*But he must ask in faith without any doubting, for the one who doubts is like the surf of the sea, driven and tossed by the wind.*" James also talked about reptiles in James 3:7,"*For every species of beast and birds, of reptiles and creature of the sea is tamed and has been tamed by the human race.*" James talked about the outdoors when he said in James 5:18,"*Then he prayed again and the sky poured rain and the earth produced its fruit.*" This is fitting to one who spent a great deal of time outdoors. Apart from a handful of references in the Gospels, the main sources for his life story are the Acts of the Apostles, the Epistles of Saint Paul, the historian Josephus, and the early Christian author Hegesippus. After Jesus' instructions recorded in Acts 1:4,"*Gathering them together He commanded them not to leave Jerusalem but to wait for what the Father had promised, "Which", He said, you heard of from me*". James accompanied the apostles, the women who had followed Jesus, his mother and his brothers to the upper room, where they prayed and waited patiently for the gift of the Holy Spirit which is speaking about in Acts 1:14."*These all with one mind were continually devoting themselves to prayer, along with the women, and Mary the mother of Jesus, and with His brothers.*" James was present when God sent the Holy Spirit to the small group, at which point the New Testament Church was born. From Jesus' resurrection on, James gave himself entirely to God and soon became an important figure in the early Church. His role was so important that Peter told others to report to James of his miraculous release from prison. He apparently became the overseeing pastor of the Jerusalem church, because in Acts 15:12-21 we see him making the final declaration during this early ministerial conference," *All the people kept silent and they were listening to Barnabas and Paul as they were relating what signs and wonders God had done through them among the Gentiles. After they had stopped speaking, James answered saying, "brethren listen to me. Simeon has related how God first concerned Himself about taking from among the Gentiles a people for His name. with this the words of the Prophets agree, just as it is written, "After these things I will return and I will rebuild the Tabernacle of David which has fallen, and I will rebuild its ruins, and I will restore it, so that the rest of mankind may seek the Lord, and all the Gentiles who are called by my name, Says the Lord who makes these things known from long ago." Therefore it is my judgment that we do not trouble those who are turning to God from among the Gentiles but that we write to them that they abstain from things contaminated and from what is strangled and from blood. For Moses, from ancient generations has in every city those who preach him since he is read in the synagogues every Sabbath.*" The apostle Paul, after his conversion, met with Peter and James before seeing any of the other apostles. Later we see James advising Paul, and Paul then acting on that advice as told about in Acts 21:17-26,"*After we arrived in Jerusalem, the brethren received us gladly, and the following day Paul went in with us to James and all the elders were present. After he had greeted them he began to relate one by one the things which God had done among the Gentiles through his ministry. And when they heard it they began glorifying God and they said to him, you see brethren how many thousands there are among the Jews of those who have believed and they are all zealous for the law, and they have been told about you, that you are teaching all the Jews who are among the Gentiles to forsake Moses, telling them not to circumcise their children nor to walk according to the customs. What then is to be done? They will certainly hear that you have come. Therefore do this that we tell you. We have four men who are under a vow take them and purify yourselves along with them and pay their expenses so that they may shave their heads, and all will know that there is nothing to the things which they have been told about you, but that you yourselves also walk orderly keeping the law. But concerning the Gentiles who have believed we wrote having decided that they should abstain from meat sacrificed to idols, and from blood and from what is strangled and from fornication. Then Paul took the men, and the next day purifying himself along with them, went into the temple giving notice of the completion of the days of purification until the sacrifice was offered for each one of them.*" He is believed to be the author of the Epistle of James in the New Testament, the first of the Seventy Apostles, and the author of the Apostolic Decree of Acts 15: 23-29, "*.... The Apostles and the brethren who are elders, to the brethren in Antioch and Syria and Cilicia who are from the Gentiles, greetings, Since we have heard that some of our number to whom we gave no instruction have disturbed you with their words, unsettling your souls, it seemed good to us, having become one in mind, to select men to send to you with our beloved Barnabas and Paul, men who have risked their lives for the name of our Lord Jesus Christ. Therefore we have sent Judas and Silas, who themselves will also report the same things by word of mouth. For it seemed good to the Holy Spirit and to us to lay upon you no greater burden than these essentials; that you abstain from things sacrificed to idols and from blood and from things strangled and from fornication; if you keep yourselves free from such things, you will do well. Farewell.*" In the Epistle to the Galatians, Paul of Tarsus describes his first visit to Jerusalem where he met James and stayed with Cephas (Simon Peter). Paul met James a few times over the years. The first meeting was about 3 years after his conversion. Roughly two decades after the event, Paul briefly mentions meeting "James, the Lord's brother" in Galatians 1:18-19,"*Then three years later I went up to Jerusalem to become acquainted with Cephas and stayed with him fifteen days. But I did not see any other of the apostles except James, the Lords brother*". Paul refers to James, at that time the only prominent Christian James in Jerusalem, as an Apostle. The second time Paul writes about meeting with James, was again many years later, during a dispute over acceptance of Gentiles in the church, possibly the same incident as the Council of Jerusalem described in the Acts of the Apostles. When Paul arrives in Jerusalem to deliver the money he raised for the faithful there, it is to James that he speaks, and it is James who insists that Paul ritually cleanse himself at Herod's Temple to prove his faith and deny rumors of teaching. This James is obviously the Lords brother, the head of the Jerusalem church. Hegesippus describes James as a vegetarian, who spent a great deal of time outdoors. He was also the brother of Jude, as it is explained in Matthew 13:55, "*is not this the carpenter's son? Is not his mother called Mary, and his brothers, James and Joseph, and Simon, and Judas?*" James had first rejected Jesus as Messiah, as the story is told in John 7:5,"*for not even His brothers were believing in Him*". As with the crowds in Jerusalem and Galilee even his own brothers did not believe in Jesus at first. They did not become His followers until after the resurrection. Later James believed that Jesus was and is the Messiah, as told about in 1 Corinthians 15:7,"*then He appeared to James, then to all the apostles*". James is mentioned in Paul's First Epistle to the Corinthians, as one to whom Jesus appeared after his resurrection. This is generally taken as an indication that this James is the same as James the younger brother of Jesus. Paul mentions James in a way that suggests James had possibly been married, as it says in 1 Corinthians 9:5,"*Do we not have a right to take along a believing* *wife, even as the rest of the apostles and the brothers of the Lord and Cephas?"* When the Christians of Antioch were concerned over whether Gentile Christians need be circumcised to be saved, they sent Paul and Barnabas to confer with the Jerusalem church. James played a prominent role in the formulation of the council's decision as it is discussed in Acts 15:13, *"After they had stopped speaking, James answered, saying, "Brethren, listen to me".* James delivers the third speech in defense of salvation by faith alone by relating how God's future plans for Gentile salvation agreed with his current work. James was the last named figure to speak, after Peter, Paul and Barnabas; he delivered what he calls his decision in Acts 15:19,*"Therefore it is my judgment that we do not trouble those who are turning to God from among the Gentiles".* The Greek word for trouble means to throw something in the path of someone to annoy them. The decision of the Jerusalem Council, after considering all the evidence was that keeping the law and observing rituals were not requirements for salvation. The Judaizers were to cease troubling and annoying the Gentiles. A Judaizer was someone who comformed to the spirit, character, principles, and practices of Judaism. When the controversy arose over certain Judaizers who were demanding the circumcision of Gentle Christians, Paul and Barnabas met in Jerusalem with the apostles and elders, and James played a significant role in that meeting. It was James who reminded them of Peter's encounter with Cornelius and how the Gentiles were to be brought into the kingdom. He further argued that this was in agreement with what the prophets had predicted. He then recommended they write a letter to Gentile churches in which they would be told to abstain from pollutions of idols, and from fornication, and from things strangled, and from blood. The apostles, elders and the whole church agreed. This became the ruling of the Council, agreed upon by all the apostles and elders, and sent to the other churches by letter. James explains that one of the most valuable things we can do for fellow-followers of the way of God is to bring them back from error. It is a practice that produces great reward. This confirms James's concern for the community of believers he had become a part of and led following the death and resurrection of Jesus. It is an early and powerful letter from one whose life was lived in the shadow of Jesus of Nazareth. James the servant of God the Father, a preacher of the gospel, and an apostle of Christ, wrote with the authority of one who had personally seen the resurrected Jesus Christ, who was recognized as an associate of the apostle and who was the leader of the Jerusalem church. James issues a warning against pursuing materialistic goals as if nothing can go wrong. It is foolishness to act as if we know what tomorrow will bring. Life itself is momentary. We are dependent on God's mercy and His will and should recognize Him in all our planning. Knowing the right way and failing to practice it is sin. This is an evil that will not go unpunished. Similarly, wealthy people are cautioned to get their priorities right. Gold and silver will be worthless one day. Then all of the material goods will be of no benefit. Too often they have been gained at the expense of hired workers, but fraud and self-indulgence will have their end. In such a world the followers of James's elder Brother are to demonstrate patience until His return. Like the farmer who must wait for his crops to receive seasonal rains and then mature, so they must hold fast to their belief and practice until "the coming of the Lord" as it explains in James 5:7–8,*"Therefore be patient, brethren until the coming of the Lord. The farmer waits for the precious produce of the soil being patient about it until it gets the early and late rains. You too be patient, strengthen your hearts for the coming of the Lord is near."* The word patient emphasizes patience with people, not trials and circumstances. James has in mind patience with the oppressive. Realizing the glory that awaits them at Christ's return should motivate believers to patiently endure mistreatment. The early rain falls in Israel during October and November and softens the ground for planting. The late rain falls in March and April, immediately before the spring harvest. Just as the farmer waits patiently from the early rain to the latter rain for his crops to ripen, so must Christians patiently wait for the Lord's return. Strengthen your hearts is a call for resolute, firm courage and commitment. James exhorts those about to collapse under the weight of persecution to strengthen their hearts with the hope of the second coming. The immanency of Christ's return is a frequent truth in the New Testament. There is no time for the petty grumbling and complaining against each other that we so easily do. If they need a model of patience in suffering, they should reflect on the history of the prophets. For examples of perseverance in difficult circumstances, they should consider Job, knowing that God is compassionate and merciful. Their commitment should be simple and sincere, represented by honest communication. How do we manage to guard the tongue? It requires a special kind of wisdom that has to be acted out in everyday life. James shows that it's only by connection with God that we can attain this wisdom. Jealousy and selfish ambition find expression through the tongue, but the wisdom that comes from above produces an attitude that is pure, then peaceable, gentle, open to reason, full of mercy and good fruits, impartial and sincere. This prevents earthly, unspiritual, and demonic behavior. Peacemaking brings with it an abundance of right action. Yet James's audience is experiencing quarrels and strife. He asks where such problems originate in James 4:1,"*What is the source of quarrels and conflicts among you? Is not the source your pleasures that wage war in your members?*" These quarrels and conflicts are between people in the church, not internal conflicts in individual people. Discord in the church is not by Gods design but results from the mix of false beleivers and truly redeemed people that makes up the church. James, like Paul uses "members" to speak of sinful, fallen human nature. His answer is that they come from within the human heart that is frustrated by not getting what it wants, though too often it wants what it ought not to have. To achieve its ends it will murder fellowman or go to war. This approach has no possibility of bringing satisfaction. Even when they do ask God for things, they do not receive them because they are asking from wrong motivations or for wrong things. If they follow the world's ways to gain their desires, they can only be enemies of God, the equivalent of adulterers in their commitment toward Him. James exhorts them to become humble, submit to God, resist the devil, in essence, to change their ways. One of the problems they have is speaking evil of and judging each other. They are rather to judge themselves. James had a devotion to direct statements on wise living. He stressed Godly behavior. James had a passion for Jesus' followers to be uncompromisingly obedient to the Word of God. James had a passion for justification by faith and on spiritually demonstrating true faith. The law of God covers all aspects of behavior in us and others. James gives several examples of how belief should result in changed, law-abiding behavior. First, he writes that favoring one person over another according to his or her wealth and status has no place in the godly value system as explained in James 2:1–9,"*My brethren do not hold your faith in our glorious Lord Jesus Christ with an attitude of personal favoritism. For if a man comes into your assembly with a gold ring and dressed in fine clothes and there also comes in a poor man in dirty clothes and you pay special attention to the one who is wearing the fine clothes and say you sit here in a good place and you say to the poor man you stand over there and sit down by my footstool, have you not made distinctions among yourselves and become judges with evil motives? Listen, my beloved brethren did not God choose the poor of this world to be rich in faith and heirs of the kingdom which He promised to those who love Him? But you have dishonored the poor man. Is it not the rich who oppress you and personally drag you into court? Do they not blaspheme the fair name by which you have been called? If however you are fulfilling the royal law according to the Scripture, "You shall love your neighbor as yourself", you are doing well. But if you show partiality, you are committing sin and are convicted by the law as transgressors."* When this speaks of your faith, it refers not to the act of believing, but to the entire Christian faith which has as its central focus Jesus Christ. Christ is the one who reveals the glory of God. In his incarnation, He showed only impartiality. Originally the word favoritism referred to raising someone's face or elevating the person but it came to refer to exalting someone strictly on a superficial, external basis, such as appearance, race, wealth, rank, or social status. James does not condemn believers for distracting dress, but the churches flattering reaction to it. James feared that Christ followers would behave just like the sinful world by catering to the rich and prominent while shunning the poor and common. After all, he says, it is too often the wealthy that exploit the poor. They may even criticize the name of Jesus. James's example involves two men coming into the meeting of Jesus' followers as visitors. One is well dressed and wealthy, the other shabbily dressed and poor. James says that respecting the first over the other because of wealth and social standing would be wrong. It would be dishonoring and humiliating the poor. Showing partiality is breaking one part of the law by not loving neighbor as self, one of the two great overall principles of the Ten Commandments, and breaking law is sin. It is a biblical concept that keeping all but one law still makes us accountable. For example, James says, by refusing to commit adultery, but on the other hand committing murder, it is as if we are guilty of breaking the whole law God does not consider one law any better or any worse than another, as he explains in James 2:10–11,"*For whoever keeps the whole law and yet stumbles in one point, he has become guilty of all. For He who said, "Do not commit adultery," also said, "Do not commit murder," now if you do not commit adultery, but do commit murder you have become a transgressor of the law.*" The idea here is that the law cannot be divided into important and less important commands. We must adhere to all of it, realizing that God will judge us according to its principles, which, if kept in the spirit, free us from the penalty of sin which is eternal death. James concludes by stating that those who show mercy love and justice will receive mercy in the judgment. He gives a second example of the requirement for faith to be demonstrated in action, pointing out the needs of those members of the believing community who are going hungry. It is a form of hypocrisy to hear their pleas, express hope for their eventual nourishment, and yet do nothing practical to help. Faith must be proven by works. Without them faith is dead. Faith alone is insufficient. James was not only the servant of God the Father, but of His Son Jesus Christ, who laid claim to his servanthood of Jesus Christ by saying in James 1:1,"*James, a bond servant of God and of the Lord Jesus Christ, to the twelve tribes who are dispersed abroad: Greetings.*" James opens by emphasizing his submission to "God and . . . the Lord Jesus Christ," addressing his audience across a wide geographic area: "To the twelve tribes in the Dispersion: Greetings". Coming from a Jewish background, James was aware of the history of ancient Israel and its origins with the 12 sons of Jacob. That many of their descendants, not just those from the tribe of Judah, had been dispersed through captivity, persecution and migration explains his reference. James was writing to Church members descended from these tribes in what was considered the area of the Diaspora, today's Mediterranean and Middle Eastern regions. The followers of Jesus in any age have one experience in common, they face trials of faith for a great purpose, and James addresses this in James 1:2-4, "*Consider it all joy, my brethren, when you encounter various trials, knowing that the testing of your faith produces endurance. And let endurance have its perfect result so that you may be perfect and complete, lacking nothing.*" The Greek word for consider may also be translated count or evaluate. The natural human response to trials is not to rejoice therefore the believer must make a conscious commitment to face them with joy. The Greek word for trials is translated trouble, or something that breaks the pattern of peace, comfort, joy, and happiness in someone's life. James wrote to his countrymen giving practical instruction about Christian life. He taught about wisdom and careful use of the tongue and reminded them that true godly service consists of active love and purity. He wrote at length about *patience*—patience in trial, patience in good works, patience under provocation, patience under oppression, patience under persecution. The foundation of patience, he wrote, is the knowledge that Christ will come to right all wrongs. He taught godly wisdom in James 1:5, "*If any of you lacks wisdom, let him ask of God, who gives to all liberally and without reproach, and it will be given to him*". When we ask, we must believe beyond any doubt that what God has promised He will deliver. God is pleased to freely give to anyone who truly believes He is able to deliver on His promises as James teaches in James 1:6-8, "*But let him ask in faith, with no doubting, for he who doubts is like a wave of the sea, driven and tossed by the wind . . . He is a double-minded man, unstable in all his ways*" James addressed a crucially important topic, *sin*. Today the world has developed a bad habit of scorning anyone who speaks of sin. Yet God scorns anyone who refuses to stand against it. James tells us how sin develops and where it leads. It begins with lust, the desire to have or do something we should not have or do. If we don't control our thoughts, our desires eventually develop into sinful actions. When such desires are full grown—when they start controlling us rather than our controlling them—sin ends in the ultimate penalty of eternal death. God brings such tests to prove, and increase the strength and quality of ones faith and to demonstrate its validity. Every trial becomes a test of faith designed to strengthen, if the believer fails the test by wrongly responding, that test then becomes a temptation or a solicitation to evil. Testing means proof, or proving. Through all this a Christian will learn to withstand tenaciously the pressure of a trial until God removes it at His appointed time and even cherish the benefits. This in turn brings spiritual completion in the form of eternal life. Trials cause us to recognize our need for wisdom and we should ask God for help in confidence. Double-mindedness achieves nothing; quiet trust in God's guidance and help is the key. Wealth affords little protection against these kinds of problems. The rich will eventually fade like the grass of the field. James further cautions against falling into the trap of blaming God for the difficulties we bring on ourselves by succumbing to sin. God gives good gifts to His children, not the evil consequences of our own wrong actions. Thankfully, He is "the Father of lights with whom there is no variation or shadow due to change." We can rely on Him implicitly if we so choose. He is the one who has willed that His people be given truth in *this* life, before others receive it, so that they will become a kind of first fruits of his creatures. James is so very much concerned with our walk with God that in his mind, he believes that if you say you live like you should then why do you behave like you shouldn't? James conveys to us to put the genuine article back into our lives. James attitude was, keep it genuine or get out. If your faith is genuine then your works will be real. Real faith produces genuine works. The person who really found the way genuinely walks in it. If you are the one who genuinely claimed to have come to Jesus Christ and He is Lord and Savior, then let your life show that is true. The Apostle James' ministry was difficult among a multitude of the most intense enemies of Christianity. But he acted with such good sense and fairness, that not only Christians esteemed him, but also Jews, and they called him the support of the people and a righteous man. He spread and established the holy faith in Jerusalem and in all of Palestine. When the Apostle Paul visited the Apostle James on his final journey, at that time the people gathered together unto him and told him of the successes of the Christian preaching among the Jews as it is described in Acts 21:20,"*And when they heard it they began glorifying God and they said to him, "You see brother how many thousands there are among the Jews of those who have believed and they are all zealous for the law*." One day after his arrival in the city he reported to James and the elders what God had accomplished through him among the Gentiles. It is not surprising that James is again singled out among those in the church at Jerusalem. It was Paul who referred to James, along with Peter and John, as pillars in the church who had extended to him and Barnabas the right hand of fellowship, and encouraged their work. But, it is for the New Testament epistle which bears his name that James is most remembered. Paul had written that Abraham was justified by faith in Romans 3:28,"*For we maintain that a man is justified by faith, apart from works of the law*." James asserted that Abraham was justified by works in James 2:23-24,"*And the Scriptures was fulfilled which says," and Abraham believed God, and it was reckoned to him as righteousness", and he was called a friend of God. You see that a man is justified by works and not by faith alone*." Indeed, James was crystal-clear about another subject fundamental to true Christianity, that a Christian must prove his faith by his actions and that works perfect one's faith. Today we might say "put your money where your mouth is" or "talk is cheap; prove your words by your actions." Jesus said people would recognize His disciples by God's love expressed through them. Similarly, James said Christ's disciples would prove their faith by their works. *Talking* about Christianity is one thing. *Acting* on it is quite another. James lived by his brother's teachings and taught other Church members to do the same. This passages is not contradictory as some would believe, it is complementary. Together they underscored the necessity of a living faith which always produces active obedience. This idea is plainly set forth in Hebrews 11 where believers were commended for demonstrating faith through action or deeds. Abel's faith produced an acceptable sacrifice. Enoch's faith led to a walk with God. Noah's faith built an ark. Abraham's faith caused him to pack up and move at God's bidding, and, ultimately led him to the point where, at God's command, he was prepared to offer his son, Isaac. Both Paul and James understood the relationship between faith and works (obedience) in regard to man's relationship with God. Other themes which James touched upon in his epistle included the nature of temptation and its source, pure religion, the dangers of the tongue, true and false wisdom, the source of discord among brethren, the future and how to face it, the dangers of wealth, and patience, prayer and confession. James has a practical emphasis, stressing not theoretical knowledge, but Godly behavior. Addressed to the twelve tribes of the dispersion, it was among the most practical epistles of the New Testament. According to Josephus, the high priest, Ananus, a man bold in temperament and very slothful, convened the judges of the Sanhedrin and brought before them a man called James, the brother of Jesus who was called the Christ, and certain others. He accused them of having transgressed the law and delivered them up to be stoned. Many of the Jews were converted to the Church by trusting the word of the righteous one alone. According to a passage in Josephus's Jewish Antiquities, "the brother of Jesus, who was called Christ, whose name was James" met his death after the death of the procurator Porcius Festus, yet before Lucceius Albinus took office which has thus been dated to 62. The High Priest Ananus ben Ananus took advantage of this lack of imperial oversight to assemble a Sanhedrin who condemned James on the charge of breaking the law," then had him executed by stoning. When Ananias became High Priest, he decided, along with other of the Jewish elders, to kill James as a preacher of Christ. One day, at Easter, when many people were gathered in Jerusalem, the elders told him to climb up onto a roof and speak against Christ. James climbed up there, and began to speak to the people about Christ as the Son of God and the true Messiah, and of His Resurrection and eternal glory in heaven. The infuriated priests and elders cast him down from the roof, and he was badly injured though still alive. A man then ran up and gave him such a vicious blow on the head that his brains spilled out. Thus this glorious apostle of Christ died a martyr's death and entered into the Kingdom of his Lord. James was sixty-three years old when he suffered for Christ. Although at first unwilling to accept Jesus as the Son of God, James came to be a staunch believer and a respected leader in the early church. Ultimately, he died for his faith. Josephus reports that Ananus' act was widely viewed as little more than judicial murder, and offended a number of "those who were considered the most fair-minded people in the City, and strict in their observance of the Law," who went as far as meeting Albinus as he entered the province to petition him about the matter. In response, King Agrippa replaced Ananus with Jesus, the son of Damneus. James suffered martyrdom and they buried him on the spot, and the pillar erected to his memory still remains close by the temple. This man was a true witness to both Jews and Greeks that Jesus is the Christ. Josephus does not mention in his writings how James was buried, which makes it hard for scholars to determine what happened to James after his death. James's letter closes with the same emphasis on practical expressions of faith: If there are those among the believers who are suffering, they should pray to God about it. If there are those who are happy, they should express praise to God. Those who are ill should call for the elders of the Church and ask for prayer and anointing so that God may heal them. If sin has caused their illness, they will be forgiven; prayer and the confession of sin are essential to healing. The prayers of the righteous for others are very effective. His life and death were a shining example of what it means to live—and die—by true faith. Of course, that is not the end, for James the Just will be brought back to life at the resurrection of the just when Christ returns, when he will continue to follow His brother's perfect example through all eternity. May we all do the same.

Chapter 8

Jude

Jude describes himself in Jude 1:1,"*Jude, a bond servant of Jesus Christ and brother of James, to those who are the called, beloved in God the Father and kept for Jesus Christ*!" The author of this epistle is the same who is called Judas, who was one of the twelve apostles of Christ, whose name was also Lebbaeus, and whose surname was Thaddaeus. Judah comes from a word that signifies "to praise" or "confess". Labbaeus means courageous, and Thaddaeus in Syriac, means praising or confessing, amiable or loving. So according to the definitions of his names he was a giving man who was very courageous in his praise, worship, and confessions. He describes himself as "Jude, the servant of Jesus Christ," by which is meant an apostolic minister or laborer. Jesus and His brothers and sisters, grew up in a sizable family that included four half brothers—James, Joses, Simon and Juda, and His sisters, showing there were at least two. Because the names of Christ's brothers are passed down to us in their Greek forms, it's easy to lose sight of how typically Jewish Jesus' family was. Jesus Himself was Jewish, because both Mary and Joseph were descended from the Israelite tribe of Judah. Jesus' Hebrew name *Yeshua* (or Joshua)—the same as the Israelite hero who conquered the Promised Land—means "God is salvation". The name of Jesus' mother, Mary, is a shortened form of *Miriam*, the sister of Moses and Aaron. Joseph (*Yosef* in Hebrew), Jesus' stepfather, was ultimately named for the Hebrew patriarch *Joseph*, one of the 12 sons of Jacob and father of the Israelite tribes of Ephraim and Manasseh. As for Jesus' half brothers, James is the anglicized Greek form of the Hebrew Ya'akov, or Jacob, the same name as that of the Hebrew patriarch who was the son of Isaac and the grandson of Abraham. Joses is another form of Joseph. Simon's Hebrew name was Simeon, the name of another of Jacob's sons and father of one of the 12 tribes of Israel. The Hebrew name of Judas (or Jude) was *Yehudah* (rendered Judah in English), the name of another of Jacob's 12 sons, from which the word *Jew* is derived. The popularity of these names is evident in that all of them are used, often repeatedly, for other people mentioned in the New Testament. From his early childhood Jude had the privilege of being in frequent association with the boy Jesus. He and the other members of the family had a great influence on Jude, the future Apostle, who, like his Master, was dominated by the virtue of love. Nothing is heard of him in the Gospel until we find him numbered among the Apostles. Jude was the brother of James and James was the well known and recognized head of the church in Jerusalem, the writer of the Letter of James, and a brother of the Lord Jesus Christ. Being a brother of James, Jude was also a half brother of our Lord Jesus Christ. Jude was one of the 4 half brothers of Jesus. Jude was a common name in Palestine. Why does Jude call himself "the brother of James" rather than "the brother of Jesus"? As some scholars points out, "Palestinian Jewish-Christian circles in the early church used the title 'brother of the Lord' not simply to identify the brothers, but as ascribing to them an authoritative status, and therefore the brothers themselves, not wishing to claim an authority based on mere blood-relationship to Jesus, avoided the term." The very self-identification which opens this epistle not only indicates humility on Jude's part, but also speaks of authenticity. Jude was not the same as the Apostle Judas, the son of James. What leads to this conclusion is

 1.) Jude's appeal to being the brother of James, the leader of the Jerusalem Council and another half brother of Jesus.

2.) Jude's salutation being similar to James

3.) Jude's not identifying himself as an apostle but rather distinguishing between him and the apostles.

Jude was a Jewish Christian, whom just like James he was a Hellenized Galilean Jew who wrote with a cultivated Greek style. Hellenization is a term used to describe the spread of ancient Greek culture, and, to a lesser extent, language. Hellenic philosophy and Christianity refers to the complex interaction between Hellenistic philosophy and early Christianity during first four centuries A.D. Jesus of Nazareth lived in Israel-Judah, an Aramaic culture with traditional Jewish philosophies and modes of thought. However Israel was an occupied territory of the Roman Empire, and had, moreover, already been Hellenized for many years before Roman occupation. Jude encouraged the followers of Jesus for the battle they were to wage against the false teachers by holding before them the love of God who would keep them in Jesus Christ for their eternal salvation. The author of this epistle is the same who is elsewhere called Judas as explained in John 14:22,"*then Judas, not Judas Iscariot, said: "but, Lord, why do you intend to show yourself to us and not to the world?"* Jude asked this question from ignorance of what Christ was meant to do. After the last Supper when Christ promised to manifest Himself to everyone who should love him, Jude asked him why He did not manifest himself to the whole world. Christ answered that he would visit all those who love him and would join themselves to intimate communion of grace with Him. Jude had an honest hearty desire that the glory of Christ might not be confined to a few only; but that the whole world might see it, and be filled with it. In Jude's modesty, and the sense he had of his own and the rest of the apostles unworthiness he wanted all of them to have a manifestation of Christ to them. He also knew they were no more deserving of the manifestation in them than any one else. This question is asked by Jude with admiration and astonishment for the amazing grace of Christ, and for his free favor and sovereign will and pleasure. During the three years of Jesus' public ministry, Jude did not believe that his brother Jesus was the Christ and Son of God. His brothers James, Joseph, and Simon did not believe this about Jesus either. Jude, like his brothers and sisters, thought Jesus was out of his mind and had lost his senses as it talks about in Mark 3:20-21,"*and He came home and the crowd gathered again to such an extent that they could not even eat a meal, when His own people heard of this they went out to take custody of Him, for they were saying, He had lost His senses.*" This refers to Jesus' return to Capernaum. Jesus' relatives evidently heard the report of this and came to Capernaum to restrain Him and His many activities and bring Him under their care and control, all supposedly for His own good. Jesus family could only explain His unconventional lifestyle, by saying He was irrational or had lost His mind. That is a reasonable reaction. How would you feel if your brother said things like, John 14:6,"*Jesus said to him, I am the way, and the truth and the life, no one comes to the Father but through Me*". However, after Jesus' resurrection James, Jude and his brothers joined the company of believers, now convinced Jesus was indeed the promised Messiah and Son of God. A special appearance by Jesus to James, and Jude, probably played a major part in James' and Jude's' change of heart. When James and Jude wrote their epistles some years later, their humility is evident by the way they saw themselves. James and Jude identified themselves as the *servant* of Jesus rather than as a close relative. Jude was not willing to boast that he was one of the half brothers of the Son of God. He may also have remembered how shamefully he had treated Jesus by rejecting Him in previous years. Jude did not likely become a believer in Jesus until after Jesus had risen from the dead. What led Jude to his conversion is not known. Since Jesus appeared to his brother James, perhaps James was instrumental in Jude's conversion. What caused their change in attitude about their brother Jesus? Paul gives us a hint in 1 Corinthians 15:3-7,"*for I delivered to you as of first importance what I also received that Christ died for our sins according to the Scriptures and that He was buried and that He was raised on the third day according to the Scriptures and that He appeared to Cephas then to the twelve, after that He appeared to more than five hundred brethren at one time most of whom remain until now, but some have fallen asleep, then He appeared to James, then to all the apostles.*" This is what changed Jesus' brother's minds,

1.) Christ died for our sins, just as in the Scripture He said He would.

2.) He was buried.

3.) He was raised from the dead on the third day, just as He said in the Scripture He said would happen.

4.) He appeared to Peter.

5.) Then he appeared to the Twelve.

6.) After that, he appeared to more than 500 believers at the same time...

7.) He appeared to James.

8.) Then he appeared to all the apostles.

Christ established his Church on earth and endowed it with every means of sanctity and grace. He selected twelve men whom he specially trained for the ministry, and these were to be his College of Apostles who were to preach the Gospel to all the nations. After Pentecost we see these Apostles animated with a deep love for their Divine Master, facing endless persecutions, and preaching Christ crucified throughout the world. They detached themselves from worldly affairs, and in fact, left all things, for the sake of Christ. It was quite clear to them that in order to love God and to taste of His love they had to disentangle themselves from all attachment to created things; in short they had to die to themselves before living for him. This was the mystery which Christ unfolded to Jude, His kinsman and one of the twelve Apostles. In any case, Jude, as well as his brothers Joseph and Simon, became missionaries who traveled about to spread the gospel of Jesus. It is said that Jude not only brought Christianity to Mesopotamia, but civilized the people of that country who were living like wild animals. He then joined Simon in Libya where the two Apostles spread the light of the Gospel. With Simon, Jude then set out for Persia where he worked zealously and converted thousands who were sunk in degrading and idolatrous practices. Sun worshippers were soon taught to worship the Living God and Christian charity prevailed in a once barbarous country. The Apostles were, however, hampered by two magicians named Zaroes and Arfaxat, who determined to uphold the worship of idols. But the Apostles were more than a match for them. In the presence of the Apostles the idols refused to answer, but when the Apostles in the name of God commanded them to speak, they were forced to acknowledge the Saints as the Disciples of the True God. The evil spirits possessing the idols then fled uttering horrible cries and shattering the images. The content of Jude's letter reveals certain traits of his Christian character. He was zealous for the gospel and teachings of Jesus Christ, for the church, and for preserving the true Christian faith and life. In Jerusalem and throughout Galilee, the family members of Jesus were well known and were the most influential and respected leaders of the Jewish community. Most scholars assume Jude addressed to Jewish Christians, because they evidently come within the area of Jude's pastoral concern and responsibility, and also because Jude had a high degree of familiarity with Jewish literature and traditions. Mary, Jude and his brothers laid the foundation of Christianity. Of the five sons of Joseph and Mary, three - Jesus, Joses-Barnabas, and Simon-Silas - turned to Roman culture, and two - James and Jude - remained attached to Jerusalem and its traditions. Jesus, the eldest, was intellectually brilliant, creative and innovative, and in his youth accused of arrogance. Joses-Barnabas was in sympathy with him, especially on his valuing celibacy. The youngest, Simon-Silas, became a close associate of Paul in his denial of Judaism. All were affected by the intense political climate of their day, when Judaism was in the process of becoming so Hellenized that it was on the verge of losing its Jewish identity. Jude, who believed that "the faith was once for all delivered to the saints", became antagonistically abusive of the pro-Rome party, pouring out biblical insults. Before the crucifixion and resurrection, Jude along with James had denied Jesus as Messiah as explained in the previous chapter. But afterward came to humbly acknowledge himself as his slave, having submitted to Christ's Lordship. Peter and the brothers of the Lord appear to share a certain connection in Acts 1:13-14,"*When they had entered the city, they went up to the upper room where they were staying, that is Peter and John and James and Andrew, Philip, and Thomas, Bartholomew and Matthew, James the son of Alphaeus and Simon the Zealot, and Judas the son of James. These all with one mind were continually devoting themselves to prayer, along with the women, and Mary the mother of Jesus, and with His brothers*", also in Matthew 28.10,"Then *Jesus said to them, "Do not be afraid go and take word to My brethren to leave for Galilee, and there they will see me*". They are all here mentioned but Judas the betrayer, who was dead, to show, that though one had disbelieved the resurrection of Christ, another had denied him, and all of them had forsook him, and fled; yet they were together again, and were firm and steadfast in the faith of Christ, waiting for the outpouring of the Holy Spirit. Christ has appointed a time and place to show the grace of God, and love of Christ towards His people. Jude was married and traveled around with his wife, and James was also married and traveled around with his wife on various mission trips as told about in 1 Corinthians 9:5,"*Do we not have a right to take along a believing wife, even as the rest of the apostles and,*" the brothers of the Lord and Cephas.". Jude was a traveling preacher who traveled with his wife. They both traveled beyond Jerusalem to work among Jewish Christians. What this suggests is that Jude and his wife may well have spent most of their time in Palestine, or perhaps among the Diaspora Jewish Christians. Diaspora is a Greek word for dispersion. It is the Jews who were expelled and living outside the land of Israel. Jesus' brothers were part of the praying group that awaited the coming of the Holy Spirit as explained in Acts 1:14,"*These all with one mind were continually devoting themselves to prayer, along with the women, and Mary the mother of Jesus, and with His brothers*". Christ had promised that they would be preserved from their enemies therefore this gave them reason to keep faithful to their Lord; and to keep preaching the Gospel. This gave them hope and comfort, and knit all of them together in love. They were unanimous in their strength and confirmation in the faith of Christ. Jude originally intended to write to the church at Ephesus to encourage the saints there to continue in the faith. His goal seemed to have been to make sure that they were not discouraged in light of the recent deaths of Paul and Peter. This should not be understood to mean that all the apostles were dead when the letter was written. The apostle John was still living and working in Ephesus at the time the letter was written. But some of the apostles may have died before Jude wrote his letter. Paul is believed to have died a martyr's death around A.D. 67 to A.D. 68. Peter is thought to have suffered martyrdom around that same time in A.D. 66 to A.D. 67. A date that has been suggested for the writing of the Letter of Jude is around A.D. 70 and possibly as late as A.D. 80. Jude and the apostles had pressing concerns of the false teachers, as Mark 13:22 speaks about," *for false Christ's and false prophets will arise, and will show signs and wonders, in order to lead astray, if possible, the elect.*" The false teachers believed that Christians are freed from the moral law by virtue of grace. Jude wanted to make sure that the church would stay grounded in the apostles' teaching. This goal also was woven into the fabric of the letter which he now found was necessary to write. Jude opens his letter by greeting his audience with three characteristics of the faith: they have been "called," "loved," and "kept". Perseverance sets the tone for the whole epistle all the way to the end. Jude wrote to these believers a discussion on theology, as a reminder that the gospel they learned from Paul was the true gospel. But news of heretics infiltrating the church changed his plans: he now wrote to them, appealing to them to stand their ground and fight for the faith they had learned. These heretics who now threatened them believed that Christians are freed from the moral law by virtue of grace, which technically is abusing God's grace. Jude points out that this kind of false teacher was not new. Three examples of false teachers are, the Old Testament story of the unbelieving Israelites who doubted God's promise to bring them into Canaan, angels who disobeyed God and are now kept in darkness, and the Old Testament story of the citizens of Sodom and Gomorrah who engaged in sexual immorality. The false teachers Jude is dealing with act "in the very same way". The implication is that they deserve the same fate. Their rejection of authority and slanderous speech contradict Michael, one of the archangels, who would not even slander the devil (presumably because of his former authority). Yet these false teachers slander all authority, revealing their lack of understanding. Jude lived at a time when Christianity was under political attack from Rome by corrupt people who had saturated the church with their heresy that God's grace gave Christians the freedom to commit immoral acts, who sowed abundant seed for a gigantic harvest of doctrinal error. It could be that this was the sign to full blown immorality which the apostle John would confront over 25 years later in his epistle. He was clearly agitated with the false teachers who had secretly crept into the church to turn the grace of God that forgives sins into a freedom and license to commit immoral acts and to sin all the more. Jude was not a man to mince words. He forcefully exposed the false teachers as godless men, blemishes, ungodly individuals who were guilty of ungodly acts and words which were done in an ungodly manner. He accused them of being grumblers, faultfinders, boasters, flatterers, scoffers, and divisive individuals. He exposed them as ones who were without the Spirit of God. He exposed these people as ones who change the grace of God, which forgives sins, into a license and freedom to sin all the more and commit immoral acts. Jude accused them of denying Jesus Christ our Lord. Having described these heretics in terms clear to his audience, Jude now addresses their fate as Jude 14-19 explains, "It was also about these men that Enoch, in the seventh generation from Adam, prophesied, saying, "*Behold, the Lord came with many thousands of His holy ones, to execute judgment upon all, and to convict all the ungodly of all their ungodly deeds which they have done in an ungodly way, and of all the harsh things which ungodly sinners have spoken against Him.*" These are grumblers, finding fault, following after their own lusts; they speak arrogantly, flattering people for the sake of gaining an advantage. But you, beloved, ought to remember the words that were spoken beforehand by the apostles of our Lord Jesus Christ, that they were saying to you, "In the last time there will be mockers, following after their own ungodly lusts." These are the ones who cause divisions, worldly-minded, devoid of the Spirit". Enoch the son of Jared, whose name means one "instructed", or "trained up". Which he was instructed and trained up by his father, in the true religion, in the nurture and admonition of the Lord; and was one that had much communion with God; he walked with him. The original purpose for writing was altered when news of the false teachers infiltrating into the church at Ephesus reached Jude. The tone of the letter probably changed because of this as well. Jude's purpose now was to "appeal to you to contend for the faith which was once for all delivered to the saints" because false teachers had crept into the church, just as Peter and Paul had predicted they would. Jude speaks decisively about his desire that the church use the writings of Peter and Paul to discern the ungodliness of the false teachers. In the Old Testament Enoch predicted that the day would come when the ungodly would be judged and Paul and Peter had even written to these believers, prophesying of false teachers. Jude now reminds them of the apostolic writings of Paul's gospel and therefore of his apostleship and authority. Further, he speaks about the faith, because he wants the church to use the writings of Paul and Peter to combat the ungodliness of the false teachers. Jude speaks of false teachers as "[dangerous] reefs at your love-feasts." The first metaphor Jude uses to describe the false teachers is found in Jude 8-13,"*Yet in the same way these men, also by dreaming, defile the flesh, and reject authority, and revile angelic majesties. But Michael the Archangel, when he disputed with the devil and argued about the body of Moses, did not dare pronounce against him a railing judgment, but said, "the Lord rebuke you!" but these men revile the things which they do not understand and the things which they know by instinct, like unreasoning animals, by these things they are destroyed. Woe to them! For they have gone the way of Cain, and for pay they have rushed head long into the error of Balaam and perished in the rebellion of Korah. These are the men who are hidden reefs in your love feasts when they feast with you without fear, caring for themselves, clouds without water, carried along by winds, autumn trees without fruit, doubly dead, uprooted, wild waves of the sea. Casting up their own shame like foam, wandering stars, for whom the black darkness has been reserved forever".* The imagery is that of danger lurking beneath the surface, able to sink casting up the foam of their own shame," a vivid picture of the filth that they bring with them. The final image is that of "wandering stars," suggesting that they are unreliable guides to sailors who depend on the sure guidance that the stars provide. Thus the false teachers are seen in these pictures to be dangerous, immoral, and untrustworthy as leaders. Jude has gone out of his way to introduce this nautical imagery. The best explanation for this nautical imagery is that he is writing to a church on the coast of the Mediterranean Sea. Once again, Ephesus seems to be the most likely candidate. The exact audience of believers with whom Jude corresponded is unknown but seems to be Jewish in light of Jude's illustrations. He undoubtedly wrote to a region plagued by false teachers. Thus the body of the letter begins and ends with an appeal to contend for the faith handed down once for all to the saints. Jude's purpose was to expose the false teachers and their audacity, to urge the members of the church to contend for the faith that had been entrusted to them, and to encourage the members to remove those in their midst who had fallen prey to the anarchy. Jude was one of the only ones who confronted apostasy. Apostasy is the defection from the true biblical faith. Jude condemned the apostates and to urge believers to contend for their faith. Jude called for discernment on the part of the church and a rigorous defense of biblical truth. Jude described the apostates in terms of their character and unconscionable activities. He borrowed from nature to show the futility of their teaching. It was enough to demonstrate that their degenerate personal lives and fruitless ministries betrayed their attempts to teach error as though it were truth. This emphasis on character repeats the constant theme regarding false teachers. Their personal character is corrupted. While their teaching is clever, subtle, deceptive, enticing, and delivered in many different forms, the common way to recognize them is to look behind their false spiritual fronts and see their wicked lives as described in 2 Peter 4-10," *for if God did not spare angels when they sinned but cast them into hell and committed them to pits of darkness reserved for judgment, and did not spare the ancient world but preserved Noah a preacher of righteousness with seven others, when He brought a flood upon the world of the ungodly, and if He condemned the cities of Sodom and Gomorrah to destruction by reducing them to ashes having made them an example to those who would live ungodly lives thereafter, and if He rescued righteous Lot, oppressed by the sensual conduct of unprincipled men, (for by what he saw and heard that righteous men while living among them, felt his righteous soul tormented day after day by their lawless deeds), then the Lord knows how to rescue the Godly from temptation and to keep the unrighteous under punishment for the day of judgment, and especially those who indulge in flesh in its corrupt desires and despise authority".* Though God has no pleasure in the death of the wicked, He must judge wickedness because His holiness requires it. False teachers are slaves to the corrupt desires of the flesh. Jude called the church to fight for the truth, in the midst of intense spiritual warfare. Jude condemned the heretics who defect from the true biblical faith. He urged believers to contend for the faith. He called for discernment on the part of the church and a rigorous defense of biblical truth. Through his blistering condemnation of the false teachers in his letter shines Jude's love and pastoral concern for his fellow Christians' faith and salvation. He was concerned that they be preserved from falling prey to the corrupt teachings in their midst, and that those who had fallen for it be delivered from it. He called on his fellow Christians to contend for the faith entrusted to them. Christians are called out of the world, from the evil spirits of it, called above the world, to higher and better things, to heavenly things unseen and eternal. Christians are called from sin to Christ, from vanity to seriousness, from uncleanness to holiness, and this according to the divine purpose and grace. As it is God who begins the work of grace and mercy in the souls of men, so it is He who carries it on and perfects it. Let us not trust in ourselves but in God alone. The mercy of God is the spring and fountain of all the good we have or hope for, as it speaks about in Ephesians 2:4-5,"*But God, being rich in mercy, because of His great love with which He loved us, even when we were dead in our transgressions made us alive together with Christ (by grace you have been saved)*". Next to mercy is peace, which we have from the sense of having obtained mercy. For peace springs love: Christ's love to us, our love to him, and our brotherly love to one another, as it talks about in Philippians 4:6-7,"*Be anxious for nothing, but in everything by prayer and supplication with thanksgiving, let your requests be known to God, and the peace of God which surpasses all comprehension, will guard your hearts and your minds in Christ Jesus.*" The apostle prays, not that Christians may be content with a little but that their souls may be full of these things, as taught in Hebrews 13:5,"*make sure that your character is free from the love of money, being content with what you have, for He Himself has said, "I will never desert you, nor will I ever forsake you."* None are shut out from gospel invitations, but only those who shut themselves out by their own wickedness as spoke about in Ephesians 6:12,"*for our struggle is not against flesh and blood but against the rulers, against the powers, against the world forces of this darkness, against the spiritual forces of wickedness, in the heavenly places.*" The gospel is available to all believers. It is to the weak as well as to the strong. Those who have received the doctrine of salvation must contend earnestly for it. Lying for the truth is bad, debating for it is not any better. Those who have received the truth must contend for it, as the apostle did by suffering with patience for it, not by making others suffer if they will not embrace every notion we call faith, as important. We ought to contend earnestly for the faith, in opposition who would corrupt or deprave it, who glides in like serpents. Those are the worst of the ungodly who take encouragement to sin boldly because the grace of God has abounded, and still abounds so wonderfully. The design of grace is to deliver men from sin and bring them unto God. Jude now returns to the positive note with which he began his letter, reminding the church to continue in faith, love, and mercy. Except for John who lived at the close of the century, all of the other apostles had been martyred, and Christianity was thought to be extremely vulnerable. One of the most commonly asked questions about the followers of Jesus are "How did the Apostles die"? This is a difficult question to answer as there is a lack of information on this subject. The Bible only mentions the deaths of two apostles and additional information about the deaths of the Apostles come from early Christian writers. The two Apostles whose deaths were mentioned in the Bible were those of Judas Iscariot who committed suicide following his betrayal of Jesus and also the death of James, not the Lords brother, who was put to death by Herod Agrippa I in 44 AD. The world in which the Apostles lived was ruled by the Romans who looked to leaders of the Jews to help to maintain peace in the provinces. Any new religious cults were seen as a threat to traditional beliefs and discontent within the population. They viewed Jesus' teachings and Jesus' followers as a cult. In such a volatile religious and political climate the teachings of the Apostles would have been viewed with contempt by both the Jews and the Romans. It is therefore likely that most, if not all of the Apostles were killed and died the deaths of martyrs, with the exception of John. Many other early Christians were persecuted due to the commands of various Roman Emperors. These early Christians were tortured and sentenced to terrible deaths, as was the custom of the times. The Jewish historian Josephus reports that priestly authorities executed James around the year AD 66. We have no record of how or when the other three brothers died. Though the time soon arrived when Jude, who was so closely related to his Lord and Master and who had been an intimate friend of his from boyhood, and a faithful follower all through his life was to join him once more. Historians say that Jude, also known as Thaddaeus was crucified at Edessa, in the first century, as he was stoned to death while preaching. Jude preached amongst untold sufferings and persecution in Judea, and Samaria, impressing upon the people the beauty of Christian charity. No doubt God glorified Jude by giving him special power to aid all those who wish to preserve their purity. According to the Armenian tradition, Jude suffered martyrdom together with the apostle Simon the Zealot, with whom he is usually connected

Chapter 9

Titus

Titus was a thoroughly Gentile Pagan until he met the apostle Paul. Titus is born of completely Gentile parents, who come from a pagan background. Titus, who was Greek, was an uncircumcised gentile, and so remained that way as Galatians 2:3 says," *But not even Titus, who was with me, though he was a Greek, was compelled to be circumcised*". The apostles did not circumcise him, as they did Timothy, when he became their companion. The probability that they did not circumcise Titus is that up to the time of his conversion, he had lived as other Gentiles, and had not been converted to the Jewish faith. The apostles at Jerusalem did not force him to be circumcised. If Titus had been converted to the Jewish faith, it is to be presumed that he would have been circumcised. There is not a lot known of Titus except what we find in the epistles of Paul. It is somewhat remarkable that there is no mention of him in the Acts of the Apostles; nor does his name occur in the New Testament anywhere except in the writings of the apostle Paul. Through Paul's random mention of Titus, we learn the following particulars respecting him.

1.) He was a man of great grace, who was very dear to the Apostle Paul.
2.) The Apostles called him their brother, their partner and fellow helper, who walked in the same spirit as they did.
3.) Titus had become a beloved disciple and fellow worker of the gospel.
4.) He had been converted to Christianity by the assistance of Paul himself. It is possible that Titus, a Gentile, met and may have been led to faith in Christ by Paul, before or during the apostle's first missionary journey. Paul was with Titus since the beginning of Titus's salvation experience. Paul would not have revealed this information about Titus if He was converted by the assistance of another. But where he lived, and when or how he was converted, is for the most part, unknown. As to the time when he was converted, it is known only that this occurred before the fourteenth year after the conversion of Paul; for at that time Titus, a Christian, was with Paul at Jerusalem as explained in Galatians 2:1," *Fourteen years later I went up again to Jerusalem, this time with Barnabas. I took Titus along also*".

It is safe to assume that the place where he lived was in some part of Asia Minor, for the Greeks abounded there. Paul worked hard there, and there were numerous converts made to the Christian faith, still this is not certain. Paul referred to Titus as "my brother", and "my partner and fellow worker". Paul referred to Titus as, my true child in a common faith in 2 Corinthians 8:23-24,"*As for Titus, he is my partner and fellow worker among you; as for our brethren, they are messengers of the churches, a glory to Christ. Therefore openly before the churches, show them the proof of your love and of our reason for boasting about you*". , Paul refers to Titus as his true son in our common faith. In our culture today, we would have made Paul a superstar but here Paul refers to his faith as being held in common with the faith of Titus. The word, in common, literally means that which belongs to several. Jesus prayed in John 17:20-21,"*I do not ask on behalf of these alone but for those who also believe in Me through their word, that they may all be one even as you, Father, are in Me, and I in You, that they also may be in Us. So that the world may believe that You sent Me.*" The biblical model is unity within diversity. I am not better than you and you are not better than me. He was quite often sent into various parts of the region on different occasions by the apostles. He becomes one of Paul's traveling companions. Titus went with Paul to Jerusalem when he was assigned by the church at Antioch with Barnabas, to ask questions before the apostles and elders there in reference to the Gentile converts. It is not known why he took Titus with him on that occasion; it is possible that he was taken with him to Jerusalem because Titus was not compelled to be circumcised, and the case came up for discussion, and that strenuous efforts were made by the Judaizing portion there to have him circumcised, as explained in Galatians 2:1-4,"*Then after an interval of fourteen years, I went up again to Jerusalem with Barnabas, taking Titus along also. It was because of a revelation that I went up and I submitted to them the gospel which I preach among the Gentiles, but I did so in private to those who were of reputation for fear that I might be running or had run in vain. This matter arose because some false brothers had infiltrated our ranks to spy on the freedom we have in Christ Jesus and to make us slaves*". Paul and Barnabas, however, were able to handle the situation in such a way that the people saw that it was not necessary that the heathen converts should be circumcised as explained in Acts 15:19-20,"*It is my judgment, therefore, that we should not make it difficult for the Gentiles who are turning to God. Instead we should write to them, telling them to abstain from food polluted by idols, from sexual immorality, from the meat of strangled animals and from blood.*" As an uncircumcised Gentile, Titus was fitting proof of the effectiveness of Paul's ministry. We then see him in the ministry of Corinth, where he is with Paul during that 18+ month of time, where the apostle forces himself into the lives of the people of Corinth. Titus watches Paul and studied Paul, and learns from him as they minister together. After the council at Jerusalem, it seems possible that Titus returned with Paul and Barnabas, accompanied by Silas and Judas as explained in Acts 15:22,"*Then the apostles and elders, with the whole church, decided to choose some of their own men and send them to Antioch with Paul and Barnabas. They chose Judas (called Barsabbas) and Silas, two men who were leaders among the brothers*". Afterwards Titus stayed with the apostle for a considerable amount of time in his travels. Even though Titus had been with Paul; he was not well known; and that the fact that he had been seen with him had led others to inquiry as to who he was, and what was his purpose for being with Paul. They saw that he was a companion of Paul, and quite essential to Paul's comfort. Titus encouraged them with the information that he brought from Corinth as explained in 2 Corinthians 7:6-15,"*But God who comforts the depressed, comforted us by the coming of Titus, and not only by his coming but also by the comfort with which he was comforted to you, as he reported to us your longing, your mourning, your zeal for me, so that I rejoiced even more. For though I caused you sorrow by my letter, I do not regret it, though I did regret it, for I see that, that letter caused you sorrow, though only for a while. I now rejoice, not that you were made sorrowful to the point of repentance for you were made sorrowful according to the will of God so that you might not suffer loss of anything through us. For the sorrow is that according to the will of God produces repentance with out regret, leading to salvation, but the sorrow of the world produces death. For behold what earnestness this very thing, this Godly sorrow, has produced in you, what vindication of yourselves, what indignation, what fear, what longing, what zeal, what avenging of wrong! In everything you demonstrated yourselves to be innocent in the matter. So although I wrote to you, it was neither for the sake of the offender nor for the sake of the one offended. But your earnestness on your behalf might be made known to you in the sight of God. For this reason we have been comforted. And besides our comfort we rejoiced even much more for the joy of Titus because of his spirit has been refreshed by you all. For if anything I have boasted to him about you, I was not put to shame but as we spoke all things to you in truth, so also our boasting before Titus proved to be the truth. His affection abounds all the more toward you as he remembers the obedience of you all, how you received him with fear and trembling.”* The Greek word for “coming” refers to the actual presence of Titus with Paul. Comforting Paul with the arrival of Titus was a huge blessing. More than that was the encouraging report he gave regarding the repentance of the Corinthians and their positive response to Paul’s letter carried by Titus. Paul was encouraged by the manner in which the Corinthians comforted Titus, since he brought them such a confrontational letter. Paul also describes how he and Barnabas partnered with the apostles and elders, whom one was Titus, to defend the faith against the false teachers and apostates in Acts 15:1-2,”*Some men came down from Judea and began teaching the brethren, “unless you are circumcised according to the customs of Moses, you can not be saved”. And when Paul and Barnabas had great dissension and debate with them, the brethren determined that Paul and Barnabas and some others of them should go up to Jerusalem to the apostles and elders concerning this issue.”* Although his name nowhere occurs in the Acts of the Apostles, he appears to have been mainly commissioned by God to minister to the Gentiles. There is reason to believe that Titus spent some time with the apostle in Ephesus because the First Epistle to the Corinthians was written at Ephesus, and was hand delivered by Titus. It is to be presumed, that Paul would, send some one with the epistle in whom he had entire confidence, and who had been so long with him as to become familiar with his views. For Titus, on this occasion, was sent not only to bear the epistle, but to strive to heal the divisions and disorders there, and to complete a collection for the poor saints in Jerusalem, which the apostle had himself initiated on behalf of the poor saints at Jerusalem as explained in 2 Corinthians 8:6,”*So we urged Titus that as he had previously made a beginning, so he would also complete in you this gracious work as well*”. Paul encouraged him to help the believers finish the collection of the money for the support of the poor saints in Jerusalem. Paul’s opponents circulated a vicious rumor, that he was using craftiness and cunning practices to deceive the Corinthians. The false apostles accused Paul of sending his assistants, whom one of them were Titus, to collect the Jerusalem offering from the Corinthians while intending to keep some of it for himself. Thus according to his opponents Paul was both a deceitful hypocrite (because he really did take money from the Corinthians after all), and a thief. This charge was all the more painful to Paul because it attacked the character of his friends. Outraged that the Corinthians could believe such ridiculous lies Paul pointed out that his associates did not take advantage of the Corinthians during their earlier visits regarding the collection. The simple truth was that neither Paul nor his representatives of whom Titus was one of them, had in any way defrauded the Corinthians. Titus was then sent to Dalmatia (modern day Yugoslavia), to witness the state of the saints there, and to encourage them in the faith. He was with Paul in Rome during his second imprisonment there, but then left him and went into Dalmatia as it say in 2 Timothy 4:9-10,"*Make every effort to come to me soon, for Demas, having loved the present world has deserted me and gone to Thessalonica, Crescens has gone to Galatia , Titus to Dalmatia.*" He returned to Crete, and preached the gospel there and in the neighboring islands. Titus becomes the poster child of grace. When Paul went to Jerusalem to carry the message of grace, he took with him uncircumcised Titus. A man whose life was transformed by the gospel of Jesus, a man who does not have to live in obedience to mosaic law, because he is righteous in God's eyes. Titus becomes a wonderful example of a Gentile believer who becomes someone full of grace, allowed by the Lord to live the life called the Christian life. As Paul looked at Titus he saw in him the ability to be a trusted troubleshooter. When they traveled together, they stopped to minister on the island of Crete. This Roman province had a hundred cities, many of which were heavily populated and very independent. By Titus' example we see what the Lord can do by grace in the life of a pagan who came to the saving knowledge of Christ. Paul left Titus in Crete to organize the people of the church in Crete, as is explained in Titus 1:5,"*For this reason I left you in Crete, that you would set in order what remains and appoint elders in every city as I directed you*". Here Paul preached the Gospel to the conversion of many. It is safe to assume that Paul had tried to accomplish some important task there, but that something had prevented it from happening so he left Titus there to finish it. Why Paul left Crete without completing the work which was to be done, and especially without ordaining the elders himself, is not known. There is evidently a striking resemblance between the circumstances which motivated him to leave Titus there, and those which existed at Ephesus when he left Timothy there to complete an important work. We know that Paul was driven away from Ephesus before he had finished the work there which he had purposed to accomplish, and it is not at all improbable that some such disturbance took place in Crete. When he left, he committed to Titus the work which he had designed to accomplish, with instructions to finish it as soon as possible, and then to come to him at Nicopolis. The gospel had had an extensive effect on the island, since he was to ordain elders "in every city." It is not easy to determine what Nicopolis is meant, for there were many cities of that name. The person, who added the subscription at the end of the epistle, affirms that it was "Nicopolis of Macedonia;" but, as has been frequently remarked in these notes, these subscriptions are of no authority. The name Nicopolis means a city of victory and was given to several places. There was a city of this name in Thrace, on the river Nessus, now called Nikopi. There was also a city of the same name in Epirus, two in Moesia, another in Armenia, another in Cilicia, and another in Egypt, in the vicinity of Alexandria. It is by no means easy to determine which of these cities is meant, though, as Paul was accustomed to travel in Greece and Asia Minor, there seems to be a probability that one of those cities is intended. The only way of determining this with any degree of probability, is, to identify what city was best known by that name at the time when the epistle was written, or what city one would be likely to go to, if he were directed to go to Nicopolis, without any further specification-as if one were directed to go to Philadelphia, London, or Rome. In such a case, he would go to the principal city of that name, though there might be many other smaller places of that name also. But even this would not be absolutely certain, for Paul may have specified to Titus the place where he expected to go before he left him, so that he would be no doubt where the place was. But if we were to allow this consideration to influence us in regard to the place, there can be little doubt that the city which he meant was Nicopolis in Epirus; and the common opinion has been, that the apostle alludes to this city. This Nicopolis was situated in Epirus, in Greece, north-west of Corinth and Athens, on the Ambracian gulf, near its mouth. On the same gulf, and directly opposite to Nicopolis, is Actium, the place where Augustus achieved a signal victory over Mark Anthony. The city of Nicopolis was built in honor of that victory. Augustus was anxious to raise this city to the highest rank among the cities of Greece, and caused games to be celebrated there, with great pomp, every few years, just like the Olympics. Having fallen into decay a few years later, the city was restored by the emperor Julian. Modern travelers describe the remains of Nicopolis as very extensive: the site which they now occupy is called Prevesa Vecchia. It should be said, however, that there is no absolute certainty about the place where the epistle was written. If the epistle were written from the Nicopolis, then it was probably after Paul's first imprisonment at Rome. If so, it was written about the year 63 or 64. It is of no material importance to be able to determine the exact time. Paul had left Titus in Crete, to set in order the things which were wanting, and to ordain elders in every city, and as he had himself, perhaps, been called to leave suddenly, it was important that Titus should have more full instructions than he had been able to give him on various issues; he should have permanent instructions to which he could refer. This was clearly a temporary arrangement, for there is no evidence that it was designed to be a permanent situation. Titus was not design to be a permanent bishop of that island, for it is clear from Titus 3:12,"*As soon as I send Artemas or Tychicus to you, do your best to come to me at Nicopolis, because I have decided to winter there*". Paul tells Titus that he should send Artemas to take his place, to come to him to Nicopolis. If Titus were to be a bishop, the apostle would not have removed him from his diocese. Paul who mentored Titus in Corinth took him to Jerusalem to prepare him to stand alone, to be God's spokesman, and to handle the errors that would be the lifestyle in Crete. Titus ministered for a period of time with Paul on the island of Crete and was left behind to continue and strengthen the work. At this period of time, the island appears to have been inhabited by a mixed population of Greeks and barbarians. After the Trojan War, the principal cities formed themselves into several republics, for the most part independent, while some of them were connected with federal ties. In ancient time the Crete's were in favor of liberty and equality of rights. Its great aim was to promote social harmony and peace, by enforcing self-control and moderation. After many years the Cretans had reverted from their ancient character; to the grossest immorality, and depraved indecency. To be known as a Cretan was not a good thing. The Cretan people were known as liars, evil brutes, and lazy gluttons. The Philistines, who were the arch enemies of Israel throughout the Old Testament, hailed from this island. Cretans were also steeped in pagan superstition and false religion, believing that Zeus was born on one of their mountains. Crete had a pagan influence which became stronger because it became a Roman soldiers training center and all that went with the lifestyle of a soldiers in training. It was also a stopping off point for sailors traveling across the Mediterranean on great trade ships. A large population in Crete was Judiazers. Jews who believed that if you really wanted to be spiritual you must be circumcised and you must obey the Law of Moses. The influence of Judaizing teachers was to be guarded against. It is probable that it was the Jews who were residing in Crete went from Crete to Jerusalem to attend the feast of the Pentecost, and who had been converted, introduced the gospel to the residence of Crete. From this epistle, also, it is clear that one of the great dangers to obedience in the churches of Crete arose from the efforts of such teachers, and from the logical arguments which they would use in favor of the Mosaic law as it says in Titus 1:10,"*for there are many rebellious men, empty talkers and deceivers, especially those of the circumcision*", also Titus 1:14-16,"*Not paying attention to Jewish myths and commandments of men who turn away from the truth. To the pure all things are pure, but to those who are defiled and unbelieving, nothing is pure, but both their mind and their conscience are defiled. They profess to know God, but by their deeds they deny Him, being detestable and disobedient and worthless for any good deed*", also Titus 3:9,"*But avoid foolish controversies and genealogies and strife and disputes about the law, for they are unprofitable and worthless.*" To counteract the effect of their teaching, it was necessary to have ministers of the gospel appointed in every important place, the kind of ministers who are qualified in their work. Titus was left there to make these arrangements, and to give him full information as to the kind of ministers which was needed. God wanted Titus to give a message to the people of Crete that was much different than what they believed and who better to do it than Titus, who was quite possibly a native of Crete. The people of Crete were tough to deal with. Titus will be dealing with rebellious people, empty talkers, deceivers, the circumcised (Jews) who must be silenced because they were upsetting everyone, teaching things they should not teach for the sake of corrupt gain, they are in it for the money; they are in it for the notoriety. Cretans had a bad reputation; they are always liars, evil beasts, and lazy gluttons. Titus was left in Crete to rebuke the Cretans for their immorality, their noisy, vain, and deceitful talk, they were hurtful, they were greedy and lustful. Do you ever feel like you have"Cretans" all around you? Perhaps you wonder if your co-workers are from Crete. Maybe you have some Cretans for neighbors, or you see a couple hanging from one of the branches in your family tree. Or, maybe you're sitting next to one today. Actually, there's a little Cretan in each one of us. The challenge for us, as it was for young Titus, is to stand for the truth so we won't fall for something else. As we minister in our Crete, we must never forget the importance of sharing the good news. Paul put it this way, "through the preaching entrusted to me by the command of God our Savior." People must hear the gospel before they can respond. We must earn the right to be heard and live a lifestyle that makes people thirsty, but we must also proclaim the message with our mouths. Romans 10:14,"*How then will they call on Him in whom they have not believed? How will they believe in Him whom they have not heard? And how will they hear without a preacher?*" Some Crete's came to Christ at Pentecost and returned to the Island to preach. We have no certain information in regard to the time when the gospel was first preached in Crete, nor by whom it was done. Cretans are mentioned to be among the people who were in Jerusalem on the day of Pentecost, and who were converted there. This conversion of the Cretans is explained in Acts 2:1-13,"*When the day of Pentecost had come, they were all together in one place, and suddenly there came from heaven a noise like a violent rushing wind and it filled the whole house where they were sitting. And there appeared to them tongues as of fire distributing themselves, and they rested on each one of them. And they were all filled with the Holy Spirit and began to speak with other tongues, and the Spirit was giving them utterances. Now there were Jews living in Jerusalem, devout men from every nation under heaven. And when this sound occurred, the crowd came together and was bewildered because each one of them was hearing them speak in his own language. They were amazed and astonished saying," Why, are not all these who are speaking, Galileans? And how is it that we each hear them in our own language to which we were born? Parthians and Medes, and Elamites, and residence of Mesopotamia, Judea, and Cappadocia, Pontus, and Asia, Phrygia and Pamphylia, Egypt and the districts of Libya around Cyrene, and visitors from Rome, both Jews and Proselytes, Cretans and Arabs, we hear them in our own tongues speaking of the mighty deeds of God. And they all continued in amazement and great perplexity, saying to one another, "what does this mean?" But others were mocking and saying," They are full of sweet wine."* It is highly probable that, when they returned to their homes, they made the gospel known to their countrymen. Yet history is wholly silent as to the method by which it was done, and as to result of the inhabitants of Crete. As no visit of any of the apostles to that island is mentioned by Luke in the Acts of the Apostles, it may be presumed that the gospel there had not produced any success; and the early history of Christianity there is unknown. The problem was they were not well taught. So they were off and running, starting churches, developing ministries not being rooted and grounded in a solid biblical thinking based on the truths of the Old Testament and teaching of the apostles. The basis for our belief is grounded in God himself. This truth about God that He can not lie is in direct contrast to the Cretan culture which is spelled out in Titus 1:12,*"One of themselves, a prophet of their own said," Cretans are always liars, evil beasts, lazy gluttons."* The Cretans were prone to see God in their image and therefore think that He is less than truthful. God is free from all deceit. The Greek literally reads, *"The non-lying God."* Numbers 23:19,*"God is not a man that He should lie, nor a son of man, that He should repent; has He said, and will He not do it? Or has He spoken, and will He not make it good."* 1 Samuel 15:29,*"Also the glory of Israel will not lie or change His mind: for He is not a man that He should change His mind."* Hebrews 6:18,*"So that by two unchangeable things in which it is impossible for God to lie, we who have taken refuge would have strong encouragement to take hold of the hope set before us."* God is the very essence of truth. In direct opposition is the devil who is described by Jesus in John 8:44,*"You are of your father the devil and you want to do the desires of your father. He was a murderer from the beginning and does not stand in the truth, because there is no truth in him. Whenever he speaks a lie he speaks from his own nature, for he is a liar and the father of lies."* God's character backs up the hope of eternal life. Because He said it, it's true, and it will happen. Even in eternity past God pledged with certainty what he was going to do. God is a promise keeping God. What He has said, He will do. You can count on His character. As Joshua reminded the people before he died in Joshua 23:14,*"Now behold, today I am going the way of all the earth, and you know in all your hearts and in all your souls that not one word of all the good words which the Lord your God spoke concerning you has failed; all have been fulfilled for you, not one of them has failed"*, also in 2 Peter 3:9,*"The Lord is not slow about His promises, as some count slowness, but is patient toward you, not wishing for any to perish but for all to come to repentance.*" The reason for all this is explained in Psalm 145:13,"*Your kingdom is an everlasting kingdom, and Your dominion endures throughout all generations.*" We are to do what Psalm 106:12 says,"*Then they believed His words; they sang His praise.*" What promise do you need to believe today? Is there something you're struggling with? Is doubt causing you some distress? Claim the promises of God and then sing His praise. The character of the Cretans themselves was a people of insincerity, falsehood, and gross living. There was great danger, therefore, that their religion would be hollow and insincere, and great need of caution lest they should be corrupted from the simplicity and purity required in the gospel, as Titus 1:13 says," *This testimony is true. For this reason, reprove them severely so that they may be sound in the faith.*" Titus had to teach Crete's who were young immature believers, strong and stubborn legalists, passive and lazy island dwellers, false teachers who stood against the truth which stand against him, and those who taught truth but lived a lie. Titus lived a strong life in righteousness and godliness. Life should copy doctrine and belief. Biblical grace spiritually strengthens. Titus was to rebuke these false teachers and those that had been corrupted. He was to teach them that they had to regard sound doctrine and not Jewish fables. He was to teach them that they could not listen to the commandment of misguided men. They were to listen to those who were pure in heart, and sound in faith. Those who were impure, whose minds and conscience were defiled, and were unbelieving, nothing was pure to them, they were practically deniers of God, and was disobedient to the law and to the Gospel, and unfit for any good work. In order to impact our world, we have to first stand on the truth if we hope to saturate those around us with the truth. Paul, later in a letter, gives personal encouragement and counsel to Titus, who though well trained and faithful, faced continued opposition from ungodly men within the churches where he ministered. Titus was to pass on that encouragement and counsel to the leaders he was to appoint in the Cretan churches. Paul had full confidence in Titus's theological understanding and convictions, evidenced by the fact that he entrusted him with such a demanding ministry. Titus was a Greek by race, and early on in his life an idolater before he met Paul. But having believed in Christ through the Apostle Paul, he became Paul's disciple and follower and labored with him greatly in the preaching of the Gospel. When Paul ordained him Bishop of Crete, he later wrote to him the Epistle which bears his name. Having shepherded in an apostolic manner the flock that had been entrusted to him, and being full of days, he rest in peace, at the age of ninety-four years old.

Are you growing in godliness?

Are you living with a mindset that everything you do, do it before the face of God?

If you want to impact the Cretans around you, you must remember that they are reading you a great deal more than they are reading the Bible.

The boy stood with back arched, head cocked back and hands clenched defiantly: *"Go ahead, give it to me."* The principal looked down at the young rebel: *"How many times have you been here?"* The child sneered rebelliously, *"Apparently not enough."* The principal gave the boy a strange look and asked: *"And you have been punished each time, have you not?"* *"Yeah, I've been punished, if that's what you want to call it."* He threw out his small chest, *"Go ahead I can take whatever you dish out. I always have. I do whatever I want to do. Ain't nothin you people gonna do to stop me either."* The principal looked over at the teacher who stood nearby: *"What did he do this time?"* The teacher said, *"Fighting. He took little Tommy and shoved his face into the sandbox."* The principal turned to look at the boy, *"Why? What did little Tommy do to you?"* The boy responded angrily: *"Nothin, I didn't like the way he was lookin' at me, just like I don't like the way you're lookin' at me! And if I thought I could do it, I'd shove your face into something."* The teacher stiffened and started to rise but a quick look from the principal stopped him. He contemplated the child for a moment and then quietly said, *"Today my young student is the day you learn about grace."* *"Grace? Isn't that what you old people do before you sit down to eat? I don't need none of your stinkin' grace."* The principal studied the young man's face and whispered, *"Oh yes, you truly do..."* The boy continued to glare as the principal continued, *"Grace, in its short definition is unmerited favor. You cannot earn it; it is a gift and is always freely given."* The boy looked puzzled and asked, *"You're not gonna whup me? You just gonna let me walk?"* The principal looked down at the unyielding child. *"Yes, I'm going to let you walk."* The boy studied the face of the principal, *"No punishment at all? Even though I socked Tommy and shoved his face into the sandbox?"* *"Oh, there has to be punishment. What you did was wrong and there are always consequences to our actions. Grace is not an excuse for doing wrong."* *"I knew it,"* sneered the boy as he held out his hands, *"Let's get on with it."* The principal nodded toward the teacher, *"Bring me the belt."* The teacher presented the belt to the principal. He carefully folded it in two and then handed it back to the teacher. He looked at the child and said, *"I want you to count the blows."* He slid out from behind his desk and walked over to stand directly in front of the young man. He gently reached out and folded the child's outstretched, expectant hands together and then turned to face the teacher with his own hands outstretched. One quiet word came forth from his mouth: *"Begin."* The belt whipped down on the outstretched hands of the principal. Crack! The young man jumped ten feet in the air. Shock registered across his face, *"One"* he whispered. Crack! *"Two."* Crack! *"Three..."* He couldn't believe this. Crack! *"Four."* Big tears welled up in the eyes of the rebel. *"OK stop! That's enough. Stop!"* Crack! The child flinched with each blow, tears beginning to stream down his face. Crack! Crack! *"No please,"* the former rebel begged, *"Stop, I did it, I'm the one who deserves it. Stop! Please. Stop..."* Still the blows came, Crack! Crack! One after another. Finally it was over. The principal stood with sweat glistening across his forehead and beads trickling down his face. Slowly he knelt down. He studied the young man for a second and then his swollen hands reached out to cradle the face of the weeping child. He looked at him and said, *"That's what grace is..."*

Chapter 10

Peter

Peter is the author of the book of the bible that bears his name, 1st and 2nd Peter. Peter is described first by his names, Simon Peter. Simon had 3 names. Each one of his names is in a different language, Aramaic, Jewish, Greek, and Syriac, but meaning the same. The authenticity of 1st and 2nd Peter has been severely attacked by modern critics, although the problems connected with each of the critics are essentially different. In 1st Peter it is claimed to be addressed to readers in Pontus, Galatia, Pamphylia, Pisidia, part of Lycaonia, Cappadocia, Asia, Caria, Lydia, Mysia, probably Phrygia, and Bithynia. There is no reason to suppose, that the books of 1st and 2nd Peter were intended solely, or even primarily, for Jewish Christians, especially as the only known churches in Asia Minor were the gentile congregations established by Paul and his associates as well as in view of Peter's own attitude toward gentile Christians. It is clear that the two books were addressed to recent converts from paganism, not to Jewish Christians. The gentile Christians were regarded as the true Israel who were scattered among the heathens, even though Peter plainly considered these gentile churches as daughters of the mother church at Jerusalem. The two books imply that the gentile Christians of Asia Minor had already been assaulted by their pagan countrymen. Although the apostle evidently regarded acts of violence as a very real possibility, at that time the only dangers were taunts and insults, and they were charged of being evil-doers, based on their rejection of heathen corruption. This attitude is attributed to their enemies in the fact that their enemies hated the human race. That attitude also was one which might have lead to theft or murder. Such accusations, generally speaking, were unjust, but it is clear, from Peter's heartfelt counsel to integrity of life, that he feared that the charges might prove real, and was also apprehensive to the notion that the Christians would relapse into pagan abominations to gain the friendship of the world. Which Peter did not want to see happen. The general situation described in these two books points to the period of Nero's persecution. Christianity had not yet been made a crime against the State and obedience to temporal superiors could still be urged. Apart from these sufferings of the Christians of Asia Minor, and their consequent trials, nothing is known regarding their condition. It was these distresses and these dangers which had provoked these letters. The contents of 1 Peter and 2 Peter is a general warning to us to have an righteous life, to show brotherly love, to be obedient to earthly superiors, even though they may be oppressive, to have mutual respect between husbands and wives, and to abstain from revenge, to have patient endurance in suffering, and most of all to imitate Christ. The Christian must not relapse into pagan immorality, but must show sobriety, service, and affection, as well as endurance through undeserved trials. Old and young are admonished to perform their God given service, and all must trust in God and be ever watchful. In both 1st and 2nd Peter there is the same basic concept of Christianity as the realization of the Old Testament kingdom of God, harmonizing with prophecy and brought into being by the crucified but risen Christ. Faith is not so much an acceptance of the forgiveness of sins based on the death of Christ upon the cross, as in Paul's teachings, but as a trust in God grounded on the recognition of Jesus as the glorified Messiah who shall be revealed in the fullness of time. The moral life is regarded as connected with faith rather than as a mere fruit of faith. The close union of prophecy and the entire Old Testament teachings leads Peter to the conclusion that the salvation sought by the prophets has become the possession of the Christian, while the spirit which worked in the prophets was the same as the spirit of Christ. The ideal of the Old Testament saints of God is realized in the Christian Church, which includes all gentiles called of God. The sufferings of Christ are not only the model for the Christian's patience under affliction, but, since they most clearly reveal His moral greatness, they inspire all Christians to self-denial and to conquer sin. Redemption from the power of sin is founded in the redemptive work of the death of Christ, which has crushed sin forever. The books of 1st and 2nd Peter teaches that Christ is the great shepherd of his flock, that the salvation of the risen Lord extends even to the dead, that the moral effect of baptism, and the answer of a good conscience toward God is given through the resurrection of Christ, and that the sufferings of the Christians mark the beginning of the judgment. The result of all this is hope in the Christian, who is but a pilgrim and a stranger in this world, a situation which should only inspire him to still greater moral perseverance. At the time of the Apostle Peter birth his name was Simon (or Simeon) then he was given the name Peter which was translated into Greek and its Greek equivalent is *Petros*. Christ Jesus called Simon "Cephas", which means 'rock' and is translated "Peter". This was probably meant as a title or nickname, as 'Cephas' was not previously used as a name. The name Peter comes from the Aramaic term for "rock". Both Peter and Cephas signify a rock or stone, for the main reason that he was built upon Christ, the rock and foundation and chief cornerstone. With Christ as his rock his future was solid, firm, and he had a sure devotion to Christ. Jesus chose the name Cephas (or Peter) which means "rock" as a symbolic name for the first of his followers. The name Peter, meaning 'rock', was selected by Jesus to indicate the he would be the rock-like foundation on which the Church would be built. Let us begin the examination of Peter's early life before the wonderful day when he was introduced to the Messiah. It is true that the Bible is somewhat silent on the issue of Peter's early life. Indeed the Gospels mention very little of Jesus' own early life, and even less of the lives of his disciples. No specific date is available for the birth of Peter. One may assume that since he was running a fishing business when he met Jesus that he was in his early thirties, born, like Jesus, some time before the turn of the century. Regardless of when he was born his original name was Simon or Symeon. If his name was Symeon which is used of Peter only in Acts 15:14,"*Simeon has related how God first concerned Himself about taking from among the Gentiles a people for His name*", and 2nd Peter 1:1,"*Simon Peter, a bond-servant and apostle of Jesus Christ, To those who have received a faith of the same kind as ours, by the righteousness of our God and Savior, Jesus Christ*", then it is clear that his parents named him with a Hebrew name. It has been supposed the Simon was merely a adaptation of the Hebrew name Symeon, however, a strong case can be made for Simon being Hellenistic. According to the Gospel of John, Peter was from the city of Bethsaida. He was also the son of a certain Jonah, or perhaps John. Bethsaida was raised to the status of city by Phillip the Tetrarch; he was a Hellenizer who furthered Graeco-Roman culture throughout his area of influence. It may then have been quite likely that Peter was acquainted well with Hellenistic culture and the Greek language. It may also be safe to assume that Peter had some knowledge of both Aramaic and Hebrew, as well. It is also likely that he had received the standard education that any Jewish male might have in the first century which consisted of education in reading, writing and, of course, memorization of the Torah. It may also be possible that Peter had some connection to the Zealots, who are a radical, warlike, diligently patriotic group of Jews in Judea, particularly prominent from a.d. 69 to 81. They advocated the violent overthrow of Roman rule and vigorously resisting the efforts of the Romans and their supporters to heathenize the Jews. In the gospels, Simon Peter is present at every event during Christ's earthly ministry although his name is not mentioned in all of the passages relating these events. We can easily surmise from the verses themselves, however, that Peter was present along with the other eleven, and later, with the Seventy [Seventy-Two in some readings]. There are also remarkable events during Christ's ministry where only Peter, John and James are present with the Lord. According to the book of Matthew, the Lord Jesus Christ began His teaching ministry soon after having been baptized by John the Baptist in the Jordan River. Matthew informs us that Jesus left His hometown of Nazareth and went to stay in Capernaum--the hometown of Peter and Andrew. It was from this fishing village of Capernaum that the Lord called Peter [and Andrew] to be His disciple. The Bible tells us that Capernaum was a place by lake, in the area of Zebulun and Naphtali. This area had become so spiritually [and perhaps even morally] darkened in its way of life that scripture refers to it as the Galilee of the Gentiles. These two regions are prophesied in the Bible book of Isaiah as the places in darkness whereupon the light would dawn. We have to marvel at the fact that this is the very first region to which Jesus comes to call his disciples. The verses in which we find this account is Matthew 4:12-13,"*Now when Jesus heard that John had been taken into custody, He withdrew into Galilee ; and leaving Nazareth, He came and settled in Capernaum, which is by the sea, in the region of Zebulun and Naphtali*", also in Matthew 4:18-20,"*Now as Jesus was walking by the Sea of Galilee, He saw two brothers, Simon who was called Peter, and Andrew his brother, casting a net into the sea ; for they were fishermen. And He said to them, "Follow Me, and I will make you fishers of men." Immediately they left their nets and followed Him*". Peter was a faithful follower of Jesus although at the Last Supper Jesus predicted that Peter would deny Him three times following His death. Jesus said unto him, "Verily I say unto thee, that this night, before the cock crow, thou shall deny me thrice." At the time of the arrest of Jesus, Peter cut off the ear of a servant of the high priest with a sword but then, as had been predicted, he denied three times that he had ever known Jesus. Peter then traveled to spread the Gospel and was in Rome in 64AD during the rule of the Roman Emperor Nero. He was called Simon from infancy by his parents and by that name he was known when Christ called him to be a disciple and follower of Him. The name Simon is the same as Simeon, a name common with the Jews. Simon comes from the Greek for "hearing, and later is what was given him by Christ at his conversion. He also answered to Cephas in the Syriac language. Peter was originally known as Simon, which is Greek, or Simeon, which is Hebrew, as explained in Mark 1:16,"*as he was going along by the sea of Galilee, He saw Simon and Andrew, the brother of Simon casting a net in the sea for they were fishermen*", also John 1:40-41,"*one of the two who heard John speak and followed Him, was Andrew, Simon Peter's brother. He found first his own brother Simon and said to him, "we have found the Messiah" which translates means Christ*". Peter was the son of Jonas, which was also known as John as explained in John 1:42," *he brought him to Jesus. Jesus looked at him and said "you are Simon, the son of John; you shall be called "Cephas" which is translated Peter"*. Integrating the accounts of Jesus' first meeting with Peter is the first task in discussing Peter's life as a disciple of Jesus. The two brothers, Peter and Andrew are featured as the first of Jesus' disciples whom he calls "on the shores of the Sea of Galilee," as described in Mark 1:16, "*As He was going along by the Sea of Galilee, He saw Simon and Andrew, the brother of Simon, casting a net in the sea; for they were fishermen*", and Matthew 4:18,"Now as Jesus was walking by the Sea of Galilee, He saw two brothers, Simon who was called Peter, and Andrew his brother, casting a net into the sea; for they were fishermen". John 1.35-42 also seems to indicate that Peter was among the first disciples, "*Again the next day John was standing with two of his disciples, and he looked at Jesus as He walked, and said, "Behold, the Lamb of God !" The two disciples heard him speak, and they followed Jesus. And Jesus turned and saw them following, and said to them, "What do you seek?" They said to Him, "Rabbi (which translated means Teacher), where are You staying?" He said to them, "Come, and you will see." So they came and saw where He was staying; and they stayed with Him that day, for it was about the tenth hour. One of the two, who heard John speak and followed Him, was Andrew, Simon Peter's brother. He found first his own brother Simon and said to him, "We have found the Messiah" (which translated means Christ). He brought him to Jesus. Jesus looked at him and said, "You are Simon the son of John; you shall be called Cephas " (which is translated Peter)"*. However not everyone agrees that Peter was among the disciples of John. Regardless, it would appear that Peter was one of the first, if not the first, of the disciples who were called by Jesus. Encyclopedia Britannica agrees with this fact that Peter was called by Jesus "at the beginning of his ministry." Jesus bestows the title "Cephas," (meaning "Rock") on Peter at their first meeting with the words, "So you are Simon the son of John? You shall be called Cephas". On the other hand the first occurrence of the name in the Gospel of Mark, which may have been compiled from source material given to John Mark by Peter himself, is in a list of the disciples. The account recorded in the Gospel of Matthew has Jesus bestowing the name on Peter after the latter confesses, "You are the Christ, the son of the living God," as told in Matthew 16:16-17, "*Simon Peter answered, "You are the Christ, the Son of the living God." And Jesus said to him, "Blessed are you, Simon-Barjona, because flesh and blood did not reveal this to you, but My Father who is in heaven*". Peter is present with John and James when Christ becomes transfigured on the mountain. He recognizes Moses and Elijah who are with the glorious Lord. In a trance or dream-like state, Peter offers to prepare a tent for them and Christ. The Apostles are greatly terrified and fall facedown to the ground when they hear the voice of God speaking to them of His love for His Son, as explained in Matthew 17:1-9, "*After six days Jesus took with him Peter, James and John the brother of James, and led them up a high mountain by themselves. There he was transfigured before them. His face shone like the sun, and his clothes became as white as the light. Just then there appeared before them Moses and Elijah, talking with Jesus. Peter said to Jesus, "Lord, it is good for us to be here. If you wish, I will put up three shelters—one for you, one for Moses and one for Elijah." While he was still speaking, a bright cloud enveloped them, and a voice from the cloud said, "This is my Son, whom I love; with him I am well pleased. Listen to him!" When the disciples heard this, they fell facedown to the ground, terrified. But Jesus came and touched them. "Get up," he said. "Don't be afraid." When they looked up, they saw no one except Jesus. As they were coming down the mountain, Jesus instructed them, "Don't tell anyone what you have seen, until the Son of Man has been raised from the dead."* Peter was married and his wife apparently accompanied him in his ministry as told about in Mark 1:29-31,*"and immediately after they came out of the synagogue, they came into the house of Simon and Andrew with James and John. Now Simons' mother in law was lying sick with a fever and immediately they spoke to Jesus about her. And He came to her and raised her up, taking her by the hand, and the fever left her, and she waited on them"*, and 1Corinthians 9:5 explains, *"do we not have a right to take along a believing wife even as the rest of the apostles and the brothers of the Lord and Cephas?"* Peter was a member of a family of fishermen who lived in Bethsaida and later in Capernaum. Andrew, Peter's brother, brought Peter to the saving knowledge of Christ. He was born in Bethsaida (meaning 'place of nets'), near the Sea of Galilee, although Mark makes him a resident of Capernaum, the apparent contradiction being understandable by the fact that at his marriage he had moved to Capernaum to make his living by fishing in the Sea of Galilee, along with his younger brother Andrew, and his father John, both were fishermen. Andrew, the brother of Simon Peter, was first a follower of John the Baptist and then became the first apostle of Jesus. Peter was originally a fisherman from the village of Capernaum and was known as Simon in that village. Capernaum would become an important center of Jesus' ministry; the gospels report that He returned there often. The gospels also indicate that Peter was a native of Galilee, based upon his having an accent typical of the region. Unlike other disciples in the early church, Peter doesn't appear to have stayed in Jerusalem. Despite his apparently important status there, he traveled around the empire and eventually ended up in Rome. His brother Andrew introduced him to Jesus and was himself a disciple of John the Baptist. Andrew had become one of the disciples of John the Baptist, and it was this younger brother who brought Peter into contact with Jesus. Peter became a constant follower of Jesus throughout all his travels. Peter was son of Jona (or Jonah), and his mother's name was never mentioned in the bible. Simon Peter, who was sometimes called Simon Cephas, after his name in Hellenized Aramaic, was a leader of the early Christian Church. He is featured prominently in the New Testament Gospels and the Acts of the Apostles. Peter was one of the most important of Jesus' twelve apostles. Peter's name appears on all of the lists of apostles and his being called by Jesus appears in the gospels of Matthew, Mark, Luke, and John, as well as Acts. While Matthew and Luke ascribe a slightly more marked influence to Peter among the apostles than does Mark there is no real difference between them. Peter is important for the history of Christianity for the main reason he is generally treated as a model for Christians to follow. This may sound strange at first because the gospels relate many examples of Peter's faithlessness, for example, his three denials of Jesus. Because of the varied traits ascribed to Peter, he may be the most animated character in the gospels by the way he act and spoke before thinking about his speech or actions first and their consequences. Yet Peter's failings are treated as symptoms of man's state of sinfulness or weakness which can be overcome through faith in Jesus. Peter did this because, after Jesus' resurrection, he traveled widely to preach Jesus' message and convert people to Christianity. Some argue that Peter being an uneducated fisherman could not have written in sophisticated Greek especially in light of the less classical styles of Greek employed in his writing. However this argument is not without a good answer. In the first place that Peter was uneducated does not mean that he was illiterate, but only that he was without formal rabbinical training in the scripture. Moreover though Aramaic may have been Peter's primary language, Greek would have been a widely spoken second language in Palestine. It is also apparent that at least some of the authors of the New Testament, though not highly educated could read the Greek of the Old Testament. In Acts, Peter is portrayed as a model disciple for others to imitate. He is also important because the gospels describe Jesus as calling Peter his "rock" upon which the future church would be built. This account can be found at Matthew 16:13-20. It states, *"When Jesus came to the region of Caesarea Philippi, he asked his disciples, "Who do people say the Son of Man is?" They replied, "Some say John the Baptist; others say Elijah; and still others, Jeremiah or one of the prophets." "But what about you?" he asked. "Who do you say I am?" Simon Peter answered, "You are the Christ, the Son of the living God." Jesus replied, "Blessed are you, Simon son of Jonah, for this was not revealed to you by man, but by my Father in heaven. And I tell you that you are Peter, and on this rock I will build my church, and the gates of Hades will not overcome it. I will give you the keys of the kingdom of heaven; whatever you bind on earth will be bound in heaven, and whatever you loose on earth will be loosed in heaven." Then he warned his disciples not to tell anyone that he was the Christ"*. During this private discussion whereby the Lord Jesus questioned His Apostles about His identity, Peter made the confession that earned him the title, "the rock." His immediate response was, "You are the Christ, the Son of the Living God." Christ instantly recognized this as knowledge coming only from His Father in Heaven. Christ then gave Simon Peter the role of leadership in the church and called him "Peter" for he was now "the rock" upon which Christ would build His church on earth. The Gospel of Matthew portrays Peter's great statement regarding the divinity of Jesus in the context of a question asked by Jesus. A discussion takes place between Jesus and his disciples near the city of Caesarea Philippi; this discussion begins with Jesus asking the question, "Who do people say that the Son of Man is". The disciples proceed to explain the various opinions that the people have in the next verse before Jesus interjects with, "But who do you say that I am". It is at this point that Peter is singled out in Matthew's Gospel as he replies, "You are the Christ, the Son of the living God". This is of great interest to the student of Peter's life. Here, for the first time recorded in the Gospels, the flamboyant Peter tactfully proclaims that Jesus is the Christ, the son of God. Jesus appears pleased with this statement and blesses Peter in the following verse. It quickly becomes clear that Peter's idea of a Messiah did not include the idea of a suffering servant because a short six verses later Peter takes Jesus aside and begins rebuking him for the idea that Jesus would die. Here Jesus rebukes Peter, calling him an adversary and saying that his mind is set on the things of man and not on the things of God. This is typical of Peter's interaction with Christ. He will take a great step of faith or make a great proclamation only to not quite get the full impact of what he just did or said. This is not something that Peter should be harshly judged on; rather it shows his own faith journey and humanity. Similarly Peter shows his faith a few chapters earlier in the Gospel of Matthew as when Jesus' was walking on the water. However, only in Matthew is Peter's role mentioned. In this narrative Jesus comes to the disciples, who are in a boat fighting against the wind and waves, walking on the water. At first the disciples are terrified by this sight and cry out in fear that it is a ghost. Once Jesus assures them that it is him, and not a ghost, Peter asks Jesus to command him to join him on the water. Jesus responds with the simple word, "come". Peter obeyed, got out of the boat, "walked on the water and came to Jesus". Peter followed Jesus' example, and walked on water towards Him as explained in Matthew 14:22-26 where it says, *"Immediately Jesus made the disciples get into the boat and go on ahead of him to the other side, while he dismissed the crowd. After he had dismissed them, he went up on a mountainside by himself to pray. When evening came, he was there alone, but the boat was already a considerable distance from land, buffeted by the waves because the wind was against it. During the fourth watch of the night Jesus went out to them, walking on the lake. When the disciples saw him walking on the lake, they were terrified. "It's a ghost," they said, and cried out in fear. But Jesus immediately said to them: "Take courage! It is I. don't be afraid."" Lord, if it's you," Peter replied, "tell me to come to you on the water." "Come," he said. Then Peter got down out of the boat, walked on the water and came toward Jesus. But when he saw the wind, he was afraid and, beginning to sink, cried out, "Lord, save me!" Immediately Jesus reached out his hand and caught him. "You of little faith," he said, "why did you doubt?" And when they climbed into the boat, the wind died down. Then those who were in the boat worshiped him, saying, "Truly you are the Son of God "Truly you are the Son of God". When they had crossed over, they landed at Gennesaret"* This is, perhaps, more than can be said for the other disciples who remained in the boat. Peter, in this passage, takes part in an event that he surely remembered for the rest of his life. It is important to remember at this point that Peter did not lack faith; he merely lacked enough faith to successfully stay on top of the water. As the story goes Peter saw the wind and became afraid, only then did he begin to sink. Still though, he cries out to Jesus for help which his Lord readily gives with the gentle rebuke, "O you of little faith, why did you doubt". So, at this point in his life Peter is revealed to be a man of faith, even if it was only a little faith. Perhaps the most endearing event in the Gospel is the time when the Apostle Peter made the attempt to walk across the lake in order to meet up with the Lord. His willingness to take such a great risk in order to please Jesus was a clear manifestation of his great love and adoration for Him, a deep and overwhelming love that would drive him to try to do what no one else would dare. Even at this early stage of his calling, Peter was willing to risk his life, if it meant pleasing God. He was the first to begin preaching to the gentiles. Because of Peter's martyrdom in Rome, traditions developed which led to the belief that the most important Christian church organization was located in Rome, not in cities like Jerusalem or Antioch where Christianity was older or where Jesus actually visited. Because Peter was given a unique leadership role, the places where he was martyred has taken that role over and popes today are regarded as the successors of Peter, first leader of the Roman church. He is described by his character as a servant, not of sin, nor satan, nor man, but Jesus Christ whose servant he was not only by creation but by redemption and grace. Peter was not merely a servant of Christ in common with other believers but also in the ministry. Peter was a man with a past. He was no one special; he was just a fisherman, and a rather rough, crude, and abrasive one at that. Most of Jesus' twelve apostles remain largely silent in the gospels; Peter, however, is often characterized as speaking out. He is the first to confess that Jesus is the Messiah as well as the only one pictured as actively denying Jesus later. In Acts, Peter is represented as traveling widely to preach about Jesus. Little information about Peter is contained in these early sources, but Christian communities filled in the gaps with other stories. Peter was a model for Christian faith and activity, and it is important for Christians to know about his background and personal history. Generally speaking, the character of Peter is described as being in one accord with all the Apostles. He is an admirable Galilean, well-meaning, confiding, freedom-loving, and courageous, yet changeable, and erratic. At first glance, it seems strange that Jesus should have given the epithet of "Rock" to one of such character, yet he saw far beneath the surface and grasped the inherent strength and stability that underlay the changing and inconstant exterior, and Peter prove unworthy of this confidence. Peter was bold and not afraid of change, but he also had many faults. As in the time when Jesus was explaining to His followers that He was about to be crucified and Peter was trying to correct Jesus in Matthew 16:22-23,"*Peter took Him aside and began to rebuke Him, saying," God forbid it, Lord, this shall never happen to you!" But He turned and said to Peter, "get behind me satan, you are a stumbling block to Me for you are not setting your mind on God's interests, but mans.*" Peter thought more highly of himself than he should have as explained in Matthew 26: 31-35,"*Then Jesus said to them, you will all fall away because of Me this night for it is written," I will strike down the Shepherd and the sheep of the flock shall be scattered". But after I have been raised I will go ahead of you to Galilee. But Peter said to Him, even though all may fall away because of You. I will never fall away. Jesus said to him, "Truly I say to you that this very night before the rooster crows you will deny Me three times. Peter said to Him, even if I have to die with You I will not deny You." All the disciples said the same thing too.*" He had a pride issue and saw himself as better than other men. It is recorded that Peter denied even knowing Jesus in Matthew 26:69-75,"*Now Peter was sitting outside in the courtyard and a servant-girl came to him and said, "you too were with Jesus the Galilean". But he denied it before them all saying" I do not know what you are talking about." When he had gone out to the gateway another servant-girl saw him and said to those who were there," This man was with Jesus of Nazareth" and again he denied it with an oath, "I do not know the man." A little later the bystanders came up and said to Peter, "Surely you too are one of them for even the way you talk gives you away." Then he began to curse and swear," I do not know the man." And immediately a rooster crowed. And Peter remembered the word which Jesus had said, "Before a rooster crows, you will deny me three times." And he went out and wept bitterly.*" Peter is well-known for rashly stating that he would die before denying Christ, to which our Lord replied, 'I tell you Peter, before the rooster crows you will have disowned me three times'; a prophecy which was fulfilled soon after Jesus was arrested in the Garden of Gethsemane. Once Peter realized the depth of his sin, he wept bitterly which showed he had a repentant heart. God is merciful and understands our weaknesses. Peter was the first to declare publicly that Jesus was the Messiah as told in Matthew 16:16,"*Simon Peter answered, "You are the Christ, the Son of the living God*". Peter's trust became intense devotion; and his quick resolution was strengthened and steadied. Yet in the account of his walking on the water, his natural instability of character, even after being long under the influence of Jesus, comes clearly to the forefront; while his denial of Christ still more strongly marks his wavering and his weakness. Nevertheless, he had already shown himself worthy of his title, as when at Caesarea Philippi he boldly declared Jesus to be the Christ, not a mere forerunner of the Messiah, especially as this was the very time when many men who were followers of Jesus were disappointed in Jesus and were abandoning him. Peter incurred the severe rebuke of his master by objecting to the necessity of Jesus' sufferings, yet on the mount of transfiguration when Moses, Elijah, and Jesus was illuminated Peter again wished to make permanent the glory there revealed by suggesting that they make 3 tabernacles in honor of Moses, Elijah, and Jesus as the bible tells in Matthew 17:1-9,"*Six days later Jesus took with Him Peter and James and John his brother, and led them up on a high mountain by themselves. And He was transfigured before them; and His face shone like the sun, and His garments became as white as light. And behold, Moses and Elijah appeared to them, talking with Him. Peter said to Jesus, "Lord, it is good for us to be here; if You wish, I will make three tabernacles here, one for You, and one for Moses, and one for Elijah." While he was still speaking, a bright cloud overshadowed them, and behold, a voice out of the cloud said, "This is My beloved Son, with whom I am well-pleased; listen to Him!" When the disciples heard this, they fell face down to the ground and were terrified. And Jesus came to them and touched them and said, "Get up, and do not be afraid." And lifting up their eyes, they saw no one except Jesus Himself alone. As they were coming down from the mountain, Jesus commanded them, saying, "Tell the vision to no one until the Son of Man has risen from the dead*". Equally typical was his desire to extend forgiveness as far as possible, though he still fell far short of the Christian ideal. The same statement holds true of the words in which he reminds Christ how both he and the other disciples had left all to follow him. As the time that Jesus was to be crucified approached, Peter's foolhardiness is revealed, as well as a certain lack of understanding of the love of Jesus which was to reach its completion. Immediately afterward he vowed, despite the prophecy of the denial, to remain faithful to Jesus even unto death. He overestimated his strength; he even could not keep awake for his master's sake in the garden of Gethsemane as the bible tells in Matthew 26:36-46,"*Then Jesus came with them to a place called Gethsemane, and said to His disciples, "Sit here while I go over there and pray." And He took with Him Peter and the two sons of Zebedee, and began to be grieved and distressed. Then He said to them, "My soul is deeply grieved, to the point of death; remain here and keep watch with Me." And He went a little beyond them, and fell on His face and prayed, saying, "My Father, if it is possible, let this cup pass from Me; yet not as I will, but as You will." And He came to the disciples and found them sleeping, and said to Peter, "So, you men could not keep watch with Me for one hour?" Keep watching and praying that you may not enter into temptation; the spirit is willing, but the flesh is weak." He went away again a second time and prayed, saying, "My Father, if this cannot pass away unless I drink it, Your will be done." Again He came and found them sleeping, for their eyes were heavy. And He left them again, and went away and prayed a third time, saying the same thing once more. Then He came to the disciples and said to them, "Are you still sleeping and resting? Behold, the hour is at hand and the Son of Man is being betrayed into the hands of sinners. "Get up, let us be going; behold, the one who betrays Me is at hand!"* It is true that he drew his sword when Jesus was seized, but when he saw that this was useless, he fled with the other disciples as described in Matthew 26:51-56,"*And behold, one of those who were with Jesus reached and drew out his sword, and struck the slave of the high priest and cut off his ear. Then Jesus said to him, "Put your sword back into its place; for all those who take up the sword shall perish by the sword., "Or do you think that I cannot appeal to My Father, and He will at once put at My disposal more than twelve legions of angels? "How then will the Scriptures be fulfilled, which say that it must happen this way?" At that time Jesus said to the crowds, "Have you come out with swords and clubs to arrest Me as you would against a robber? Every day I used to sit in the temple teaching and you did not seize Me. "But all this has taken place to fulfill the Scriptures of the prophets." Then all the disciples left Him and fled.*" Nevertheless, he made his way into the palace of the high priest, where he was put to the real test, only to deny Jesus with the utmost fervor. Yet in all this he never really lost faith in Christ for an instant, and when he became aware of what he almost unconsciously done, his remorse and shame, kept him away from Christ until after the resurrection. Then, however, his old energy reappeared, and though at the tomb the younger disciple John and Peter ran to the tomb John out ran him, he was still the first to find that the grave was empty. In the account of the appearance of the risen Christ at the Sea of Tiberias, the old character of Peter once more becomes manifest. The temperament of Peter, as here outlined, was inseparably connected with his position of distinction among the apostles. Not only was he closely associated with the two sons of Zebedee, James and John, and once with his own brother, Andrew, as one of the favorite and most trusted disciples of Jesus, and not only were he and John commissioned to make preparations for the Last Supper, but the entire content of the Gospels make him predominant over the other disciples. This position seems to have been due, mainly to his quick resolution and to his energy. It was confirmed by Jesus for the present and for the future; for the present by addressing to him questions and answers which concerned the other disciples as well. We learnt that when Jesus sent a message to His disciples that He was risen from the dead, His messenger, the angel, especially mentioned Peter by name saying, "tell the disciples and Peter, He goes before you into Galilee" as it says in Mark 16; 1-7,"*When the Sabbath was over, Mary Magdalene and Mary the mother of Jesus and Salome, bought spices so that they might come and anoint Him. Very early on the first day of the week they came to the tomb when the sun had risen, they were saying to one another, "who will roll away the stone for us from the entrance of the tomb?" Looking up, they saw that the stone had been rolled away, although it was extremely large. Entering the tomb they saw a young man sitting at the right wearing a white robe and they were amazed. And he said to them do not be amazed you are looking for Jesus the Nazarene who has been crucified, He has risen, He is not here, behold, here is the place where they laid Him. But go tell His disciples and Peter, He is going ahead of you to Galilee, there you will see Him, just as He told you.*" I can just imagine the joy Peter felt when he was told that Jesus had sent him a personal message. His heart must have leaped for joy, his countenance rose, and he must have been greatly encouraged. Peter had been included in Gods plan for the future even though he had a past record of foolish behavior and many failures. Peter had denied Christ and yet he became one of the best known apostles. Peter could have spent his entire life feeling bad and depressed about his denial of Jesus but he pressed past the failure and became valuable to God's kingdom. In keeping with His belief that one should pay Caesar's things to Caesar and God's things to

God, Jesus has Peter pay the tax collector the payment he demanded. This tax payment is recorded at Matthew 17:24-27 and reads, "*After Jesus and his disciples arrived in Capernaum, the collectors of the two-drachma tax came to Peter and asked, "Doesn't your teacher pay the temple tax?" "Yes, he does," he replied. When Peter came into the house, Jesus was the first to speak. "What do you think, Simon?" he asked. "From whom do the kings of the earth collect duty and taxes—from their own sons or from others?" "From others," Peter answered. "Then the sons are exempt," Jesus said to him. "But so that we may not offend them, go to the lake and throw out your line. Take the first fish you catch; open its mouth and you will find a four-drachma coin. Take it and give it to them for my tax and yours.*" He had so much Holy Spirit power that when his shadow fell on people they were healed as explained in Acts 5:15,"*to such an extent that they even carried the sick out into the streets and laid them on cots and pallets, so that when Peter came by at least his shadow might fall on any one of them*". God is willing to forgive those who make mistakes but they must be willing to receive His forgiveness. They must also forgive themselves. God promises to forget our past mistakes as Jeremiah 31:34 says," *They will not teach again, each man his neighbor and each man his brother, saying, 'Know the Lord,' for they will all know Me, from the least of them to the greatest of them," declares the Lord, "for I will forgive their iniquity, and their sin I will remember no more*". Stop remembering what God has forgotten! The apostles had extreme humility and a sense of obligation to Christ. They acknowledged Him as Lord and that Peter considered it an honor to be one of God's chosen. He was one that was sent by Christ, and had his commission and doctrine directly from Him to go everywhere and preach the gospel, plant churches, and put the churches in order, and place proper persons over the churches. Peter identifies himself with a balance of humility and dignity, as explained in 1 Peter 1:1-2," *Peter an apostle of Jesus Christ: to those who reside as aliens, scattered throughout Pontus, Galatia, Cappadocia, Asia, and Bithynia, who are chosen according to the foreknowledge of God the Father, by the sanctifying work of the spirit to obey Jesus Christ and be sprinkled with His blood: May grace and peace be yours in the fullest measure*". As a servant he was on equal basis with other Christians. He was an obedient slave of Christ. As an apostle, he was unique, divinely called and commissioned as an eyewitness to the resurrection of Christ. Peter was one of a unique group of men who were personally called as it is explained in Matthew 10:1-4," *Jesus summoned His twelve disciples and gave them authority over unclean spirits, to cast them out, and to heal every kind of disease and every kind of sickness, now the names of the twelve apostles are these: the first, Simon, who is called Peter, and Andrew his brother, and James the son of Zebedee, and John his brother, Philip and Bartholomew, Thomas and Matthew the tax collector, James the son of Alphaeus, and Thaddaeus, Simon the Zealot, and Judas Iscariot, the one who betrayed Him*". Peter was also commissioned by Jesus Christ and who ministered with Christ after His resurrection as explained in John 20:19-22," *So when it was evening on that day, the first day of the week, and when the doors were shut, where the disciples were, for fear of the Jews. Jesus came and stood in their midst and said to them Peace be with you and when He had said this He showed them both His hands and His side. The disciples then rejoiced when they saw the Lord. So Jesus said to them again Peace be with you as the Father has sent me, I also send you and when He had said this He breathed on them and said to them "Receive the Holy Spirit*". The church was built upon the foundation of their teaching. Peter was the leader among Christ's apostles. The gospel writers emphasize this fact by placing his name at the head of each list of apostles. Peter was soon the leader of the twelve, often speaking for them. He was also one of the three closest to Jesus (with John, 'the one Jesus loved', and James). Peter was called to follow Christ early in his ministry and was later appointed to apostleship, as explained in Mark 3:13-19,"*and He went up on the mountain and summoned those whom He Himself wanted, and they came to Him, and He appointed twelve so that they would be with Him and that He could send them out to preach, and to have authority to cast out the demons. And He appointed the twelve, Simon, to whom He gave the name Peter, and James the son of Zebedee, and John the brother of James, to them he gave the name Boanerges, which means sons of thunder, and Andrew, and Philip, and Bartholomew, and Matthew, and Thomas, and James the son of Alphaeus, and Thaddaeus, and Simon the Zealot: and Judas Iscariot, who betrayed Him*". The Lord clearly singled out Peter for special lessons throughout the gospels. He was the spokesman for the twelve, articulating their thoughts and questions as well as his own. His triumphs and weaknesses are chronicled in the gospels. Peter's evangelistic activity in Judea and the neighboring cities after the resurrection of Jesus is recorded in Acts, although 1st and 2nd Peter contains a few valuable implications. There is no reason to doubt the essential authenticity of Peter's speeches in Acts, the facts there recorded. After the ascension, Peter's courageous evangelistic work of proclaiming the gospel, was undismayed by the threats of the Sanhedrin at Jerusalem. He preached and worked in Samaria and along the Syro-Phenician coast, especially in Lydda, Joppa, and Cassarea, performing many miracles. When Peter Returned to Jerusalem, he was imprisoned under Herod Agrippa after the death of James, the brother of John, but escaping, he left the city, though he seems again to have taken up his residence there after Herod's death. Paul visited him there three years after his conversion, and he was there at the time of the council of the apostles. With Jerusalem as a base, he visited other churches, accompanied by his wife. Despite the existence of the evangelistic Christians in Corinth, there is no reason to suppose that Peter ever labored in Jerusalem. The Book of Matthew, Mark, Luke, John and Acts are in full agreement as to the position of Peter as the leader of the apostolic church. He was the most outspoken in the meeting of the Apostles when they chose Matthias to succeed Judas Iscariot. He was the most outspoken of the whole company of apostles in winning a large body of Jewish converts to Christ and in defending the Gospel against the Jewish hierarchy. He improved conditions within the church at Jerusalem, he watched over relations with other Christian communities, and he was the first to receive a pagan into the new church. On the other hand, he enjoyed no absolute control. He labored in Samaria together with John. Paul at first describes Peter as the leader of the church at Jerusalem, but by the time of the apostolic council he was, only one of the three pillars of the church, the other two being James and John. After the resurrection and ascension, and after the coming of the Holy Spirit, Peter initiated the plan for choosing a replacement for Judas as told about in Acts 1:15-16,"*at this time Peter stood up in the midst of the brethren, a gathering of about one hundred and twenty persons was there together and said, brethren the scripture had been fulfilled which the Holy Spirit foretold by the mouth of David concerning Judas, who became a guide to those who arrested Jesus*". He was empowered to become the leading gospel preacher from the day of Pentecost on. After Jesus' ascension, Peter and John took the lead of the early Church. Later, Peter had a vision from the Holy Spirit which led him to approve of evangelism to the Gentiles, though he later reverted to more Jewish ways under pressure from strict Jewish Christians. Peter was imprisoned under King Herod Agrippa the First, but was led out of the cell by an angel of the Lord the night before he was to be executed as explained in Acts 12:7,"*Suddenly an angel of the Lord appeared and a light shone in the cell. He struck Peter on the side and woke him up. "Quick, get up!" he said, and the chains fell off Peter's wrists*". We read the story of Peter's deliverance in Acts 12:7 and King Herod Agrippa I is the same person who is the grandson of Herod the Great, who tried to kill the infant Jesus in Matthew 2. He was the nephew of Herod Antipas, who killed John the Baptist and examined Jesus on Good Friday. He is the father of Herod Agrippa II, who heard the defense of Paul before Festus, and who put the Apostle James bar-Zebedee to death, and imprisoned Peter with the intent of killing him also. As Peter slept, chained to guards, an angel jabbed him in the ribs and said, "Get up, get dressed, and follow me." He led Peter out of the prison and a few blocks away and there left him. Peter went to a house where many Christians had gathered to pray for him, got an interesting reception, gave them a message for James, kinsman of Jesus and head of the Jerusalem community, then he left Jerusalem for a while. Soon after all this occurred Herod died suddenly. These events took place around Passover time, but to remember them would be a distraction from the Crucifixion and Resurrection of Our Lord. During all three of the famous missionary journeys of Apostle Paul, he kept in touch with the churches he'd established along the way, by sending them letters, called "epistles." Many of these epistles have been preserved, and are now chapters of the New Testament. The letters from the missionary journeys of the Apostle Paul date from a period between 50 and 60 A.D. and are the earliest books of the New Testament. In his letters, Apostle Paul rallied his followers in times of discouragement and persecution, and instructed the communities that he found to continue in ethical behavior, he offered advice and he also corrected their failures. The first extended missionary journey of the Apostle Paul occurred when Paul was probably in his 40's. He sailed out on a ship with Barnabas and Barnabas' cousin Mark (the same Mark of the second book in the New Testament), but Mark returned home only part way through. Apostle Paul and Barnabas continued in their missionary journey by first establishing churches on the island of Cyprus and then on the coast of Asia Minor. At the time of Apostle Paul's first mission, Greek and Roman religions were beginning to lose their appeal and people were ready for a new faith. Paul the Apostle preached a sermon in a synagogue on this trip that was said to be an especially superb presentation of the Christian faith to a Jewish audience. How many converts from this journey were Jews and how many were Gentiles is unknown, but the Apostle Paul had special appeal to Gentiles because he didn't require circumcision or observance of the Jewish law. Therefore Gentiles felt free to flock to the synagogues to hear him speak. In some places the new congregations may have been almost entirely Gentile. At the end of the first missionary journey of the Apostle Paul, Paul returned to Antioch, where he found that an order had been sent from Jerusalem insisting that all Gentile converts be circumcised. This triggered the second missionary journey of the Apostle Paul to Jerusalem, which Paul said was inspired by a revelation. He took with him Barnabas Titus, and a Gentile Paul had added to his missionary team. The year was then about 50 A.D. First Paul and Barnabas had a private meeting with the apostles Peter, James and John, in which they compared their missions and what they were preaching, and concluded they were acting in accord with each other. Paul felt supported in his belief that Gentile converts didn't require circumcision. While he was in Jerusalem, there was a determined effort on the part of Jewish Christians to have his new colleague Titus, circumcised, which Paul firmly resisted. Next came a council of the apostles, the purpose of which was to settle disputes over how much of Jewish law Christians were required to uphold. At the meetings Apostle Paul opposed the circumcision of Jewish Christians, repeating his belief that the ritual would make Christianity a Jewish sect. a strong point was made of the success of his missions, and how that success depended in part on the confidence of Gentiles that they wouldn't be required to follow Jewish traditions. In the end, the council decided that the missionary should continue without pressure on Gentiles to adopt Jewish ways. Apostle Paul would continue his missionary work, using Antioch as a base. Peter would continue his missionary work among Jews, using Jerusalem as a base. The issue of Judaism would rise again and again, however – throughout his life, Paul had to persevere in his efforts to prevent Jewish tradition from altering the Christian Religion along its own natural lines of development. He was asked to bear in mind, the sensitivity of Jewish converts in Jerusalem. Antioch also received a letter that included some minimal rules for Gentile converts:

1.) They could not eat meat obtained in pagan sacrifices;
2.) They could eat only kosher meat according to Jewish custom; and
3.) They were expected to observe restrictions on sexual relationships established by Jewish religious law.

It's believed that Paul the Apostle never saw the contents of this letter and that it arrived when he was out of the area on missionary work and had ceased to have close contact with Antioch. He also performed notable miracles in the early days of the church and opened the door of the gospel to the Samaritans, and to the Gentiles. Perhaps the greatest show of Peter's maturity in the book of Acts is his vision in Joppa and the conversion of the gentile Cornelius. This narrative takes place near the end of Peter's recorded ministry in Acts, but it reveals much light on how Peter had grown over the years since the night when he denied his Lord. In the vision that Peter has, recorded in Acts 10:16, a voice commands him to eat unclean animals. Peter refuses in his classic manner by proclaiming that he has "never eaten anything unholy and unclean". Yet verse seventeen is the first real light that is shed upon Peter's growth and maturity. In this verse Peter is greatly perplexed at the vision, and verse nineteen elaborates this point by saying that Peter was reflecting on the vision. He was thinking! At some point Peter had gone from an action-taker who did not think, or at the least thought only briefly and often came to wrong conclusions, to an action-taker (as can be seen in the fact that he does go and preach to Cornelius) who thought through things. In Apostle Peter's vision on the rooftop, Peter having climbed to the roof to pray in privacy, he began feeling hunger pangs. His mind wandered, he fell into a trance, and then an appalling scene played out before him. A large sheet descended from heaven, overflowing with "unclean" mammals, reptiles, and birds. Acts 10 does not get more specific, but a good clue to the species can be found in Leviticus 11: pigs, camels, rabbits, vultures, ravens, horned owls, screech owls, storks, bats, ants, beetles, bears, lizards, skinks, weasels, rats, and snakes. Simon Peter's mother would have told him, "Simon, that's nasty! Don't even touch it! Go wash your hands this instant! Why? Because we are different, that's why we don't eat pigs. They're nasty, unclean. God told us not to touch them". To Peter, as to every Jew in Palestine, such foods are more than distasteful; they are taboo, even abominable. God had said, "You are to detest them". If during the course of a day, Peter happened to touch the carcass of an insect he would wash himself and his clothes and remain impure till evening, unable to visit the temple in such a state. If a gecko or a spider happens to fall from the ceiling onto a clay cooking pot, he would have to discard the pot contents and smash it. Now these disapproved items were descending in a sheet, with a celestial voice commanding, "Get up, Peter, kill and eat". Peter reminded God of his own rules. "Surely not, Lord", he protested. I have never eaten anything impure or unclean". The voice replied "do not call anything impure that God has made clean". Twice more this scene repeated itself until Peter, shaken to the core, descended the stairs to encounter the next jolt of the day: a group of "unclean" Gentiles who wanted to join the band of Jesus-followers. That was the kind of conviction Peter had against unclean food, as explained in Acts 10:9-19,"*On the next day, as they were on their way and approaching the city, Peter went up on the housetop about the sixth hour to pray. But he became hungry and was desiring to eat ; but while they were making preparations, he fell into a trance ; and he saw the sky opened up, and an object like a great sheet coming down, lowered by four corners to the ground, and there were in it all kinds of four-footed animals and crawling creatures of the earth and birds of the air. A voice came to him, "Get up, Peter, kill and eat!" But Peter said, "By no means, Lord, for I have never eaten anything unholy and unclean." Again a voice came to him a second time, "What God has cleansed, no longer consider unholy." This happened three times, and immediately the object was taken up into the sky. Now while Peter was greatly perplexed in mind as to what the vision which he had seen might be, behold, the men who had been sent by Cornelius, having asked directions for Simon's house, appeared at the gate ; and calling out, they were asking whether Simon, who was also called Peter, was staying there. While Peter was reflecting on the vision, the Spirit said to him, "Behold, three men are looking for you."* Peter's reflection is interrupted by the men Cornelius has sent, or more accurately, his reflection is interrupted by the Spirit telling him that men are looking for him and that he should accompany them Acts 10:19-20,"*While Peter was reflecting on the vision, the Spirit said to him, "Behold, three men are looking for you." But get up, go downstairs and accompany them without misgivings, for I have sent them Myself.*" This narrative proceeds with Peter traveling to Cornelius' house and speaking the Gospel to all who were there Acts 10:34-43,"*Opening his mouth, Peter said : "I most certainly understand now that God is not one to show partiality, but in every nation the man who fears Him and does what is right is welcome to Him. "The word which He sent to the sons of Israel, preaching peace through Jesus Christ (He is Lord of all)- you yourselves know the thing which took place throughout all Judea, starting from Galilee, after the baptism which John proclaimed. "You know of Jesus of Nazareth, how God anointed Him with the Holy Spirit and with power, and how He went about doing good and healing all who were oppressed by the devil, for God was with Him." We are witnesses of all the things He did both in the land of the Jews and in Jerusalem. They also put Him to death by hanging Him on a cross. "God raised Him up on the third day and granted that He become visible, not to all the people, but to witnesses who were chosen beforehand by God, that is, to us who ate and drank with Him after He arose from the dead. "And He ordered us to preach to the people, and solemnly to testify that this is the One who has been appointed by God as Judge of the living and* the dead. *"Of Him all the prophets bear witness that through His name everyone who believes in Him receives forgiveness of sins"*. The narrative ends with the new convert's speaking in tongues and being baptized Acts 10:44-48, *"While Peter was still speaking these words, the Holy Spirit fell upon all those who were listening to the message. All the circumcised believers who came with Peter were amazed, because the gift of the Holy Spirit had been poured out on the Gentiles also. For they were hearing them speaking with tongues and exalting God. Then Peter answered, "Surely no one can refuse the water for these to be baptized who have received the Holy Spirit just as we did, can he?" And he ordered them to be baptized in the name of Jesus Christ. Then they asked him to stay on for a few days"*. Some discount the miracles, and indeed the entire Cornelius narrative as nothing more than an attempt by the writer of the book of Acts to include Peter in a more favorable light towards the gentiles. However, with the belief that Acts is an accurate historical source, one may see how Peter has come to the right conclusion this time. In Acts 10:28,*"And he said to them, "You yourselves know how unlawful it is for a man who is a Jew to associate with a foreigner or to visit him; and yet God has shown me that I should not call any man unholy or unclean"*. Peter explains that God has shown him that no man should be called unclean. This is undoubtedly an important revelation for Peter. It is of great importance to the modern reader, in the fact that it shows that Peter has truly thought things through. In the time period between Christ's death and Peter's vision the apostle has gained understanding. Perhaps we see in Peter, more than any of the other disciples, a man who has grown through his relationship with Jesus. The teaching of Peter, as recorded in Acts, was essentially apologetic, and practical. The narrative of Acts shifts from a focus on Peter to a focus on Paul half way through chapter twelve when the author reports that after escaping imprisonment and almost certain death Peter "left and went to another place" Acts 12:17,*"But motioning to them with his hand to be silent, he described to them how the Lord had led him out of the prison. And he said, "Report these things to James and the brethren." Then he left and went to another place"*. This is the last appearance of Peter in the book of Acts except for a brief speech during the Jerusalem Council. This then nearly exhausts the information contained within the New Testament regarding Peter. It is true that he is mentioned by Paul in both Galatians and 1 Corinthians, but chronologically speaking Peter is largely out of the picture aside from the prior appearance at the Apostolic Council. Peter's leaving for "another place" can possibly be dated to AD 41 or 42, this dating would also satisfy an command of Jesus that the Apostles should remain centered in Jerusalem for twelve years. It is possible that after departing from Jerusalem Peter visited Antioch, as well as several towns in Asia Minor. He may have visited Corinth, which would explain the reference that Paul makes to a "Cephas group" within that church as described in 1 Corinthians 1:12-14,*"Now I mean this, that each one of you is saying, "I am of Paul," and "I of Apollos," and "I of Cephas," and "I of Christ." 13 Has Christ been divided? Paul was not crucified for you, was he? Or were you baptized in the name of Paul? 14 I thank God that I baptized none of you except Crispus and Gaius"*, also 1 Corinthians 9:5,*"Do we not have a right to take along a believing wife, even as the rest of the apostles and the brothers of the Lord and Cephas?"* It is important however to keep in mind that all of Paul's references to Cephas in Galatians and 1 Corinthians are distant and somewhat guarded. Any discussion of Peter's later missionary activity, indeed any discussion of his whereabouts and activities after Acts 15 must eventually come to a discussion of his alleged stay in Rome. Some have purposed that Peter had two stays in Rome, the first of which began in the winter of AD 42 and was interrupted when Peter returned to Jerusalem after Herod Agrippa's death. The question of whether or not Peter ever went to Rome has been questioned off and on for that past 800 years. The Biblical record remains silent regarding this issue, the only arguments that may be made from the book of Romans on this issue are arguments from silence, such as the fact that "Peter was not one" of the persons listed by Paul at the end of Romans. The only other possible reference to Peter in Rome in the New Testament is found in 1 Peter 5.13 which says," *She who is in Babylon, chosen together with you, sends you greetings, and so does my son, Mark*", where the writer sends greetings from the saints in "Babylon." Some scholars have taken Babylon to be a "cryptic name for Rome". If this is the case then it makes at least some argument for Peter having stayed in Rome, though a single reference is far from conclusive. As has already been assumed one must move outside the realm of Scripture for an answer to the question of Peter's stay in Rome, and indeed for an explanation of Peter's martyrdom in general. At least one scholar has commented that all the "earliest extant sources which commented on Peter's death agreed that it happened in Rome". These earliest sources include Dionysius of Corinth dated to sometime between AD 166 and 174. However Dionysius contradicts Paul's statement in Romans that he has not yet visited Rome, Romans 1:9-10, "*For God, whom I serve in my spirit in the preaching of the gospel of His Son, is my witness as to how unceasingly I make mention of you, always in my prayers making request, if perhaps now at last by the will of God I may succeed in coming to you*". This has caused some scholars to be unclear as to the accuracy of the remainder of what he has to say, even with obvious objections being raised as to the historicity of Peter's stay in Rome "there is a large measure of agreement that Peter did go to Rome". Assuming that this large measure of scholarship is correct, and that Peter did indeed stay in Rome there are certain other traditions regarding his stay. There is one strong tradition that he lived with Aquila and Priscilla during his time in the Imperial Capital of Rome. There is also a tradition that says Peter lived with Senator Pudens during this period. The final and perhaps most important tradition regarding Peter in Rome is his martyrdom. It is now necessary to turn to Church history, tradition, and various writings for an understanding of the later years of Peter's life. Paul stressed the sufferings of Christ was undeserved and the unrighteous act of murder on the part of the Jews through pagan hands. Christ was more than a true prophet; Christ was anointed by the Holy Ghost, and was proven by miracles, wonders, and signs. Christ's' death was due not to chance, but to the divine plan as foretold by the prophets, the purpose being the first of all the blessings of the Messianic kingdom, including the forgiveness of sins. The proof of the Messianic kingship of Jesus, even during his human life and suffering, was sought in the fact that, in harmony with prophecy, he had been raised by God from the dead on the third day, had been manifested to chosen witnesses, and had been exalted to the right hand of God. This resurrection, of which it was an essential duty of the apostles to be witnesses, had made Jesus the Messianic king, the cornerstone of the divine kingdom, Lord of all, the perfection of the divine kingdom established since the days of the Old Testament patriarchs, and the perfection of the Messianic days foretold by the prophets. He promised all the blessings of the perfect kingdom of God, forgiveness of sins, peace, the gift of the Holy Spirit, salvation from a perverse generation, physical health, all salvation, and every divine blessing. On the condition in which man shares in these blessings is repentance, which first becomes fully possible through the death and resurrection of Christ, as well as obedience to God and acceptance of the divine revelation that Jesus is the Christ, the pledge and the expression of acceptance on both sides being baptism in the name of Christ. The fullness of the divine kingdom will be impossible until the last judgment, when God will send Jesus as the judge of the quick and the dead, and to bring to the faithful of all ages rest from the affliction of the present. While Peter realized that, in accordance with his divine promises, God would extend the blessings established in Christ to the entire world and would call all the gentiles, despite their unbelief and rejection of Jesus to Himself, in the hope that they might still be won for Christ. He was certain that he and the other apostles were ordained to preach solely to the Jews, and so strong was his aversion to the gentiles that only special divine commands could make him enter the house of the Roman centurion Cornelius in Caesarea and preach the Gospel to him and his family, concluding by baptizing them. Saint Peter supported Paul's view of not imposing Jewish law on Gentile converts. When Peter visited Antioch, Paul insisted on disregarding the law that forbade Jews to eat with Gentiles, and all the members of his community, Jew and Gentile alike, sat down to share a meal. Peter had no difficulty joining in. But when hard-line members of the Jewish congregation from Jerusalem arrived, Peter backed off from the mixed meals, and so did Barnabas. Both Paul and Peter had assumed the purity laws wouldn't be allowed to interfere with fellowship at the tables, but the Jerusalem visitors applied vigorous pressure, and they were forced to relent. If they didn't, it seemed the Jerusalem contingent would demand a split into two groups, and that any return to unity would then depend on meeting their demands that Gentiles obey all Jewish law. During this visit, Paul insisted on sticking to his own understanding of the agreements reached in Jerusalem, and eventually the visitors left. As a point of interest, the problem was resolved when Peter had a vision in which he was told to eat foods that Jewish law said were unclean. Peter proclaimed as he understood the vision, "of a truth I perceive that God is no respecter of persons." The growth of the Church in non-Jewish territory, however, forced Peter and other Judeo-Christians to modify their views, and at the council convened at Jerusalem to decide on the requirements to be laid upon gentile converts to Christianity. Peter disapproved of excessive ritual requirements of the converts, though agreeing with James that the gentile Christians should refrain from all things forbidden in the Noachian laws binding on every gentile. Further light is cast upon this council by the account given by Paul, according to which the final conclusion was complete harmony, and it was decided that James, Peter, and John should preach to the Jews, and Paul and Barnabas to the gentiles. Neither does the disagreement between Paul and Peter recorded by Paul as taking place at Antioch point to any opposition of principle between the two, particularly as they both agreed that true righteousness was to be sought, not in works of the law, but solely in faith in Christ. There can be little doubt that Peter's sudden change of attitude at Antioch was hypocritical, although at the same time it must be remembered that some uncertainty as to the proper course to be pursued may have existed in Peter's own mind. According to tradition Peter had to watch as his wife was crucified, but encouraged her with these words, "Remember the Lord". When it came time for him to be crucified, he reportedly pled that he was not worthy to be crucified like his Lord but rather should be crucified upside down, which tradition says he was. Christians believe Peter died in Rome during the persecution of Christians around 64 CE under Emperor Nero. Legend has it that Peter

was to be crucified but begged to be crucified upside down instead, in order that he may not be blessed to die in the same way as the Lord. In 64 AD Nero set fire to Rome and blamed the Christians for its destruction. Peter was one of the Christians who was taken prisoner and was sentenced to death by crucifixion. He was crucified with his head downwards because he did not consider himself worthy to die in the same manner and posture as Jesus. Constantly it is Peter who is singled out as the disciple of action. It is he who walks on water, he who proclaims Jesus as the son of the living God, he who proposes that tents be pitched for Jesus, Moses and Elijah, and it is he who cuts off Malchus' ear. Throughout the Gospels, Peter acts. Most often these actions are undertaken on Peter's part with a lack of full understanding regarding what Jesus is doing. Nevertheless Peter does act, and it is he who receives the command to feed Jesus' sheep as described in John 21:15-17,"*When they had finished eating, Jesus said to Simon Peter, "Simon son of John, do you truly love me more than these?" "Yes, Lord," he said, "you know that I love you." Jesus said, "Feed my lambs." Again Jesus said, "Simon son of John, do you truly love me?" He answered, "Yes, Lord, you know that I love you." Jesus said, "Take care of my sheep." The third time he said to him, "Simon son of John, do you love me?" Peter was hurt because Jesus asked him the third time, "Do you love me?" He said, "Lord, you know all things; you know that I love you." Jesus said, "Feed my sheep"*.
Interestingly, Peter receives this command after jumping out of a boat to get to Jesus and then hauling 153 large fish ashore in a net single handedly, or so the text would seem to indicate in John 21:1-14, "*Afterward Jesus appeared again to his disciples, by the Sea of Tiberius. It happened this way: Simon Peter, Thomas (called Didymus), Nathanael from Cana in Galilee, the sons of Zebedee, and two other disciples were together. "I'm going out to fish," Simon Peter told them, and they said, "We'll go with you." So they went out and got into the boat, but that night they caught nothing. Early in the morning, Jesus stood on the shore, but the disciples did not realize that it was Jesus. He called out to them, "Friends haven't you any fish?" "No," they answered. He said, "Throw your net on the right side of the boat and you will find some." When they did, they were unable to haul the net in because of the large number of fish. Then the disciple whom Jesus loved said to Peter, "It is the Lord!" As soon as Simon Peter heard him say, "It is the Lord," he wrapped his outer garment around him (for he had taken it off) and jumped into the water. The other disciples followed in the boat, towing the net full of fish, for they were not far from shore, about a hundred yards. When they landed, they saw a fire of burning coals there with fish on it, and some bread. Jesus said to them, "Bring some of the fish you have just caught." Simon Peter climbed aboard and dragged the net ashore. It was full of large fish, but even with so many the net was not torn. Jesus said to them, "Come and have breakfast." None of the disciples dared ask him, "Who are you?" They knew it was the Lord. Jesus came, took the bread and gave it to them, and did the same with the fish. This was now the third time Jesus appeared to his disciples after he was raised from the dead*". These examples show that it takes no stretch of the imagination to say that Peter was a man of action throughout his association with Jesus. At this point a certain amount of tension might be expected. If one has read the Gospel accounts in their entirety there is no doubt that although Peter was a man of action, his action often goes in the wrong direction. Jesus constantly rebukes Peter, sometimes harshly and sometimes gently. Yet in the beginning chapters of Acts this same disciple, the one who has been rebuked the most by Christ, even if because he acted the most in his presence, is again set

forth as the principle speaker and action-taker of the Twelve, now reduced to eleven. It is this reduction that sets forth Peter as the action-taker within the first chapter of Acts. Peter makes a good case for the choice of an unblemished successor to Judas. It is Peter who sets out the requirements for Judas' replacement, and it may even have been Peter who decided on the use of the lot to decide between the two possible replacements. So as the book that will outline the earliest history of the church begins Peter is again in the spotlight. Still taking action, and maturing along the way. Undoubtedly, the author of Acts portrays Peter as an extremely important figure of the early Christian community. Since his death, the church in Rome claimed to have special prestige from his life and death in their city, with the Vatican bascilla of St Peter's said to be built above the site of his martyrdom. Peter was given more prominence by the Church in the time of Pope Leo the Great (who died in 461), and since then all Popes claim that they are spiritual descendants of Peter. The sole remaining source is tradition, which seems to preserve a kernel of truth in the legend that the apostle went to Rome toward the close of his life and there suffered martyrdom under Nero. Thus Clement, in his first epistle to the Corinthians, written in 95-97, records: "Peter, through unrighteous envy, endured not one or two, but numerous labors; and, when he had at length suffered martyrdom, departed to the place of glory due to him". It is also noteworthy that no source describes the place of Peter's martyrdom as other than Rome, the place evidently implied by Clement, as the context shows. It would also seem that Papias of Hierapolis knew of Peter's residence at Rome. There are, however, a number of direct statements that Peter lived at Rome. Dionysius of Corinth states that Peter and Paul founded the church at Corinth and then taught in Italy, both suffering martyrdom at Rome. A similar story is told both by the late second-century Acts of Peter and by the almost contemporary Acts of Peter and Paul. Reference must also be made to a tradition that Peter carried on a conflict at Rome with Paul. Mark was his companion at Rome, where the second Gospel was written after Peter's death on the basis of his oral communications. The death of Peter, almost coincident with that of Paul, took place in 64, the year of the general persecution of the Christians instigated by the burning of Rome. Peter's life has been examined, from his humble beginnings in a back water province of the Roman Empire, to his meeting with the Son of the Living God, to his death, presumably, in the capital of the greatest of the ancient empires. Throughout his life Peter proved to be a man of faith; he stepped out on a wind-tossed sea to be with his Lord. He was often quick to act and slow to think in his early years, showing him to be a man of action. He had no qualms about cutting off the ear of someone who came to take his Lord away from him. Yet, many years later, it can be seen that Peter had matured a great deal and that, although he remained a man of both faith and action, he had brought these into at least some type of balance. Perhaps it is this human struggle and maturity, this humanity, which makes Peter one of the most interesting Biblical characters to study.

Chapter 11

Timothy

Timothy was born of Greek and Jewish parents who his mother, Eunice and grandmother, Lois gave him his name which means "one who honors God". Eunice and Lois were devout Jews who became believers in the Lord Jesus Christ and taught Timothy the Old Testament Scriptures from his childhood. His mother, Eunice, and his grandmother, Lois, are mentioned as ones who are distinguished for their obedience as 2 Timothy 1:5 explains," *I have been reminded of your sincere faith, which first lived in your grandmother Lois and in your mother Eunice and, I am persuaded, now lives in you also*". We know very little of his father except that he was a Greek as told in Acts 16:1,"*Paul came also to Derbe and to Lystra. And a disciple was there, named Timothy, the son of a Jewish woman who was a believer, but his father was a Greek*". His father was a Greek, who also was a pagan, who may have died before Timothy met Paul. Timothy was not circumcised at birth, and the reason why he was not circumcised in his infancy may be because the fact that his mother was Jewish and his father were Greek. In the Holy Scriptures, there is mention of Timothy's mother Eunice, and Grandmother Lois, as believers in Jesus Christ as savior and Lord whom when Timothy was very young, they taught him the Word of God. Timothy was pleased to stand by the side of a dear mother, and hear from her lips the great things God had done for His people in every age! Timothy was converted to Christ in the year 52 by the Apostle Paul. When the Apostle Paul and Barnabas first visited the Lycaonian cities, the Apostle Paul at Lystra healed one individual who was crippled from birth. Many of the individuals at that particular place believed in Christ, and among them was the future youthful disciple Timothy, his mother Eunice and grandmother Loida (Lois) as explained in Acts 14: 6-12,"*they became aware of it and fled to the cities of Lycaonia, Lystra and Derbe, and the surrounding region; and there they continued to preach the gospel. At Lystra a man was sitting who had no strength in his feet, lame from his mother's womb, who had never walked. This man was listening to Paul as he spoke, who, when he had fixed his gaze on him and had seen that he had faith to be made well, said with a loud voice, "Stand upright on your feet." And he leaped up and began to walk. When the crowds saw what Paul had done, they raised their voice, saying in the Lycaonian language, "The gods have become like men and have come down to us." And they began calling Barnabas, Zeus, and Paul, Hermes, because he was the chief speaker"*. The seed of faith, planted in the soul of Timothy by the Apostle Paul, brought forth abundant fruit. Paul led Timothy to Christ undoubtedly during his ministry in Lystra on his first missionary journey. Timothy is praised by Paul for his knowledge of the scriptures. With Timothy's knowledge of the scriptures from a child, Paul chose him to be his companion in his travels, and to assist him in the spread of the gospel. Paul knew it would be very disagreeable to the Jews to hear the word of God from the lips of an uncircumcised person, so Paul took him and circumcised him. Paul believed that the Apostles had to become all things to all people, so that he might gain some for Christ. According to a later tradition, Paul reportedly ordained Timothy as bishop at Ephesus in the year 65, where he served for 15 years. Timothy was Paul's dearest disciple, his most steadfast associate. He was converted during the apostle's first missionary journey. When Paul revisited Lystra, Timothy, though still very young (about twenty years old) joined him as a co-worker and companion. Timothy was a disciple and friend of the Apostle Paul. His grandmother influenced and taught him when he came to follow Christ. When the Apostle Paul visited Lystra, the young Timothy was already a full member of the Christian Church and after the two discussed the many difficulties Christianity was facing, the younger man expressed a desire to serve as a missionary, despite its hazards. It was after the departure of Barnabas and Mark that Paul summoned Timothy to accompany him as a colleague in the cause of Christ. A *disciple* means a *learner,* and a *scholar.* When Timothy was a young man, he heard the Apostle preach, and the Holy Spirit blessed what was preached and touched the heart of Timothy. From that time he loved to be with so wise and kind a teacher as Paul. Sometimes they went on long missionary journeys together, to make known the way in which sinners can be saved, through faith in our Lord Jesus Christ. There are two letters, in the New Testament which were written by the Apostle to Timothy. If you read these letters, you will see what good advice the Apostle Paul gave to Timothy, and how much he loved him. We place Timothy among the children of the Bible, because it is said of him in 2 Timothy 3:15," *and that from childhood you have known the sacred writings which are able to give you the wisdom that leads to salvation through faith which is in Christ Jesus".* Jewish children were taught by their parents at home, and were often taken by them to the temple to see the sacrifices offered. No doubt young Timothy had been told by his devout mother how God saved Noah in the ark, and Daniel in the den of lions; how David slew the giant Goliath with a sling and stone, and how Elijah was fed by ravens in a desert. These, and a hundred other beautiful stories, she told him from the sacred Book. She also must have taught him that the Passover was kept because the angel of God passed over the Hebrews, and slew the Egyptians; and that the lamb was offered every day in the temple as atonement for sin. She must also have told him of the great things God had done for their nation, and that He had promised to send them a Savior. All these instructions were very useful to Timothy when he grew up and became a preacher of the Gospel. He must often have praised God for giving him such a reverent family and friends to care for him and teach him. Timothy did not have a complete Bible, as we have, nor was his books like what we use today. It was probably made of long sheets of parchment, and was rolled upon a short stick. It was not printed, for printing was not then invented, but written with a kind of steel pen. It was too large to put into a pocket and must have cost a large sum of money. A poor child in those days did not have a copy of the Scriptures which he could call his own. He could not say, "This is my own Bible." As Timothy knew the Holy Scriptures from an early age, so it is important for us today to know the same Holy Scriptures that they might learn of God and His way of salvation through faith in His Son, the Lord Jesus Christ. The Holy Bible is God's inspired Word which He has preserved for us and we need to know it if we are to live a life pleasing to God. It is true that there are some things in the Bible hard to understand. Many years ago a devout man said, "It is like a river: so deep in the middle that an elephant may swim in it, but along the shore a lamb may wade, and not be drowned." You should be like the lamb. There are truths in the Scriptures which the wisest cannot fully understand; but if we have sincere and prayerful hearts, we may learn all that we need to know. If a child seeks to learn from the Bible, and asks God for His blessing, he will become wise, good, and happy. The Bible can make children "wise unto salvation" through faith in Christ Jesus. It teaches us many things; but its main objective is to lead a person to the salvation of the soul. It tells us of the love of a Savior, of what He is, what He has done, and what He has promised to do for those who believe in Him. Jesus says that we should "search the Scriptures," for they testify of Him. You should search with as much zeal as men seek for jewels in a mine and have as much excitement and enthusiasm as a football fan whose team just won the super bowl. It contains "the pearl of great price." You should read the Bible often, and read it daily. A wise man once said, "Get a little at a time, and as often as you can, and you will soon know a great deal." It is like a gold mine, where a man may dig every day of his life, and find much gold, and yet there will be plenty left for others. Timothy occupied a position of considerable influence and authority in Ephesus which is modern day Turkey, and was reportedly much loved by Paul, who was his mentor. Timothy is carefully instructed on how to carry out his duties, such as conducting worship, the organization of the church, dealing with false teachings, the role of women in the church, the encouragement of members not to lose their faith, and the other responsibilities of bishops and deacons. Paul and Timothy were historical people in the relationship of mentor (Paul) and student (Timothy). Paul refers to Timothy as his assistant, "fellow worker," and sometimes co-author in several of his recognized authentic letters such as 1 Corinthians, Romans, and Philippians. Timothy first met Paul during Paul's second visit to Lystra where it seems he was converted during Paul's first visit there when Paul, having been impressed by his "own son in the faith," at that time made Timothy his companion and mentored him in Christian leadership. Paul and Timothy did missionary journeys together, in Phrygia, Galatia, Mysia, Troa, Philippi, Berea, Athens, Thessalonica, as well as Corinth, Macedonia, Ephesus and greater Asia. Timothy also came to Paul's aid when Paul was put into prison. It is noteworthy that Paul reportedly decided that Timothy should be circumcised, according to Acts 16:3,"*Paul wanted this man to go with him; and he took him and circumcised him because of the Jews who were in those parts, for they all knew that his father was a Greek*". Since Timothy had a Jewish mother, he too was considered Jewish under Jewish law. Paul's motivation for circumcising Timothy may be expressed in 1 Corinthians 9:20 which states," *To the Jews I became as a Jew, so that I might win Jews; to those who are under the Law, as under the Law though not being myself under the Law, so that I might win those who are under the Law*". Others believe that Paul's well-known displeasure to the circumcision of Gentile Christians simply did not apply to Jewish Christians of whom Timothy was one, as was Paul. Still others consider Acts' account on this matter to be fictitious, believing that Paul would never consent to having his protégé circumcised. Timothy traveled and worked with the apostle Paul, and because of their shared Christian faith, Paul treated him like a son. Timothy was one of his most faithful co-workers. Timothy was from Lystra of Lycaonis, a city in the Roman Province of Galatia that today is part of modern Turkey. On the arrival of Paul at Lystra the youthful Timothy, with his mother and grandmother, eagerly embraced the faith. Seven years later, when the Apostle again visited the country, the boy had grown into manhood, while his good heart, his seriousness and zeal had won the esteem of all around him; and holy men were prophesying great things of Timothy. Paul at once saw how Timothy would fit right in for the work of an evangelist. Timothy was instantly ordained, and from that time became the constant and much-beloved fellow-worker of the Apostle. Timothy was baptized and later ordained to the priesthood by Paul. The young Galatian became Paul's missionary companion and his most beloved spiritual son. Paul showed his trust in this disciple by anointing him bishop of the great city of Ephesus. Timothy joined Paul on his second missionary journey where Timothy is said to have helped found the churches at Corinth, Thessalonica, and Philippi. Some scholars believe that he co-wrote II Corinthians, I and II Thessalonians, Philippians, Colossians, and Philemon. Timothy was with Paul at the time of his imprisonment in Caesarea and at the time of his later imprisonment in Rome. Timothy was also briefly jailed in Rome. Somehow Timothy escaped the very rough treatment suffered by Paul and Silas at Philippi. When Paul went on to Athens, Silas and Timothy stayed for some time at Berea and Thessalonica before joining Paul at Corinth. We do not know at what point in Timothy's career he was ordained by the laying-on of hands by Paul and others. We do not know whether he accompanied Paul back to Antioch between the Second and Third Journeys. But we do know that Timothy and another disciple named Erastus were Paul's 'helpers' during his long teaching ministry at Ephesus, which may well have been interrupted by some crisis involving danger. Timothy acted as Paul's messenger to carry the Corinthian correspondence from Ephesus, and his name is linked with Paul's in letters to Thessalonica, Colossae, and Philippi. At the end of Paul's Third Journey, Timothy was among the large group of disciples who met Paul at Troas and shared a Eucharist the night before Paul sailed for Jerusalem. But we do not know whether Timothy accompanied Paul or shared any of his imprisonment at Caesarea. It seems that Luke acted as Paul's secretary and companion until his arrival in Rome; from then onwards there is little evidence of Paul's movements, let alone those of his companions. If Paul's letter to Philippi or to Colossae, whether to the congregation or to Philemon, were written in Rome, then certainly Timothy was with Paul in Rome. Whether the letters to Timothy were written by Paul or not, it is certain that Paul sent Timothy as his representative to Ephesus, to teach for some considerable time. We know that Paul sent for Timothy to bring his scrolls and cloak before winter set in, but we do not know whether Timothy arrived before Paul's execution. The final chapter of the letter to Hebrew Christians may just possibly have been an appendix added by Paul himself. Its last message is that Timothy has been set free from some imprisonment and that Paul hopes he will arrive in time to be with him. Paul either sent or accompanied Timothy to Ephesus, where he became the first bishop. There existed between them a most intimate bond, as between father and son. Paul calls him his beloved child, devoted to him "like a son to his father" as it says in Philippians 2:22,"*But you know of his proven worth, that he served with me in the furtherance of the gospel like a child serving his father*". Timothy had a kindly disposition, unselfish, prudent, and zealous; he was a great consolation to Paul, particularly in the sufferings of his later years. He also assisted the apostle in the establishment of all the major Christian communities and was entrusted with missions of highest importance. As mentioned, Timothy was with Paul during his first Roman imprisonment and Paul made his self-sacrificing companion a bishop of Ephesus, but the finest monument left him by his master are the two books of the Bible bearing his name. Timothy felt the solemn honor of being the recipient of two letters from the great apostle Paul entitled First Timothy and Second Timothy. Paul wrote two letters to Timothy, one written from Macedonia and the second from Rome while he was in prison awaiting execution. While Timothy was the Pastor in the Ephesus church, Paul wanted to encourage him to continue his good works as described in Acts 19:10, "*This took place for two years, so that all who lived in Asia heard the word of the Lord, both Jews and Greeks*" also in Acts 20:31,"*Therefore be on the alert, remembering that night and day for a period of three years I did not cease to admonish each one with tears*". It is apparent that Paul is pleased that Timothy, his former student and travel companion, has risen up in the ranks of church leadership. When Paul was forced to flee Berea because of the hostility of the Jews there, Timothy remained, but after a time was sent to Thessalonica to report on the condition of the Christians there and to encourage them under persecution, a report that led to Paul's first letter to the Thessalonians when he joined Timothy at Corinth. Timothy and Erastus were sent to Macedonia then went to Corinth to remind the Corinthians of Paul's teaching, and then accompanied Paul into Macedonia and Achaia. Timothy was a young man that was greatly interested in taking up work like the Apostle Paul did. Paul, in fact, employed Timothy to stay in many congregations, to set matters right. All Christians can profit, like Paul's disciple, from Our Lord's admonition and the great Apostle's letters. It is remarkable what great stress Paul lays on the avoidance of idle talk, and on application to holy reading. These are his chief topics. He exhorts his son Timothy to "avoid tattlers and busybodies; to give no heed to novelties; to shun profane and vain chatter, but hold to sound teaching; to be an example in words and conversation; to attend to reading, to exhortation, and to doctrine." Let us faithfully follow these excellent counsels. The Book of First Timothy has 6 chapters and include the following: Paul's greetings, his warning against false teachings, the church officials, the mystery of their religion, people's turning away from their faith, Paul's advice to Timothy, how to act towards others, and true wealth including the love of money with the often quoted, 1Timothy 6:10,"*For the love of money is a root of all kinds of evil. Some people, eager for money, have wandered from the faith and pierced themselves with many griefs*". Paul charges Timothy to fight a good fight, for Christ. There are several key themes in I Timothy, for instance False Teachings. Timothy refers to false teachings as the "strange doctrines", in 1 Timothy 1:3,"*As I urged you upon my departure for Macedonia, remain on at Ephesus so that you may instruct certain men not to teach strange doctrines*". Timothy talks about meaningless talk in 1Timothy 4:7,"*But have nothing to do with worldly fables fit only for old women. On the other hand, discipline yourself for the purpose of godliness*". Timothy condemns blasphemous teaching in 1 Timothy 1:6,"*For some men, straying from these things, have turned aside to fruitless discussion*". Timothy condemned people who followed and listened to myths and endless genealogies as explained in 1 Timothy 6:3,"*If anyone advocates a different doctrine and does not agree with sound words, those of our Lord Jesus Christ, and with the doctrine conforming to godliness"*. The false teachings apparently relate to the theological basis of self-denying practices that the heathens at Ephesus engaged in, including abstinence from marriage and refraining from eating certain foods. The dietary restrictions were apparently urged by Jewish Christians called "teachers of the Law" who advocated adoption of Jewish dietary laws, as described in 1 Timothy 1:7, *"wanting to be teachers of the Law, even though they do not understand either what they are saying or the matters about which they make confident assertions"*. Paul gives to Timothy a warning not to let heresy and false doctrine take hold. Timothy also taught on the subject of the proper roles for women. This clarifies the role of Christian women as, women are not to be preoccupied with external beauty, such as braided hair, gold, pearls, or costly attire, but should be more concerned with internal qualities such as good deeds, as taught in 1 Timothy 2:9-10,*"Likewise, I want women to adorn themselves with proper clothing, modestly and discreetly, not with braided hair and gold or pearls or costly garments, but rather by means of good works, as is proper for women making a claim to godliness"*. Women must dress moderately, learn in quietness and submission, must not teach or have authority over men. The author justifies this policy on the basis that Adam was not the one deceived; it was the woman who was deceived and became a sinner. There are exhortations to a good conscience, and instructions regarding worship and organization in the congregation, and counsel on "godly devotion along with self-sufficiency". The Books of Timothy is addressed by Paul to Timothy personally, but actually it is meant for many of the concerns of the Christian church. About a quarter of a century after Christ, Timothy and Paul traveled to Europe, accompanied by Silas. In most areas theirs was at best a thankless job, but with the zeal born of a profound love of the Savior, they succeeded in securing a foothold in spiritually darkened corners. They brought this about with administrative skill in the face of odds which might have discouraged some. In a fury of religious speech, they summoned thousands to the fold and established Churches of God where for centuries people had worshipped mere objects or beasts out of fear and superstition. Timothy regulates congregational life, while relaying qualifications for the clergy, then details the admonitions of personal life and the behavior of widows and the clergy. Timothy displayed his talents to the fullest in establishing the cornerstone from which Christianity has grown to its present day proportions. Timothy appears to have been entirely at Paul's disposal from Paul's visit to Lystra on the Second Journey until the time of Paul's death in Rome, a period of perhaps 17 years. Timothy was by nature reserved, bashful, cautious and timid, and even with all of Timothy's personality traits Paul still commissioned Timothy to strengthen the insubordinate, opposing, rebellious, and stubborn Corinthians in their faith and in their loyalty to Paul. For all his shyness, Timothy could be trusted above many others for his pastoral concern and his gentle tact in dealing with awkward situations. When in prison, Paul wrote to the Christian community at Philippi about Timothy, in Philippians 2:19-22,*"But I hope in the Lord Jesus to send Timothy to you shortly, so that I also may be encouraged when I learn of your condition . For I have no one else of kindred spirit who will genuinely be concerned for your welfare. For they all seek after their own interests, not those of Christ Jesus. But you know of his proven worth, that he served with me in the furtherance of the gospel like a child serving his father"*. Although Timothy may have been subject to 'frequent ailments' he seems to have been constantly ready to undertake dangerous journeys on difficult errands for Paul, as explained in 1 Timothy 5:23, *"No longer drink water exclusively, but use a little wine for the sake of your stomach and your frequent ailments*". He was ordained and went with Paul in his journey through Phrygia, Galatia and Mysia; also to Troas, Philippi, Veria, and Corinth. He was designated to the office of an evangelist as it is told in 1 Timothy 4:14,"*Do not neglect the spiritual gift within you, which was bestowed on you through prophetic utterance with the laying on of hands by the presbytery*". Timothy went with Paul in his journey as described in Acts 17:14,"*Then immediately the brethren sent Paul out to go as far as the sea; and Silas and Timothy remained there*". There he followed Paul to Athens, and was sent with Silas on a mission to Thessalonica as described in Acts 17:15," *Now those who escorted Paul brought him as far as Athens; and receiving a command for Silas and Timothy to come to him as soon as possible, they left*", also talked about in I Thessalonians 3:2,"*and we sent Timothy, our brother and God's fellow worker in the gospel of Christ, to strengthen and encourage you as to your faith*". We next find him at Corinth with Paul as mentioned in I Thessalonians 1:1,"*Paul and Silvanus and Timothy, To the church of the Thessalonians in God the Father and the Lord Jesus Christ: Grace to you and peace*", also in II Thessalonians 1:1,"*Paul and Silvanus and Timothy, To the church of the Thessalonians in God our Father and the Lord Jesus Christ*". He now disappears for a few years, and is again noticed as being with Paul at Ephesus as described in Acts 19:22,"*And having sent into Macedonia two of those who ministered to him, Timothy and Erastus, he himself stayed in Asia for a while*", from there he was sent on a mission into Macedonia. He accompanied Paul afterward into Asia as described in Acts 20:4."*And he was accompanied by Sopater of Berea, the son of Pyrrhus, and by Aristarchus and Secundus of the Thessalonians, and Gaius of Derbe, and Timothy, and Tychicus and Trophimus of Asia*" where he was with him for some time. When the apostle was a prisoner at Rome, Timothy joined him as told about in Philemon 1:1, "*Paul, a prisoner of Christ Jesus, and Timothy our brother, To Philemon our beloved brother and fellow worker*", where it appears he also suffered imprisonment as described in Hebrews 13:23,"*Take notice that our brother Timothy has been released, with whom, if he comes soon, I will see you*". During Paul's second imprisonment he wrote to Timothy, asking him to rejoin him as soon as possible, and to bring with him certain things which he had left at Troas, his cloak and parchments, as described in 2 Timothy 4:13,"*When you come bring the cloak which I left at Troas with Carpus, and the books, especially the parchments*". Paul went on to Macedonia from where he wrote Timothy to help him carry out his task in the church. Timothy was well versed in Paul's theology; the apostle had no need to give him extensive doctrinal instruction. Timothy was distinguished for his early obedience and association with the sacred scriptures. The more we follow that which is good, the faster, and the further we shall flee from that which is evil. The keeping up the communion and fellowship of the saints, will carry us away from the fellowship with darkness. See how often the apostle cautions against disputes in religion. Religion consist more in believing and practicing what God requires. The same God who teaches the truth, by His grace brings us to acknowledge it, otherwise our hearts would continue to rebel against it. God is still in the business of pardoning those who repent, but we can not tell that He will give repentance to those who oppose His will. Sinners are taken in a snare, and in the worst snare because it is the devils, they are slaves to him. And if anyone longs for deliverance, let him remember they never can escape, except by repentance, which is the gift of God and we must ask it of Him by earnest, persevering prayer as taught in 2 Timothy

2:24,"*The Lords bond servant must not be quarrelsome, but be kind to all, able to teach, patient when wronged*". By the "servant of the Lord" is not meant any believer in common, but a minister of the word as Timothy was. One ought not to debate in a quarrelsome manner; he ought to strive for the faith of the gospel. This is praiseworthy to him, supplying him with the precious promises of truth by mild and kind instruction. They ought to be suitable to teach showing a willingness to instruct the ignorant and obstinate and making use of abilities given for that purpose. He ought to be able to bear evil so as not to be irritated and provoked, or to be discouraged from the defenses of the gospel. It is not only a privilege to receive the Christian faith; it is a duty to share it with all. All Christians must look at themselves as a link in a living chain which stretches unbroken from this present moment back to Jesus Christ. When he revisited Lystra on his second missionary journey Paul chose Timothy to accompany him. Timothy was very young, probably in his late teens or early twenties, since about fifteen years later, Paul referred to him as a young man. Timothy who had a reputation of godliness was to be Paul's disciple, friend, and co-laborer for the rest of the apostle's life, ministering with him in Berea, Athens, Corinth, and accompanying him on his trip to Jerusalem. Paul often sent Timothy to churches as his representative. He also served as a pastor of a church at Ephesus. There may be no more significant verse that Paul wrote in support of discipling than 2 Timothy 2:2,"*The things which you have heard from me in the presence of many witnesses, entrust these to faithful men who will be able to teach others also*". In addition to being an evangelist and church builder, Paul was a master disciple maker who modeled a lifelong commitment to discipling others to Christ Jesus. A few examples of God's handiwork through Paul are Luke, Titus, Timothy, Priscilla and Aquila and many others. His understanding of the discipling process is clearly stated in 2nd Timothy 2:2. In this statement, Paul shows:

1.) Demonstration of his discipled Life in Christ to the one he was discipling – Timothy
2.) The way and the life to others, Timothy's hearing the word spoken by Paul, the witness or seeing of Paul's life in action, the emphasis on a chain of reproduction
3.) Teaching of the discipling concept, scripture, lifestyle, entrust and teach the things you have heard from me
4.) Value of being with the disciple and having the disciple with you.
5.) Wise investment of discipling effort, entrust to faithful men
6.) Goal of reproduction into future generations, able to teach others also

Paul's heart was not with Timothy, the man he had invested so heavily in for between 14-18 years, spending time and effort in praying with him, teaching him, working alongside him, modeling the life of commitment to the discipling process. He knew the things he had transferred to Timothy, the things heard before many witnesses, and was confident he had made the required commitment in Timothy. Neither was his heart with the ones that Timothy was discipling. If Paul's work with Timothy was effective, and he believed it had been, then Timothy would also pass on Christ Jesus to those he had chosen to disciple. Paul's heart lay with the ones who would come as the result of the discipling work of the "faithful men" Timothy selected. In all likelihood, these were people that

Paul would never know. He knew that special truth had been committed to Timothy, not just for Paul's benefit, but so that he could invest it in others, that is where he placed his emphasis in the statement to Timothy. It would not be fair to pass by the "faithful men" Paul mentions without looking at them for a moment. What would Paul consider to be a faithful man? Most likely the faithful men would have been men like Timothy. They would have been men who were righteous, with habits and discipline that made them worthy of Timothy's time. If you think about it, no one wants to place their investment of time, effort and resources in someone who is shaky or questionable. You can be a great scientist, a famous statesman, or even a great theologian, and still fall short of God's plan for your life. If you do not understand and experience basic truths about discipleship taught by the apostle Paul and Jesus Christ, you are not his disciple, and you won't be able to disciple others. The apostle Paul wrote to his spiritual son, his disciple Timothy, in 2 Timothy 2:1-2,"*You therefore, my son, be strong in the grace that is in Christ Jesus. The things which you have heard from me in the presence of many witnesses, entrust these to faithful men who will be able to teach others also*". A disciple is one who loves God, our Lord Jesus Christ, with all his heart, soul, and mind, and tries to become more and more like him through a life of faith and obedience. The following are some characteristics of such trustworthy men,

1. A disciple must have assurance of salvation. He must know that he is a child of God that Christ dwells within him.
2. A disciple walks in the fullness and power of the Holy Spirit. The Holy Spirit is responsible for everything that happens in the life of a believer-his new birth, daily walk, understanding of Scripture, and prayers. He produces the fruit of the Spirit in us, which enables us to live holy lives and witness for Christ.
3. A disciple demonstrates love for God, his neighbor, his fellow disciples, and his enemies. Jesus commands us to love God with all of our hearts, with all of our souls, with all of our minds, and he also commands us to love our neighbors as ourselves.
4. A disciple is one who knows how to read, study, memorize, and meditate upon the Word of God, to hide its truths in his heart. It is impossible to walk in the fullness of God's Holy Spirit without an understanding of God's Word. The reverse is also true-you can't understand God's Word without the Holy Spirit.
5. A true disciple of Jesus is a man or woman of prayer. The Lord Jesus Christ, who spent 40 days in prayer and fasting in the wilderness, is our great example of this.
6. The disciple is one who is obedient, who studies the Word of God, and obeys the commands of God in a lifestyle that honors the Lord Jesus Christ.
7. A disciple is one who trusts God and lives a life of faith. Scripture reminds us that "without faith it is impossible to please God."
8. A disciple understands God's grace. God loves us unconditionally, whether we obey him or not. This is the opposite of legalism, the primary heresy of the Christian life, which urges us to try to obey God's laws in our own wisdom, our own strength, and our own power.
9. A disciple is one who witnesses for Christ as a way of life. As Christians we are to bear fruit, according to John 15:8,"*My Father is glorified by this, that you bear*

much fruit, and so prove to be My disciples". This includes the fruit of souls brought into Christ's kingdom as well as the fruit of the Spirit.

10. A true disciple of the Lord Jesus worships God in the fellowship of his church. He is involved in his church through study, worship, prayer, witnessing, and the stewardship of his time, talent, and treasure.

The word faithful has great meaning. It indicates someone who can be trusted to remain true to their calling, someone who can be trusted to stay the course and finish the race. A faithful person will continue on even when things are difficult. They go forward even when the one sending them is no longer present. You can count on a faithful person. You can put your faith in them. Paul wanted Timothy to find men of faithfulness, who were worthy of his investment of time and effort. After being released from his first Roman imprisonment, Paul revisited several of the cities in which he had ministered including the church at Ephesus, leaving Timothy behind there to deal with problems that had arisen such as false doctrines, disorder in worship, materialism, and the need for qualified leaders. This being done Timothy went along with him into several parts and Paul made great use of him, in preaching the word, planting churches, and writing epistles. Paul sent him to various places with messages from him, to Philippi, Corinth, and Thessalonica, and now had left him at Ephesus, where he appealed to Timothy to abide for a while, for that he was the bishop, pastor, or overseer, of that church is not likely, since his residence here was not constant and was afterwards called away from here by the apostle, who desired to stay there, under whom, and by whose direction, he acted while there. Timothy had to see that the churches had elders, bishops, and overseers whom the Holy Spirit had set over them, who the apostle called to him at Miletus, and gave them some advice and instructions. The design of Timothy's continuance there was to check growing errors and heresies, and to take care of and preserve the disciples of Gods house. Timothy was to teach the disciples how to behave in the church of God. He was to take interest to his doctrine and conversation, gives rules relating to the qualifications of the bishops and deacons, to take care of the widows, and to show the Christian walk and Christian conversation to all sorts of persons of every office, age, sex, rank, and order. After Paul asks Timothy to stay at Ephesus, he observes Timothy watching and taking note of the false teachers there. He gave an account of his apostleship and also of his conversation; he encouraged the sinners to stop sinning to the glory of the grace of God. Paul then closes with an exhortation to Timothy to constantly persevere in his Christian warfare, which we should also take note of. When Paul went to Macedonia, he desired Timothy to continue at Ephesus, his end was to restrain the false teachers from preaching the doctrine they did, which was contrary to the gospel of Jesus Christ. The doctrine the false teachers were teaching were useless, and unedifying. We are now approaching the climax of the Apostle Paul's second letter to Timothy. From the loneliness of his prison cell in Rome, and in view of his approaching martyrdom which he knows is coming, Paul addresses these solemn words to Timothy, who is far away in pagan Ephesus in 2 Timothy 4:1-4,"*I solemnly charge you in the presence of God and of Christ Jesus, who is to judge the living and the dead, and by His appearing and His kingdom: preach the word; be ready in season and out of season; reprove, rebuke, exhort, with great patience and instruction. For the time will come when they will not endure sound doctrine; but wanting to have their ears tickled, they will accumulate for themselves teachers in accordance to their own desires, and will turn away their ears from the truth and will turn aside to myths"*. No other passage in Scripture describes more accurately the day in which we live. This underscores again what we have seen many times already in Second Timothy, that, though this was written almost 2,000 years ago, it is highly relevant to our own day. In these words, the apostle is obviously seeking to open Timothy's eyes to the importance of what he is called to do. Paul flings back the boundaries of time and space to reveal to Timothy the unseen realities before whom every Christian lives and labors, reminding him of the great distinguished people who are involved in his witness in Ephesus: "I charge you in the presence of God and of Christ Jesus who is to judge the living and the dead," Paul says. There is nothing more helpful to us in the midst of pressure than to realize that what we are doing is a very important thing; yet there is nothing harder for us to understand about our own Christian ministry than that fact. Like Timothy, we see ourselves as a tiny minority amidst an overwhelming, mounting majority committed to evil and unbelief. Our voice seems to be a mere whisper in the commotion of chaos and the clamor of voices that speak and echo worldly things today. Most of us think of ourselves, and of our day to day commitment to walk with Christ, as being almost insignificant, that we are contributing nothing to arrest the downhill slide of our day. We think that we cannot speak with any impact at all against the voices of unbelief we hear on every side. I am sure Timothy felt that way too. As we have been seeing all through this letter, in his day there was an advance in evil and an increase in the voices that were denouncing faith and belief. Immorality was widespread in Ephesus; sexual perversions were accepted as an appropriate lifestyle in that city, just as they are in our day. Timothy must have felt that he could make no headway at all against the approaching tide of evil. What the apostle does here is roll back the separation between the visible and invisible worlds and show us in whose presence we are laboring, who are the powerful forces observing us and working with us in everything we do and say as Christians. Paul reminds Timothy that he is laboring in the presence of God the Father, the Creator, the One who holds in his hands the life breath of every human being, the One who is Sovereign over all human events. Timothy is also reminded that he carries on his ministry in the sight of Christ Jesus, the One who is to be the Judge of all men, before whom every human heart is exposed, the One before whom everyone, believer and unbeliever, must ultimately stand and give an account, although not at the same judgment. Jesus himself said that the Father had committed all judgment into his hands. So Timothy carries on his ministry before the One who thoroughly understands all of human history. This is what I hope we capture, a consciousness of who is watching, and before whom we labor. Not only do we labor in the sight of the Father and the Son, but Paul, in other passages, has told us that believers are called the "theater," the "spectacle" of the universe. In First Corinthians 4 he speaks of himself in that way in 1 Corinthians 4:9,"*For, I think, God has exhibited us apostles last of all, as men condemned to death; because we have become a spectacle to the world, both to angels and to men*". In Hebrews 12:1, the writer reminds us that we are surrounded by a great cloud of witnesses, "*Therefore, since we have so great a cloud of witnesses surrounding us, let us also lay aside every encumbrance and the sin which so easily entangles us, and let us run with endurance the race that is set before us*". In our limited, finite observation of life we often feel like we have been abandoned to labor alone, but we are not. Furthermore, not only are we being observed and helped by these powerful forces for righteousness in the universe, but we are involved, as Timothy was, with the greatest program the world has ever known. Paul charges Timothy not only in the presence of God and of Christ, but "by his appearing and his kingdom." Most of the commentators take the phrase, "by his appearing," to refer to the second coming of our Lord. It is true that the word epiphania, which is used here, from which we get the English word epiphany, is indeed used of the second coming of Christ, although here the word is a reference to the first coming of Jesus. Paul is asking Timothy to look back to that first appearing of Jesus, who by his death and resurrection brought life and immortality through the gospel and thus began in that invisible, remarkable way to spread the kingdom of God on earth. By his witness, Timothy is involved in the advance of that greatest of all tasks which God is doing in the world. That sets things in the right perspective. When we live and work and talk as Christians, we live righteously and justly, we live lovingly and compassionately before man. When we involve ourselves in the hurts of others to speak a word of comfort and relief, and especially when we point men to the Savior who can change their lives, we are involved in this greatest of all human endeavors, in a work that eclipses in significance and importance anything that has ever happened in human history. We are doing an extremely significant thing. Jesus taught us to pray in Matthew 6:7-13,"*And when you pray, do not keep on babbling like pagans, for they think they will be heard because of their many words. Do not be like them, for your Father knows what you need before you ask him. "This, then, is how you should pray: " 'Our Father in heaven, hallowed be your name, your kingdom come, your will be done on earth as it is in heaven. Give us today our daily bread. Forgive us our debts, as we also have forgiven our debtors. And lead us not into temptation, but deliver us from the evil one*". When we are living, speaking and behaving as Christians should, that is what we are doing: We are answering that prayer, we are advancing the kingdom of God, and we are causing the will of God to be done on earth as it is done in heaven. There is no higher calling. In John Pollock's new biography of Billy Graham there is recorded an incident which occurred when Lyndon Johnson was elected President. The President asked Billy Graham, with whom he had been friends for years, what particular position he would like to have in his administration. Without a moment's thought Billy said to him, "Sir, I believe that Jesus Christ has called me to preach his gospel. To me that is the highest calling any man could have on earth." That was an appropriate response. I have always been pleased that Billy Graham has turned aside from many such invitations so that he might maintain the calling to which God has called him. But we must not think of him as being unique in that regard -- every one of us is called to the task of proclaiming the gospel of the Lord Jesus Christ. That is brought out clearly in what Paul goes on to say to Timothy. He reminds him of the most essential element of a Christian witness in a dying world, as talked about in 2 Timothy 4:2,"*preach the word; be ready in season and out of season; reprove, rebuke, exhort, with great patience and instruction*". That is the one great essential that must be carried on to fulfill the prayer of our Lord and to advance the kingdom of God, to bring to fulfillment that amazing work that began by his first appearing upon the earth. When we read the phrase, "preach the word," however, most of us think that this is addressed to preachers. No, this word is not addressed to preachers only. It includes all the people of God, for it does not merely mean to preach the word, it actually means to "announce, proclaim, set it forth, deliver the truth, and make it known." It is not something you argue about; you declare it because God himself has said it. This can be done over a cup of coffee, in an office, or in a car while you are driving to work. It is something that can come up any place, anytime. Where human hearts are open, seeking, longing and hurting, there is the place, there is the opportunity to "preach the word." "Proclaim the good news," Paul says -- and it is good news. It is not news of what we have to do for God. That distortion has been widely peddled across the world and in this country, and it has resulted in a phony Christianity. But that is not the gospel. The gospel is the story of what God has already done for us. That is what ministers to the aching heart, the broken heart, the heart crying out for God. The gospel is the news that God loves us, he pities us, and he sees us in our hurt, our agony, our failure and our weakness, God also sees us in our strutting boldness and pridefulness and still he loves us. He has already done something about it, through the death and the resurrection of Jesus, in that amazing series of events that came through the appearing of Jesus on earth, he broke the stranglehold of evil upon human hearts, he found a way to set aside his own just sentence of death. Through those who open their hearts to the Savior, he has found a way not only to die for us, but to come and live in us, and start the process of renewing us, remaking us, and restoring us to our lost inheritance. That is the word we are to proclaim. That is the answer we Christians have to the increasingly obvious hurt and heartache of human need all around. It is the most effective thing we can do in our day. The darker the hour the greater it is for the need for the preaching of the Word. That is to be done by every Christian in every conceivable circumstance of life. I hope that comes through clearly because this is what the Apostle Paul is seeking to bring to Timothy's mind. Against this impressive background of the watching heavens, and in view of the paramount importance of continuing the redemptive work of Christ, Paul lays this solemn charge on Timothy's heart, as he does upon us: "Proclaim the truth; preach the word." Then he tells Timothy, and us, how to do it: First, "Be urgent in season and out of season," he says. Urgency means to do it with passion, with a deep belief in our own hearts that this is what is needed. Do not just come to somebody whose life is falling apart, and say, "By the way, I've got something that might help you. Let me see if I can remember it, wait, wait, its coming, I think it goes something like this. It has something to do with Jesus and the gospel." No, that either leaves no impression at all, or it leaves a negative impression. Rather come with a deep sense of commitment and belief in what you say, "Let me share with you something that has meant everything to me. It is my entire life and being." Then urgently, earnestly, lay it upon people's hearts, "in season and out of season." Many have been confused about what that means. Some have taken it to mean that you are to push the gospel on people whether they want it or not, to shove it down their throats, like the Boy Scout who helped the woman across the street even though she did not want to go. Some Christians take this passage to mean they have the right to impose a witness upon people whether they are ready to hear it or not. Saint Francis of Assisi once said, "Preach the Gospel at all times and when necessary use words". But, as John R. W. Stott has wisely said at this point, "This is not a biblical warrant for rudeness, but a biblical appeal against laziness." Witness whether you feel like doing it or not. Witness whether the opportunity seems good or barely feasible. In either case be ready to proclaim the Word. There is nothing else that can set human hearts free. That is why this is central and why, amidst all the other implications and exhortations of Scripture, the apostle singles this one thing out and says to Timothy, "In the light of the presence of God and the significance of the work you are doing, this is the one thing you must not neglect: Proclaim the word of God." Then do it, Paul says, with a variety of approaches. Notice how helpful and practical this is. "Convince, rebuke and exhort," he says. It is rather interesting that those words reflect three different approaches that we can use in announcing the gospel. "Convince" is a word addressed to the mind, as in argue, or reason, set it forth in a systematic, reasonable way, answering questions, removing obstacles. Present your witness, proclaim the Gospel in a way that cannot be contradicted by your life. Present it in a way that people have no doubts that the Gospel is the answer to life's questions. All of us should become experts at the reason and logic of the gospel. It is a reasonable, logical explanation of what is going on in the world, for why men act the way they do. But also there may be some who will need "rebuke." That considers someone who has fallen into sin, someone who needs a word that will appeal to the conscience because of sin which is destroying him or her and hurting others, sin which is demolishing, depersonalizing and dehumanizing those involved in it. Sometimes it is necessary to speak a word that points out the evil effects of wrongdoing, a word that seeks to address the conscience to turn away from this so that it no longer spreads evil among humanity. When you do that you are proclaiming the gospel. Then there are some who need "exhortation," encouragement; they need their wills challenged and encouraged to act. Many people are fearful to try something new, fearful to believe something that they cannot prove. Here is where the approach of encouragement comes in, exhorting them and encouraging their wills to set aside their fears and believe the truth of the gospel. We are to involve ourselves in all of these helpful approaches. Finally, says the apostle, "be unfailing in patience and in teaching" patiently keep on teaching if not in words, then in actions as what Saint Francis of Assisi said. Although Christians ought to beware of pressure tactics that seek to make people act or say they believe when they are not yet really convinced. Many evangelists and others, unfortunately, have resorted to psychological tricks and gimmicks, pressure tactics to get people to come forward and commit them in an emotional movement or mood that do not represent a real commitment of the heart. That is not a part of the gospel approach. The Spirit does move in great convicting power at times, and people respond almost against any attempts to keep them quiet. But we are not to employ pressure tactics to get people to move. Nor are we to abandon those who are slow in responding, but, as the apostle says, we are to keep on explaining; answering questions, clarifying, applying the gospel to specific situations. All of that is the work of teaching. Notice that the passage begins and ends with an admonition to "Proclaim the truth." State it first, announce it, herald it, proclaim it; and then explain it, teach it, break it down, make it clear. All this, says the apostle, is required, especially as we approach the end, because of the conditions that will obtain at that time. There will be terrible condition that will come in the church as 2 Timothy 3:2-5 explains,"*For men will be lovers of self, lovers of money, boastful, arrogant, revilers, disobedient to parents, ungrateful, unholy, unloving, irreconcilable, malicious gossips, without self-control, brutal, haters of good, treacherous, reckless, conceited, lovers of pleasure rather than lovers of God, holding to a form of godliness, although they have denied its power; Avoid such men as these*". Clearly, that is in the church. But here there is described a corresponding condition that will be evident in the world at large. At its base is a dislike of the truth: The time is coming when people will not endure sound teaching, but having itching ears they will accumulate for themselves teachers to suit their own likings, and will turn away from listening to the truth and wander into myths. 2 Timothy 4:3-4,"*For the time will come when they will not endure sound doctrine ; but wanting to have their ears tickled, they will accumulate for themselves teachers in accordance to their own desires, and will turn away their ears from the truth and will turn aside to myths"*. Surely that is descriptive of our own day. It indicates a time when the general population will forsake what is commonly called 'a Christian consensus,' an fundamental of social life by Christian principles, and substitute others. This is the time in which we live: "They will not endure sound teaching." Sound teaching is that which leads to health and wholeness of spirit, soul and body, teaching that permits human beings to live at peace, to develop them and enjoy their lives. But, Paul says, men and women will turn away from that and refuse to hear it. They will do this because truth requires the admission of human weakness, which people do not like to admit; the restraint of passions, which they do not like to do; and submission to the authority of God and other authorities under him, which they dislike and reject. They turn away from the truth, as this indicates; they will not even give it a hearing. It is not that they will listen to the truth and then decide whether it is right or wrong; no, they do not even want to hear it. They do not want you to say anything and they resist, sometimes openly, sometimes with subtle influences, every attempt to introduce the truth into any kind of social or governmental situation. Then, since they will not listen to teachers of truth, as the apostle says, they will look for others who will teach them what they want to hear. There is a disease, widespread in our day, called "itching ear disease," which Paul mentions here. This is an ear that wants to hear a particular line of things, an ear that wants to be entertained, that is always looking for something new, an ear that wants constant affirmation and does not want to hear anything negative or contradictory. People who have this disease look for teachers who will scratch that itch; and the result, the apostle says, is that they "wander into myths." What do these teachers, which such people accumulate in great numbers, teach? They cannot teach the truth because the truth is unacceptable, so they teach attractive lies, fantasies for the most part, speculative philosophies that emerge from the minds of men which have no basis in fact or history. There are many of these myths abroad today. I do not know all the myths that were taught in Timothy's day, but these errors appear again and again in the course of human history. Take the myth of reincarnation. Many people, even Christians, believe that lie, that myth which has no basis whatsoever in fact. There is no empirical evidence that can support or prove the idea that people die, then come back to earth to live another life, and then die and come back to earth again. That is the myth that says, "If at first you don't succeed, die, die again!" Reincarnation directly contradicts the evidence of revelation. It is diametrically opposite to the biblical teaching of the resurrection of the body, that the body survives life, is changed, and people go on in the same body. Reincarnation says they leave that body, never to enter it again, and come back and take another body. The two are diametrically opposed. You cannot believe in the biblical doctrine of resurrection and also believe in the widespread myth of reincarnation. That is one myth that is taught today to please the itching ears of men who will not believe what the Word of God says about the survival of the body. Take another myth widespread in our day, the myth of evolution. In the last century, this myth began to take over the scientific world, again without a shred of evidence to support it. Any attempt to try to set forth anything to the contrary is met with ridicule and mockery, put down as though those who hold any other view are village idiots, incapable of reasoning with intelligent men. Yet I find that many Christians believe the myth of evolution. They do not seem to understand the theological implications which evolution teaches, without any support from science, that our race is descended from apes and other animals so that there never was or could be a fall. By denying the fall, evolution teaches that there is no need for any redemptive act on the part of God. Why should we need to be redeemed if we have never fallen? That is the theology of the lie of evolution. Take the lie of human autonomy, which we hear on every side today. Autonomy is freedom to determine one's own actions, or behavior. We hear that man is the measure of all things; man is the ultimate intelligence in the universe; our destiny is in our own hands; we can and must work out all our own problems; there is nothing more out there. Reflected almost every time you turn on the television, pick up a newspaper or read a magazine is this underlying assumption that man is the measure of all things. Take the myth of the omnicompetence of science, that science can solve all our problems. We see pictured in the media unthreatening, very mild-looking doctors and others dressed in white coats, working away in laboratories on the basis of human existence. There, we are told, they are solving problems in the realm of the molecules that make us up, finding new bases of life and secrets of matter, discovering that science can put everything together and bring about a brave new world in which we can live free from fear and free from conflict with one another. Yet, if you look at the record of scientific achievement, all the technological advances of which we are so proud today have resulted instead in the dehumanization and depersonalization of people, the pollution of our atmosphere, the corruption of our ways of life and the increase in threat to the welfare of the world. That is the record! It speaks for itself! Yet it is all set aside in the face of this attractive lie. Take the matter of homosexuality as an accepted lifestyle. This is being taught and spread everywhere in our society by every means, at every level. We are told that homosexuality can be as satisfying, as enjoyable, and as contributive to the life and happiness of a human being as heterosexuality. That is an outright denial of all that God had in mind when he made them in the beginning male and female, and said, "These shall be one flesh," as described in Genesis 2:24.”*For this reason a man shall leave his father and his mother, and be joined to his wife; and they shall become one flesh*”. We have been saturated by a world that is committed to falsehood. That is why, as Paul says, we must increasingly proclaim the truth as it is in Jesus. As we see these things abounding around us, the temptation in our day is to start a protest movement, to organize a demonstration, to mindlessly chant slogans, or stage sit-ins. I understand the feelings of frustration that come when we see all that is dear and precious to us today being destroyed by these lies. We want to take hold of these lies and smash them. But that is not what the Word of God says will work. The apostle reminds us that the most effective thing is, preach the word, announce the truth, tell of reality, make it clear, and spread the word. All of heaven is watching, and all of God is committed to blessing, fulfilling and carrying that through until the world at last arrives at the day that God himself has designated, that final end when all creation shall bow together before the Lord Jesus and declare that Jesus is Lord, to the glory of God the Father. You and I are called to advance that work. Do not let anybody tell you that your life as a Christian does not count. It counts tremendously. It is the most significant thing taking place on this earth today, above any international program, act of Congress or decision of president, king or ruler. Glory in what God has called you to do, and be faithful to his command: Preach the word; be ready in season and out of season; convince, rebuke, and exhort; Be unfailing in patience and in teaching. After Paul's martyrdom, St John the Evangelist was Timothy's teacher. But when the Emperor Domitian exiled John from Ephesus to the island of Patmos, Timothy remained in Ephesus as bishop. Timothy completed his life as a martyr. At Ephesus the pagans made a day of feast in honor of their idols and they carried them through the city, accompanied by blasphemous ceremonies and songs. The holy Bishop Timothy, zealous for the glory of God, attempted to halt the procession and reason with the spiritually blind idol-worshipping people, by preaching the true faith in Christ. The pagans dashed angrily upon the holy disciple, they beat him, dragged him along the ground, and finally, they stoned him. The holy Disciple Timothy's death by martyrdom occurred in the year January 22, 98, just days before the day of feasts on January 26, 98. In the IV Century the holy relics of the Disciple Timothy were transferred to Constantinople and placed in the church of the Holy Apostles. His honored relics were later taken to Constantinople and buried in the Church of the Holy Apostles by the graves of St Luke the Evangelist and St Andrew the First-Called. The Feast Day of Saint Timothy is January 24. The origin of Feast Days: most saints have specially designated feast days and are associated with a specific day of the year and these are referred to as the saint's feast day. The feast days first arose from the very early Christian custom of the annual commemoration of martyrs on the dates of their deaths at the same time celebrating their graduation into heaven. St. Timothy himself not many years after the death of St. Paul won his martyr's crown at Ephesus. As a child Timothy delighted in reading the sacred books, and to his last hour he would remember the parting words of his spiritual father, "Attende lectioni - Apply thyself to reading." Paul completed Christ's command through his discipling work with Timothy. He completed the investment that Christ commanded in the Great Commission in Matthew 28:18-20,"*And Jesus came up and spoke to them, saying, "All authority has been given to Me in heaven and on earth." Go therefore and make disciples of all the nations, baptizing them in the name of the Father and the Son and the Holy Spirit, teaching them to observe all that I commanded you; and lo, I am with you always, even to the end of the age.*" The 2nd Timothy model of disciple making is "life on life" training. It is sharing your life with another so that they will know Christ, and grow, so that the process will be repeated in another. It is more than teaching words and doctrine. It is also teaching the lifestyle and commitment that go with the words and doctrine. In understanding of the full meaning of discipleship, it is transferring Christ like discipline, from one to another. Everyone who claims salvation today can trace their salvation back to these words from John's Gospel. As the Word became flesh and was shared with the first believers and was taken by them as the Word and shared with others who shared the Word with others, we have a direct link back to Christ Jesus. If you want to become a disciple of our Savior and be someone who disciples others, you can begin today. Develop the practice of spending time alone each day with God in prayer and in his Word. Pray for people who will meet weekly with you, who will commit themselves to changing the world through evangelism and discipleship. The world desperately needs such a change, but only our Lord Jesus Christ has the power and plan to change men and nations.

Chapter 12

Epaphras

There are some people in the Bible who only get the briefest of mentions; we can often miss the ones that are mentioned the least, Epaphras was one of the least mentioned. He was a man we would all do well to be a little more like. Epaphras was a Christian preacher who spread the Gospel to his fellow Colossian citizens. He is a dynamic example of discipline and love of heart to serve in the Body of Christ. Epaphras worked with the Apostle Paul in the outreach of God's Word in Asia Minor, specifically in the area of Colossae and Laodicea, which we know as Central Turkey and its southern coast. Paul saw this man as his co-worker, a fellow worker, a fellow slave of Jesus Christ, and a fellow servant with himself and with Timotheos. Paul saw Epaphras as doing the same work that he was doing as a fellow slave. In most of Paul's letters in the Holy Scriptures, he begins by referring to himself as a servant of Jesus Christ, as in the books of Romans, Titus, Philippians, II Corinthians, and Galatians. Paul describes Epaphras as doing the same work, for the same Lord, and accomplishing the same thing as the planting of local churches around the world. Paul considers Epaphras as a fellow slave of Christ. Paul, more than anyone, could appreciate the work that was involved in planting a church in a pagan land. Paul came into many cities, preached the gospel, and suffered greatly for it! He knew of the risks and the dangers. He knew of the opposition that would be faced by all the servants of Jesus Christ by the local idol makers of different districts and vicinities who have their crafts and livelihoods put in jeopardy by the witness of Christ Jesus and by those who preach Christ in different towns. Paul was stoned and left for dead in Lystra, beaten in Philippi, nearly torn in pieces in Jerusalem, and in Ephesus. Paul knew all about the danger and trouble that would face a man planting a church in such hostile territory. In fact, he wrote many of his letters from prison, for doing the very same work that Epaphras was doing in Colosse! For that fact, Paul referred to Epaphras as a fellow slave as one who was sold out to serving the Lord by preaching the gospel to the lost and supporting the planting of local churches for the glory of God. Epaphras had a completely surrendered life to the Lord. Every desire and will was surrendered to the Lord. Whatever this slave of God might have called his own, he surrendered to the Lord, placing all at the disposal of the Master, Christ Jesus. This quality should be the characteristic of every believer! Unfortunately, it is not. Not every believer is a servant of Christ, a slave, even though we ought to be. Too many believers serve other things and have other masters. Paul warns those who are servants of other masters in Romans 6:16, "*Do you not know that when you present yourselves to someone as slaves for obedience, you are slaves of the one whom you obey, either of sin resulting in death, or of obedience resulting in righteousness*". Some serve their job, some serve their family, some serve their friends, some serve the world, and some are self serving. They do not give a second thought to serving Jesus Christ as explained in Romans 1:25, "*For they exchanged the truth of God for a lie, and worshiped and served the creature rather than the Creator, who is blessed forever. Amen*" also Matthew 6:24, "*No one can serve two master; for either he will hate the one and love the other, or he will be devoted to one and despise the other. You cannot serve God and wealth*". This was not the case with Epaphras, he served Christ only, he was a slave of Christ, he had no will of his own, his meat was to do the will of the one who sent him as explained in John 4:34, "*Jesus said to them, "My food is to do the will of Him who sent Me and to accomplish His work*". A servant is to be selfless, and attending to the needs of others. Epaphras was such a man. He had the heart to only serve Christ! He is called by Paul his fellow servant or another word for fellow servant, a sun-doulos which means fellows bond servant. Fellow servant or sun-doulos is a servant, or an associate of a slave. It is someone who serves the same master with another as described in Colossians 4:12-13, "*Epaphras, who is one of your number, a bond slave of Jesus Christ, sends you his greetings, always laboring earnestly for you in his prayers, that you may stand perfect and fully assured in all the will of God. For I testify for him that he has a deep concern for you and for those who are in Laodicea and Hierapolis.*" Here he is called a "sun-doulos" which implies that he is a servant along with other servants. He served Christ, but not alone. He did so with many others, including the apostle Paul. Epaphras prayed with persistent prayers. If you think about it is it not here where we so frequently fail? We give up, instead of holding on. We should be persistent in our prayers as 1 Thessalonians 5:17 says, "*Pray without ceasing*". Epaphras' prayers were agonizing prayers. He was quite literally, striving in agony. Epaphras' prayers were intense prayers that were lead by the Holy Spirit as described in Romans 8:26,"*In the same way the Spirit also helps our weakness; for we do not know how to pray as we should, but the Spirit Himself intercedes for us with groaning too deep for words*". Epaphras was a true missionary. This man had a deep concern, not only for the Christians at Colosse, but also for those at Laodicea and Hierapolis. Have we any concern for the millions who have never heard the gospel? Do we pray for their salvation? Do we give of our own abundance for missionary work? Could we go to the foreign field, to the mission field? May God give us all a true missionary vision! The few bits of information we can gather about Epaphras make us want to learn more. Not only did Paul refer to Epaphras as Paul's fellow prisoner, but as a dear fellow servant, a faithful minister of Christ, as well as a servant of Christ. He had been a member of the church at Colosse and had eventually become associated with the apostle Paul in his ministry in that region. He had brought word to Paul concerning the church while Paul was a prisoner at Rome, and had somehow been imprisoned there himself. He had brought an encouraging testimony about the church to Paul, assuring him that the Lord will bring forth fruit in Colosse, testifying of the church's faith in Christ Jesus and love in the Spirit as described in Colossians 1:4-8, "*since we heard of your faith in Christ Jesus and the love which you have for all the saints ; because of the hope laid up for you in heaven, of which you previously heard in the word of truth, the gospel which has come to you, just as in all the world also it is constantly bearing fruit and increasing, even as it has been doing in you also since the day you heard of it and understood the grace of God in truth; just as you learned it from Epaphras, our beloved fellow bond-servant, who is a faithful servant of Christ on our behalf, and he also informed us of your love in the Spirit*". Paul reveals a deep appreciation of Epaphras. Paul shows that Epaphras was a teacher. We can see this in the words, as you also learned. He had brought the Gospel message to the Colossians and had nurtured it so that it affected their lives abundantly. The apostle describes him as a dear fellow-servant. This sets the seal of approval upon what Epaphras was teaching. As a fellow-servant or bond slave then his position in Christ was the same as that of Paul and Timothy. They were bond slaves to the same Master. Therefore, his teaching and life was geared to the word of the Lord. Epaphras was dear to them all. He was both highly esteemed and loved. Furthermore, he is described as a faithful minister on our behalf. As a representative of Paul to the Colossians, Epaphras was commended for his reliability and trustworthiness. It was also Epaphras who carried the report of their love in the Spirit to the apostle. This love is not merely human affection, but a genuine love which always seeks the best for the Lord and His people. It was a love promoted by the indwelling Spirit of God. Epaphras was faithful by the way that he taught the people how to live the love of God. He shared with them the hope of Christ's return, along with the grace of God. Another aspect mentioned here is that he was not critical of them, but shared with Paul the believer's love that they had for him. Epaphras must have been so committed that Paul figuratively labeled him as a prisoner of war with him. Paul by this time was literally a prisoner in bonds. The apostles had comfort in the communion of saints and ministers. One is his fellow-servant, another fellow-prisoner, and all his fellow-workers, working out their own salvation, and endeavoring to promote the salvation of others as described in Colossians 4:12, "*Epaphras, who is one of your number, a bond slave of Jesus Christ, sends you his greetings, always laboring earnestly for you in his prayers, that you may stand perfect and fully assured in all the will of God*". As Paul considers this church, he thanks God for their faith in Jesus, the love that they share with one another, and for the hope they demonstrate. This trio of faith, hope, and love, is repeated frequently in the New Testament. It is the fruit of a true conversion to Jesus Christ. Those who profess salvation but do not desire these fruit of the spirit in their lives have not made a true commitment to the Lord Jesus Christ. It may be these people who are entangling the Colossian church in conflict. It may be these types of people who bad mouth the modern church today. Paul is thankful that, even in the midst of their difficulties, the faithful members of the congregation are still maintaining their testimony. These characteristics of faith, hope, and love are every much the fruit of the life of a Christian as an apple is the fruit of an apple tree. God's love, present in the heart of every true believer, gives hope, and together they strengthen one's faith. A person is literally transformed when they come to Christ. A person who leaves behind a life of pointless conflict, sin, bitterness, anger, hatred, and despair find that through the power of the Holy Spirit, they now experience faith hope and love. Have you experienced faith, hope, and love, or have you experienced confusion and despair? If you experiences confusion and despair, it is possible that your profession as a Christian was premature. It is not enough to simply know who Jesus is, you must believe in who He is. Faith involves accepting Him as Lord and Savior, meaning that you place your trust wholly in Him. It involves accepting Christ as Lord of your life. It is replacing your self as the authority in your life and making Christ the ultimate authority. Often the gospel is presented in a watered-down version, or in an emotional context that draws people to make a decision out of guilt or emotional motivation. That decision may be done to comfort the plea of a religious leader rather than as a spontaneous response of recognition of God's love and desire for one's salvation. When a person responds to the true gospel, the good news that Jesus saves, it results in a changed life in God as He is given Lordship in the life of the believer. Faith is like sitting in a chair. One can believe that a chair can support their weight just as someone can believe that Jesus can save. However it is not until one sits in that chair that such belief is expressed as faith. Likewise faith in Jesus Christ involves acting on belief. The faithful Colossians had done this. Where the truth of the gospel is understood and moved upon in faith the fruit of the Spirit is a result. Paul has mentioned love, faith, and hope. James and Paul fully agree concerning the demonstration of fruit in the life of a Christian. James argues that faith without good works is dead. Paul states that faith will produce works. They are both saying the same thing, that a life that turns to Christ is transformed to one that demonstrates the fruit of love, peace, and joy. Paul also adds many of the characteristic traits of someone who demonstrates the fruit of the Spirit, such as gentleness, patience, kindness, etc. Paul showed gratitude for the Colossian's faith, love, hope and fruitfulness. The apostle, along with others is found thanking God for the Colossians as well as constantly praying for them. Prayers are request to God while thanksgiving is the return of praise for requests that were answered. God's worshippers are those who praise or thank God and offer up spiritual sacrifices while giving the honor or glory to Him. The words, the God and Father of our Lord Jesus Christ, tell us that the same Father loves us even to the degree that He loves His own beloved Son. It is through Jesus Christ that God the Father's entire counsel and purpose will be fulfilled. God the Father is to be the subject of glory and praise, the searcher of hearts, the comforter; and the merciful One who has secured our future. Like Paul, we may find fresh causes for which we can thank God for our fellow believers. The faith of the Colossian Christians, their love towards all other believers, and the hope they possessed are the three reasons given for Paul's thanksgiving. Interestingly, Paul had heard these things witnessed about the Colossians. They could not be classed as secret or passive disciples. They made, as we all should, the confession of their faith known. Furthermore, do we, like Paul, give thanks for those whom we know fully trust in the exalted Savior and act accordingly? Do we give thanks for those who have love for all their fellow Christians? Do we give thanks that Christians are encouraged by the hope of an inheritance secured for them in heaven? Peter describes it as an inheritance which is incorruptible, and undefiled, and that does not fade away. Which is reserved in heaven for us as described in 1 Peter 1:4,"*to obtain an inheritance which is imperishable and undefiled and will not fade away, reserved in heaven for you*". It is therefore an inheritance which is both everlasting and pure. This virtue of faith, love and hope marks the life of the Christian. Faith rests in Christ and all that He has done and is doing. Love works in and through our hearts today. Hope looks to certainty in the future. Paul reminds the Colossians that they had heard of this hope previously, as when Epaphras preached the Gospel to them. Paul describes this as the word of the truth of the gospel which emphasizes the truth of the good news that they had received as opposed to the false teachings that were, at that time, infiltrating their assembly. The apostle states that the word of truth of the Gospel has come to them as it has come into the entire world. The Greek word for, is come, is pareimi, which is usually reserved for the coming of a person. It emphasizes the fact that the glad tidings concern the Person of Christ. The fact that Paul refers to the entire world, shows that the range of the Gospel was universal. What had been experienced at Colossae was happening everywhere the Gospel was preached. The American Standard Version reads: "Which is come unto you; even as it is also in all the world, bearing fruit and increasing." This translation highlights the supernatural power of the Gospel. A plant does not naturally bear fruit and increase at the same time. Usually, it has to be pruned to be fruitful or else it grows wild with all of its life being used in the growth of branches and leaves. The Gospel was bearing fruit in the salvation of souls and increasing spiritually in the growth of these new Christians. It is God's sovereign display of love which saves and sanctifies those who believe. This is in contrast to the false teaching that a person's own, so-called good works or keeping of rules and ordinances are able to save them. As Paul prepares to deal with the doctrinal issues of the church, he reminds the church of their minister, Epaphras as explained in Colossians 1:7-9, "*just as you learned it from Epaphras, our beloved fellow bond-servant, who is a faithful servant of Christ on our behalf, and he also informed us of your love in the Spirit. For this reason also, since the day we heard of it, we have not ceased to pray for you and to ask that you may be filled with the knowledge of His will in all spiritual wisdom and understanding*". Paul declares him to be a fellow servant. Paul's declaration is an allusion to Epaphras' equality with Paul in the ministry. Paul was insistent that he did not lord it over any Christian, and that all Christians were his full equal, without regard to their worldly social state. Paul was concerned for the spiritual growth of the Christians at Colossae. His prayers for them express an abundance which can be seen in his use of the words "all" and "every". Broadly, his unceasing prayer was that they should:

1. Know God's will
2. Walk worthily
3. Work fruitfully
4. Grow in the knowledge of God
5. Be empowered to patience
6. Express a thankful spirit

First, he wanted them to be filled with the knowledge of God's will in all wisdom and spiritual understanding. The Holy Spirit will give the spiritual insight where we can understand the will of God for our lives through God's word. Wisdom is the application of that understanding to our lives. Obedience to His word will prove His will to be good, acceptable and perfect as described in Romans 12:2,"*And do not be conformed to this world, but be transformed by the renewing of your mind, so that you may prove what the will of God is, that which is good and acceptable and perfect*". Second, he wanted their walk that is the course and conduct of their lives, to give pleasure to God. In the way as the life of the Lord Jesus could draw forth the Father's expression of delight. Just as the way God expressed His love for His Son Jesus in Matthew 3:17, "*and behold, a voice out *of the heavens said, "This is My beloved Son, in whom I am well-pleased"*. Third, they were to do good works. A good work is one which is done to benefit others while giving the credit to God alone. His glory is the motive for good works. Only those who are new creatures in Christ are capable of doing good works as described in Ephesians 2:10, *"For we are His workmanship, created in Christ Jesus for good works, which God prepared beforehand so that we would walk in them"*, also Titus 3:8, *"This is a trustworthy statement ; and concerning these things I want you to speak confidently, so that those who have believed God will be careful to engage in good deeds. These things are good and profitable for men"*. Fourth, Paul wanted them to increase in the knowledge of God. The only way to do this is through communion with Him in prayer, studying His revealed word and living in His will as described in Hosea 6:3,*"So let us know, let us press on to know the Lord. His going forth is as certain as the dawn; and He will come to us like the rain, like the spring rain watering the earth"*. Fifth, he wanted them to be filled with all might according to God's glorious power unto all patience and longsuffering with joyfulness. This power is tapped by prayer. The purpose for it is not to create marvelous preachers or the working of miracles, but rather to produce joyfulness in our lives when we are under great trial. "Patience" is a word which speaks of endurance under pressure and "long-suffering" expresses a quiet suffering of the failings of others or their abuse. Patience means "no giving-up"; "long-suffering" means "no giving-back"; and "with joyfulness" suggests "no giving-in". Paul wants them to have thankful hearts in the light of what the Father has done for them. Oh, how I wish that our Christian lives might manifest these qualities also! The letter that Paul wrote to Philemon carried the clear message that Christians often want to separate themselves from other Christians based upon racial status, ethnic status, economic status, church position, church authority, or other reasons. When Satan separates Christians from one another, he wins. We see in Epaphras the spiritual integrity of Paul. Even as he honestly describes the state of his church, in the fact that his church is in conflict due to false teachers trying to take control, his report does not fail to recognize the love in the Spirit that is also there. When our focus is drawn towards those in a congregation that are stirring up conflict and hurt, it is easy to forget that there are always the remnant of the faithful standing on the foundation on their faith. The members of the Colossian church need to be encouraged, recognized, and prayed for as Epaphras and Paul are doing. We should be more like Epaphras and Paul. We should encourage, and pray rather than to be criticizing or condemning as we might choose to do. It is Paul's desire that the Colossian Christians be filled literally, to overflowing, with the knowledge of God's will. He desires all Christians to have an intimate and complete knowledge of Christ. Paul desires that Christians have the kind of knowledge of Christ that carries with it a portion of God's wisdom, and a full understanding of spiritual matters. This is a pretty high desire, but why should we not pray for God-sized tasks rather than tasks that we think we could otherwise accomplish on our own? Later Epaphras was sent back to Colossae bearing Paul's letter to the saints of that city. He is seen at one time to have been a fellow prisoner in Christ Jesus along with Paul, as explained in Philemon 1:23, *"Epaphras, my fellow prisoner in Christ Jesus, greets you"*. Epaphras and Aristarchus may have alternated as the Apostle's fellow-prisoners, Epaphras being a prisoner of Christ with Paul while the letter to Philemon was written and Aristarchus serving in the same capacity while Paul's letter to the Colossians was written. Whatever the circumstances may have been it was indeed an honor to have been linked with Paul as a fellow-prisoner in the Lord. One of the reasons for Epaphras' journey to Rome and his willingness to share for a time the Apostle Paul's imprisonment was his desire to acquaint Paul with the progress of the gospel in the Lycus valley and to encourage the great apostle. But the main reason was undoubtedly to solicit advice about a dangerous heresy which had arisen in Colossae and was threatening the security of the church. It is possible that Epaphras needed the greater wisdom of the apostle to assist him in dealing with these matters. Though such service was often demanding, difficult, exhausting, hard, rough and tearful, you have to consider what a blessed relationship this was, something which Epaphras must have truly cherished. Paul refers to Epaphras not only as a faithful minister of Christ, but as a servant of Jesus Christ. The words "minister" and "servant" having the same root, doulos, which means "bond slave" which is the same word is used of Christ in Philippians 2:7,"*but emptied Himself, taking the form of a bond-servant, and being made in the likeness of men*". The basic idea in regard to Epaphras' service is that he was faithful. How important this is, especially in a day where you find unfaithfulness everywhere, and how important constant and dedicated service means in the sight of God! It is required in stewards, that a man is found faithful, as explained in 1 Corinthians 4:2,"*In this case, moreover, it is required of stewards that one be found trustworthy*". When one considers the difficulties that the Colossian church members are facing, all of these traits which Epaphras manifested, would go far to render the false teachings inadequate. We need knowledge of God's will, we need wisdom, and we need spiritual understanding to deal with all of these issues. Whether the issue is large or small, people get hurt when the response to conflict is not expressed in love, and it rarely is. We see in Paul and Epaphras a response that is based upon love. They pray for the resources by which the Christians will find a way out of the conflict. They continue to love the church of Colosse and encourage them. This response is a character trait that Paul passed on to Epaphras. Paul, in turn, sent word to the Colossians that he hath a great zeal for them. Epaphras was a faithful witness and minister. In the way that he was strong in faith, great in zeal, fervent in prayer, loving in spirit, and willing to suffer for his faith. According to tradition, he later became a pastor at Colosse and eventually was martyred there. Epaphras was a great hero of the faith. His life would surely be an inspiration if we knew all aspects of his life. It will be a joy to meet him in heaven, as well as a host of other faithful believers who have served the Lord. Christians from various times and places, and through the ages, who are significant ancestors in our Christian faith. Epaphras is mentioned only three times in the New Testament, in the letters to Philemon and the Colossians which it is not too surprising that he is passed over by biblical scholars who are more interested in Paul's better-known companions. Even though Epaphras is not mentioned all that often, Colossians portrays him as an authentic interpreter of Paul and an important teacher. After all, by the time the letter to the Colossians was written, Paul was dead. Epaphras has great relevance for Christians today who seek ways to witness to the contemporary world. Epaphras is known as servant of Christ and fellow prisoner which are very worthy labels given to someone committed to doing God's will for a lifetime. He viewed himself as a fellow slave, he saw himself as one of many servants. He was not a maverick, he was not alone in his servitude, and he worked with others in this great endeavor for the Lord. He was a slave, and there were many others. Paul saw Epaphras as one of his personal colleagues, a fellow laborer, doing the same work for the Lord, but in a different location. This may have been said to help give more credibility to Epaphras in the church at Colosse. Paul sent Epaphras back to Colosse with a divinely inspired letter. In this letter, Paul puts Epaphras on the same level as himself, a fellow servant. He stood shoulder to shoulder with the great apostle. This was Paul letter of recommendation to the congregation concerning Epaphras. If the believers in Colosse were so bold as to set aside the teachings that they originally heard from Epaphras, listen and believe what the false teachers are teaching; now they were put on notice. They were warned that they not only were rejecting his authority, but also that of Paul and Timothy! Rejecting the authority of one was rejecting the authority of them all for the fact that they all agreed on the same doctrine and teachings. Not only would these words give credibility to Epaphras in the church, but it would serve to abolish the concept of a hierarchy in the local church. Paul saw himself on the same level as Epaphras. He was a fellow slave, standing shoulder to shoulder with his lesser known servant, Epaphras. According to Paul, Epaphras is a beloved fellow bond servant who faithfully served Christ Jesus by the will of God. True bond servants are to know the grace of God, believe the truth of the gospel, and to own and profess it's sincerely in which Epaphras did faithfully to the fullest extent of his abilities. The reason for referring to Epaphras as a beloved fellow worker was because at the time this epistle was written Epaphras was with Paul in prison. Epaphras brought to his friend Paul, the news from the region, including the state of the church in Colossae. Most likely, the church in Colossae was started during Paul's stay in Ephesus, about 100 miles west of Colossae. In the days of the apostle Paul, Colossae was part of the Roman province of Asia. It was situated in the Lycus Valley which was itself in a volcanic region and often subject to earthquakes. Nevertheless, the valley was one to which many Jews came because of the pleasures and prosperity the region offered. Although an important city in the Persian era, it declined when the main trade route from Ephesus to Antioch was detoured to the west, near Laodicea. The Greek historian and geographer, Strabo, who lived a couple of generations before Paul, described Colossae as merely a small town. The message that Epaphras brought described the faith and love of the Colossian Christians. However, as the community from which the body was drawn was multicultural, so was the make-up of the church. As people came from different ethnic, religious, and philosophical backgrounds, they carried their views into the church. The Jewish wanted a religion of law, tradition, and rituals. Some Greeks wanted a religion that saved one based upon knowledge and philosophy. Other Greeks thought that all physical objects are evil, and all that is spiritual is good, and therefore denied the physical existence of Jesus. This worldly doctrine was successfully invading the congregation, compromising the gospel, and creating extreme conflict with the remaining of members. It was bringing doubt into the minds of those who wanted to maintain the purity of the faith in their own lives and those who demonstrate the transformed life that is based upon true faith in Jesus Christ. Epaphras visited Paul to seek his advice and counsel concerning errors which were creeping into the church at Colosse. But he did not only seek help, he gave much help to Paul. Epaphras comforted him and ministered to him in a number of different ways. What a great privilege it was for Epaphras to minister to God's honored and suffering apostle! How natural that Paul should feel a deep affection for Epaphras! He was a faithful minister of Christ! He was undoubtedly a successful servant of the Lord, but Paul emphasizes that he was a faithful minister of Christ. Can there be a greater tribute than this? Epaphras was the minister of the church at Colosse, but more important than that, he was a minister of Christ. He was directly responsible to the Lord Himself. It was from the One who sat upon the throne that he received his orders. We are to mirror Epaphras' faithfulness to the Lord so that we may hear well done good and faithful servant, as described in Matthew 25:22."*His master said to him, 'Well done, good and faithful slave. You were faithful with a few things, I will put you in charge of many things; enter into the joy of your master."* We must show God we are faithful as explained in Luke 16:10-12, *"He who is faithful in a very little thing is faithful also in much; and he who is unrighteous in a very little thing is unrighteous also in much." Therefore if you have not been faithful in the use of unrighteous wealth, who will entrust the true riches to you? "And if you have not been faithful in the use of that which is another's, who will give you that which is your own"*. God must find us trustworthy in all things, in all aspects of our life as explained in 1 Corinthians 4:2, *"In this case, moreover, it is required of stewards that one be found trustworthy"*. Once God finds us faithful and trustworthy, He then rewards us as explained in Revelation 2:10, *"Do not fear what you are about to suffer. Behold, the devil is about to cast some of you into prison, so that you will be tested, and you will have tribulation for ten days. Be faithful until death, and I will give you the crown of life"*. Epaphras was a bearer of good news. Nobody knew the church members at Colosse better than Epaphras, yet he said all the good things he could about them. He exalted their integrity and kept silent about their shortcomings. Be careful that you are never guilty of criticizing your church or assembly; your careless criticism may breed disaffection among the members and bring dishonor upon the Name of the Lord. Notice that Epaphras was not only "of" the church at Colosse; he was "for" the church at Colosse. If you are "of" a church or if you belong to a church, be sure you are always "for" it as well, for the Lord's sake and for the sake of your fellow-believers. Serve your church or assembly with your utmost loyalty and shield the faults of someone in the assembly exposing no one's dirty laundry to the public. If you do not altogether agree with a preacher, be silent about him before the godless. Do not tear him or any of your fellow Church members to pieces. To be guilty of dragging the failure of a church, preacher or Christian before the world is to act as a traitor. Epaphras had authority in his position. The authority that Epaphras had was recognized and commended by Paul. In addition to having authority over the people, he was also very much loved by the people! Why wouldn't the people of Colosse love him? He gave his all to bring the gospel message to them and he poured his life into establishing a church there. Now he visits Paul and brings them a letter from the apostle written for their edification. They loved him and no doubt, he loved them. I think it's fair to say that many of the fellow servants we know as missionaries around the world are also dearly loved by us. We pray for them, pray with them, and hear them share their ministry during mission conferences. Epaphras was a servant of Christ and a fellow servant of the apostles, jointly engaged with them in preaching the gospel. These two terms, servant and fellow servant speak of the relationship Epaphras had with the apostles and with the Colossians. To Paul and Timothy, Epaphras was their dear fellow servant. He worked with Paul, but for the Colossians, he was their faithful minister. Epaphras was a servant or in Greek a doulos or a sun-doulos. He is here called a diakonos. Diakonos is one who executes the commands of another, for instance a master, a servant, attendant, or a minister. This is a term that is used of those who perform a service, a ministry. It is the word normally translated "deacon." Epaphras was a deacon of Christ. Both doulos and diakonos speak of a servant, but doulos is a bond servant, without a will in the matter. Diakonos speaks of willing service. This speaks of the willingness of Epaphras to put himself into subjection to the will of God in serving Christ and ministering to God's people. Paul emphasizes that Epaphras was a faithful servant. He was faithful to the task to which God appointed him. He was faithful in bringing the gospel to that city. The fact that a church existed in Colosse was a testimony to his faithfulness. In fact, it may be that Paul was also commending him for establishing churches in the nearby cities of Laodecea and Hierapolis. We know the trouble that later arose in Laodecea and we know the trouble that had already arisen at the time of the writing of this epistle in Colosse. As its leader, Epaphras could have quit when the going got tough. Many leaders do call it quits when the invasion of false teachers stirs up trouble. It seemed that there must have been several waves of false teachers, for there are quite a variety of doctrinal issues that he raises in this book. It might seem that a follower of Christ might get tired of fighting one battle after another. He could have given up and let the wolves take over, but he didn't. He stuck it out in good times and in bad times and Paul praises him for it. He was a teacher and a servant. What really made him valuable in the ministry was his faithfulness. A faithful follower of Christ is spiritual health to believers! God would much rather have each one of us to be faithful servants in whatever our ministry might be. God would much rather each one of us to be faithful, reliable, trustworthy, dependable, and consistent. God would much rather we not weary in well doing. Once again, Paul was putting the full weight of his own apostolic authority behind Epaphras. Paul let the whole congregation know that Epaphras was a faithful deacon of Christ. He is setting him apart from the false teachers, who did not serve Christ. Paul identifies him as a "faithful minister". Paul did not identify all "ministers" as "faithful" as described in 2 Corinthians 11:13-15, *"For such men are false apostles, deceitful workers, disguising themselves as apostles of Christ. No wonder, for even Satan disguises himself as an angel of light. Therefore it is not surprising if his servants also disguise themselves as servants of righteousness, whose end will be according to their deeds"*. Some in the church were unfaithful. Some in the church were actually false apostles who only posed as faithful ministers of Christ. They were in reality ministers of Satan. Paul was not afraid to identify false apostles and ministers of Satan. When there was a faithful minister of Christ, Paul stood up for him, endorsed him, stood with him, and commended him before the people. That is just what Paul did for Epaphras. Epaphras was a very influential preacher of the word. Paul considered Epaphras a precious servant of Christ and to the fellow ministers on account of the grace and gifts bestowed on him because of his usefulness in the ministry and his faithfulness and integrity. Epaphras was one whom Christ had made and not man, who God qualified, and sent forth and made successful. He preached none but Christ, and Him crucified, in the business of salvation. He was a faithful servant, one that sought not his own glory but the glory of Him who sent him. He wanted not to please men but his master. He concealed no part of this message but freely and fully declared it wholly and faithfully. He was faithful to Christ who put him into the ministry and to the souls of men to whom he ministered. It is said he was one that was for your spiritual good. He had a great zeal for others; he dearly loved others. He spent his time and strength on helping and ministering to others. He made great use of his time, gifts and talents for their use and benefit while among them. Epaphras was a native of Colosse, and one of their faithful ministers who brought the good news of Christ to his home town. He had a heart to see people saved! He was from Colosse and grew up there. He had family there. He was the perfect man for the job. He knew the language; the culture; the people; the problems; the manner of life; he was a Colossian! He knew many people in that city, and now that he was saved, he realized that all of his old friends were still unsaved. That's one of the first things a new believer realizes, that those around him are still in darkness, just as he once was. Someone brought the gospel to Epaphras and he was saved. Now he had a desire to bring the gospel to others, especially to his home town – Colosse! This was just what we saw in the lives of the other apostles. Andrew was introduced to Christ, and the first thing he thought of was bringing the good news to his brother, Peter! He was not merely a servant in the same sense as a believer, but as he was a preacher of the gospel. He faithfully served his Lord and Master Jesus Christ. Epaphras came from Colossae so the people he ministered to were his people - they would have spoken with the same accent. It would be only natural that he would have cared about their fate because he'd lived with and loved his city and the people in it. Epaphras had a particular desire that the Colossians should be blessed. Paul never was at the church at Colosse, Epaphras founded the church at Colosse, during Paul's 3 year ministry at Ephesus. Several years after the Colossian church was founded a dangerous heresy arose to threaten it. It contained elements of what later became known as Gnosticism. Gnosticism is the belief that God is good, but matter is evil and Jesus Christ was merely one of a series of emanations. Emanation means to flow out, issue, or proceed, as from a source or origin, come forth, originate. They believed that Jesus was descending from God and being less than God, a belief that led them to deny His true humanity, and that a secret higher knowledge above scripture was necessary for enlightenment and salvation. The Colossian heresy also embraced aspects of Jewish legalism, for instance the necessity of circumcision for salvation, observance of the ceremonial rituals of the Old Testament law (dietary laws, festivals, Sabbaths) and rigid asceticism. Asceticism is defined as the doctrine that a person can attain a high spiritual and moral state by practicing self-denial, and self-mortification. It also called for the worship of angels, and mystical experiences. The epistle shows us how Paul deals with the false teachings which were permeating the church. The false teachers gave an important place to the powers of the spirit world which degraded the Person and work of Christ. Paul combats this by teaching that Christ is the One in whom the fullness of the Godhead dwells, even the Creator and Lord of all things in heaven and in earth. Paul argues that it is through the work of Christ that we have peace with God. Paul urges that we should live lives in the power of the Spirit which reveal the life of Christ in and through us. Paul revealed the secret of God is found in Christ alone. Therefore, in general terms, we may say that the epistle deals with the glories of Christ as Head over all things to the church. We may certainly conclude that the threat from this false teaching was real, that an immediate response was urgent. Paul had no doubt that the church has been well instructed in the Christian faith. He had confidence in Epaphras' abilities which is the reason why Paul describes Epaphras as a faithful minister of Christ. Epaphras brought the gospel message to the city of Colosse and taught the people in that city. Epaphras also enrolled many people in his discipleship class and he began to teach them the word of the truth of the gospel. Just as when the Lord took in disciples, some received it superficially and later departed, and in others it took root in good soil and was saved! They became disciples and they produced fruit, abundant fruit! This was part of the Lord's commission to spread the good news of the resurrected Savior, make disciples of all nations, and all cities, including Colosse. God used Epaphras, to bring the gospel to Colosse. He was also used of the Lord to start the church in Laodicea and Hierapolis. Epaphras not only had a heart for the Colossians, but he also had a heart for other nearby cities of Laodicea and Hierapolis. These 3 three cities were only about 10 miles apart, a tri-city region. It is likely that Epaphras knew people in each of these other cities too, perhaps relatives, friends, or even acquaintances. He would have had many contacts and many opportunities to speak to people about Christ and the language and culture would have been the same. The Lord chose Epaphras for this ministry, the perfect man for the job. Unknown to Epaphras, God ordained him before the foundation of the earth for him to be raised in that region for such a time as this. God's plan was to use Epaphras as God's instrument to bring the gospel there! He had zeal, an excitement for these people. He was eagerly excited and full of enthusiasm to bring the gospel to these cities. He had a genuine zeal for those people and not only zeal, but great zeal, much zeal for his people. This was his character, not just a passing excitement, continual zeal! One of the first things that God puts in the heart of a new believer is a concern to see others saved. Do you have that desire? Is it zeal? Is it great zeal? Perhaps you used to but you have allowed that zeal to die down and the coals became cold. Stir up those coals! One of the best ways to stir up an interest in evangelism is to do it, take advantage of the opportunities God gives. You will soon see how exciting it is to share the good news and to point men to Christ. Who better to begin with than those closest to you? For example relatives, coworkers, neighbors, and friends! Mission boards spend lots of money and take years to train a person to go overseas, learn the language, learn the culture, make friends, and try to fit in, so that they can then have opportunities to evangelize. You don't have to worry about all that if you share the gospel with those around you! It wasn't necessary for Epaphras to learn the language or culture. He was one of them already! It is the same with you, you are one of them! You know the language, you have contacts here already. Take advantage of this great privilege and share the gospel of Christ with those around you! There is one characteristic that stands out about Epaphras and that is his prayerfulness. Unlike Paul, we don't know if Epaphras wrote anything down or sent letters; his work was prayer. He is said to have been laboring fervently, and agonizing, or wrestling in prayer. Paul says Epaphras is always laboring earnestly for others in his prayers and, he has a deep concern for others. Notice it is in the plural sense, in prayers, and always. The original word from which wrestling is translated means that he went through a struggle in prayer. The phrase deep concern implies strenuous work. The sort of work that demands putting his heart and soul into his work. Prayer makes the presence of the Lord alive and changes every work, which could have been fruitless, into light and glory to the Heavenly Father. For prayer to be fruitful as in the way Epaphras and Paul made it fruitful, we, as Christ's slaves, must struggle in prayer, in order to trust in God's will. Prayer was no passing matter to this believer; he took his prayer life seriously, which made him a prayer warrior. He sensed responsibility for others in the body of Christ, so he wrestled in prayer that the churches in the Lycus Valley might develop to their full potential in Christ. He agonized in prayer; in just the same way that Jesus did when he went to the garden of Gethsemane. Real prayer, earnest prayer, is hard work. There are so many interruptions; so many excuses for not sticking at it so it becomes harder and harder to even try a little. He's not praying for non-believers to know Jesus, he's praying for people that already follow Jesus Christ. He is praying for his own Christian brothers and sisters. Epaphras was a faithful minister to the Colossians in part because of his prayer life. He labored for them fervently in prayer. Notice what he prayed for, that they would stand perfect and complete in the will of God. Paul's prayers for the people were that they would be filled with the knowledge of His will. Imagine if all of us here were filled with the knowledge of God's will, and we walked according to Gods will! This kind of praying puts God and His will at the center of everything. Epaphras taught and led this church, but not according to his own will, not according what he thought or felt would be best. He sought the will of the Lord. In reality, it's impossible to be a faithful servant of God's people without faithfully laboring in prayer. If prayer isn't paramount, then God is not at the center of a ministry. If prayer is not paramount and in the center of a ministry then that ministry is operating in the power of the flesh which occurs far too often! Prayer is the backbone of ministries. The Body of Christ should pray together, seek God's will, God's mind, and God's guidance! It is also how the hearts of the people are knit together. The nearby church of Laodicea was described as a lukewarm church, with little passion or commitment. They certainly didn't practice what they preached. You know the type of Christian; the ones who aren't prepared to roll up their sleeves and actually do anything to build up the church. That was what Epaphras continued to pray about, that they would be excited and enthusiastic in wanting to serve Christ. You know it does seem rather intimidating the thought of building prayer into your day, seriously, where on earth do you fit it? Any one of us can work it into our day from breakfast to supper. At anytime we can say a quick, quiet prayer. We can say a quick prayer while we are working, while we are driving, while we are shopping, or while we are taking care of our families. Our prayers should be faithful. We have so many wonderful examples to serve as role models. We have wonderful examples of people of faith who persevered in prayer. A few examples of people who persevered in prayer are, David, a man after God's own heart, as it says in Psalms 55:16-17,"*But I call to God, and the Lord saves me. Evening, morning and noon I cry out in distress, and he hears my voice*". An example of a man greatly beloved by God is Daniel, as described in Daniel 6:10,"*Now when Daniel learned that the decree had been published, he went home to his upstairs room where the windows opened toward Jerusalem. Three times a day he got down on his knees and prayed, giving thanks to his God, just as he had done before*". On several occasions, Jesus warned His disciples to be watchful in prayer as explained in Matthew 26:41,"*Watch and pray so that you will not fall into temptation. The spirit is willing, but the body is weak*". Our prayers should be thankful and purposeful. Prayers are often too general in their requests, lacking specific purpose; it's far easier to pray for a specific person or situation. Epaphras prayed for the people he knew, that they would know God in new ways. He prayed constantly, he wrestled in prayer laboring fervently. He prayed personally for others. He prayed with a goal in mind, that followers of Christ may stand perfect and complete. Whenever we're not certain what to pray for, it seems like a pretty good place for us to start is to pray that followers of Christ would stand and be made perfect and complete. Epaphras bore a sincere love and healthy affection for the church of Colosse. Colosse was always in Epaphras' prayers, he never forgot his dear flock of which he was pastor. He struggled and labored with God for them, even to a point of agony. He was continually praying in earnest prayer for them. It was a type of persevering, persistent, and fervent prayer for them. He prayed for them to be filled with the Holy Spirit and have perfect knowledge of the revealed will of God. He prayed that they would understand both doctrine and practice of Christ and to be empowered to act according to it. Epaphras was constantly laboring in prayer. Paul held up Epaphras as an example of one who rightly and fervently labored in prayer. So that all of us, who are Christ's disciples, might stand perfect and complete in God's will. Epaphras had a devout prayer life. At least three basic ideas are significant in Epaphras' prayer life.

1.) He was persistent. As the Apostle Paul draws his letter to a close, he reveals the persistency and the faithfulness where Epaphras prays for the Colossian Christians. In other words, there was no letting up or letting down in his prayerful remembrance of them. An example of a persistently constant prayer life is found in Ephesians 6:18,"*With all prayer and petition pray at all times in the Spirit, and with this in view, be on the alert with all perseverance and petition for all the saints*", also in Colossians 1:3,"*We give thanks to God, the Father of our Lord Jesus Christ, praying always for you*" also Colossians 4:2,"*Devote yourselves to prayer, keeping alert in it with an attitude of thanksgiving*" also 1 Thessalonians 5:17,"*pray without ceasing*" and finally, Jude 1:20,"*But you, beloved, building yourselves up on your most holy faith, praying in the Holy Spirit*".

2.) He was persevering. Epaphras prayed things through. Prayer was not a form, but a force in his life, the very essence of his life. As conveyed by the words laboring fervently, which are but one word in the Greek text, which literally means agonized (agonizomenos**)** in the presence of God.

3.) He was particular. Epaphras did not pray generic, blanketed, nonexclusive prayers, but specifically targeted prayers. General petitions will only bring general answers, but specific petitions will bring specific answers united with the blessings which accompany such answers. Epaphras' prayed that the Colossians might be able to stand. How important it is for the people of God, individually and collectively, to both stand, and take a stand as explained in Galatians 5:1,"*It was for freedom that Christ set us free ; therefore keep standing firm and do not be subject again to a yoke of slavery*" also Ephesians 6:13-14,"*Therefore , take up the full armor of God, so that you will be able to resist in the evil day, and having done everything, to stand firm. Stand firm therefore, having girded your loins with truth, and having put on the breastplate of righteousness*", and Philippians 1:27,"*Only conduct yourselves in a manner worthy of the gospel of Christ, so that whether I come and see you or remain absent, I will hear of you that you are standing firm in one spirit, with one mind striving together for the faith of the gospel*". Much of the chaos, confusion, and corruption in this present age are directly traceable to the fact that no stand is taken for what is righteous. A good bit of the trouble and division which scars, spoil, and tarnish God's people stems from spiritual immaturity. Epaphras prayed that they might be complete in the will of God that they might be fully assured in all their associations with Him. That they may be assured of all the promises that He promised through His Word, and they are assured of their union in Christ. These things we learn by means of our Lord's revealed will through the Scriptures. Such a petition only serves to stress the importance of reading the Word of God day by day, as well as meditating upon it.

During one of D. L. Moody's Atlantic Ocean crossings a fire broke out in the hold of the ship. A friend is reported to have said to the famous evangelist, "Mr. Moody, let us go to the other end of the ship and engage in prayer." The heavenly-minded yet down-to-earth Moody replied, "Not so, sir; we stand right here and pass buckets and pray hard all the time." Such truly reflects the spirit of Epaphras and his ministry, a man of God who may be looked upon as an Elijah of the New Testament as explained in James 5:16,"*Therefore, confess your sins to one another, and pray for one another so that you may be healed. The effective prayer of a righteous man can accomplish much*". God grant that in these "last days" the Church of Jesus Christ might be blessed with many more prayer warriors such as Epaphras was in his day. Will you be one of them? Real prayer warriors are not often found, especially in this busy, fast-moving, age. An age of, hurry, worry, and bury. Yet, in every period of man's hectic life, God has always had those who have spent much time in secret communion with Him, tucked away in their prayer closet. Apart from such prayer warriors the Church of Jesus Christ would be virtually powerless. If we knew what we owe as believers to the ceaseless intercession of our Great High Priest, the Lord Jesus Christ, it would blow our minds! Jesus is united with the faithful men and women of God in intercessory prayer. If we only knew, we would surely be driven to our knees in true praise and thankfulness to our Lord, at the same time submitting ourselves more often of the priceless privilege of prayer. Epaphras was a man of prayer and though his biography is brief we are reminded of the fact that little is much when God is in it. James, the half-brother of the Lord Jesus, was called camel knees because of his calloused knees as a result of long hours spent in prayer, and Epaphras might well be thought of as another camel knee of the Bible. Epaphras was called by God to take the Gospel of Christ to the unevangelized. This is the call and responsibility of every true believer, to engage in the missionary work committed to them. It's one thing to be doctrinally sound or orthodox. But that orthodoxy ought to be accompanied by the love of God for the brethren. Without this kind of love in the Spirit the church may have all their paper work in order, sound, orthodox, fundamental, but cold! Let's not be that kind of church. God is truth, but He is also love! The Colossians had the love in the Spirit. Where the truth is received there ought to be a life filled with the love of God manifested in real deeds, and action. It is good for a church to contend for the faith. That is what this epistle is all about, but it is also important for a church to demonstrate the life and love of God towards each other in every day living. The Colossians demonstrated Spiritual fruit, produced by the Holy Spirit who indwelt them. They had love, joy, and peace. This was part of the progress report that Epaphras made to Paul as he shared what God was doing in Colosse, how the saints there had been demonstrating genuine love in the Spirit. This was not a phony, showy kind of love, done to be seen of men. This was supernatural. It was the kind of love produced in the life of a yielded believer. It was the fruit of the indwelling Holy Spirit. This was the real thing. No doubt Epaphras had told Paul many other things about the church. It is also clear that he reported about those who were teaching Jewish tradition; Greek philosophy; and pagan asceticism. Paul addressed all those issues. But for now, he seems impressed with this one fact: that the Colossians had been manifesting agape love in the spirit. Epaphras had talked much about this to Paul and he was impressed with what he heard. Thus, the apostle praises these folks for their love. Imagine getting a letter from Paul praising you for your love in the Spirit? That must have been a great encouragement to these believers! Consider also the fact that with all the problems attacking the church at the time of the writing, Epaphras' report highlights their love in the spirit in the midst of it all! That is a remarkable quality for a church to have in such a time of attack. Often when a church is attacked, and there are problems in the assembly, one might expect to see backbiting, division, gossip, and fighting amongst themselves. That was not the case in Colosse. In the midst of their attack, what impressed Paul was their love in the Spirit. This also says a lot about Epaphras. Other men might have faced all the problems and attacks in the assembly and would have become discouraged, and reported to Paul about the problems not Epaphras. Isn't that human nature to see only the problems? Some men and women have a nature that they see only the problems, and not the good, only the bad in people and not the Christ-like qualities. There were plenty of issues in the church at Colosse and they would all be dealt with in good time. But Epaphras was the kind of man who, in the midst of trying times and spiritual attacks, was still able to see the love of God being manifested in the saints. Be that kind of person! In spite of the problems that arose in that church, Paul was thanking God for its existence. He knew of their problems, he knew of the controversy brewing there. But he also knew of their faith in Christ and the love which they had to all the saints. He knew that the gospel Epaphras preached was producing fruit in that place. He knew that Epaphras was a faithful servant of Christ, and that if the saints rallied behind his leadership, refocused on Christ as Paul exhorts them, that the problems could be resolved. Paul was thanking God for them, praying always for them. Paul wanted God's best for these believers. He had never met them, but from prison he was doing what he could to encourage them in the truth, to support the man God sent there and the truth he was teaching. He was doing his best to expose and reject all those who sought to undermine the work of God. Can't you see in this man Paul a love for the local church? Can't you see in this man Epaphras a love for the work of the Lord? They were servants, slaves of Jesus Christ, servants of God's people. God was glorified through it all. May that be the case in all churches! The favorable report which Epaphras brought to Paul was a source of joy and encouragement to the Apostle. Are you consistently faithful in reading God's Word, prayer, upholding the Person and work of Christ, witnessing, assembling yourself with the Lord's people, and in every other aspect of the Christian life?

Chapter 13

Do you remember when you first said yes to Jesus? When He first knocked on your heart, and you opened the door of your heart to Him?

Revelation 3:20 "Here I am! I stand at the door and knock. If anyone hears my voice and opens the door, I will come in and eat with him, and he with me. "

Jesus is speaking to you again; He is wooing you, luring you, saying I want you to know my heart!! I want you to know that the heart beat of it all is right here! I remember the kindness of your youth, the love that you had when you went after me.

I believe God is and was fighting for your heart. I believe God is speaking to the hearts of His people calling us back to the place where we went after Him. I believe God is saying, I remember how you use to love me, I remember how you use to go after me. It's the way Mary of Bethany poured her life into a bottle and broke it at his feet. It was extravagant!! It was her worship of Him. She didn't count the cost, she didn't think about what she was giving up, she has viewed everything of her life in light of this Man and of His words, "where else have we to go Jesus, you have the words of eternal life"?

Matthew 26:6-13
"And when Jesus was in Bethany at the house of Simon the leper, a woman came to Him having an alabaster flask, of very costly fragrant oil, and she poured it on His head as He sat at the table. But when his disciples saw it, they were indignant saying, 'Why this waste? For this fragrant oil might have been sold for much and given to the poor.' But when Jesus as aware of it, He said to them, 'Why do you trouble this woman? For she has done a good work for me. For you have the poor with you always, but me you do not have always. For in pouring this fragrant oil on MY body she did it for my burial. Assuredly, I say to you, wherever this gospel is preached in the whole world, what this woman has done will also be told as a memorial to her.'"

Jesus remembers the kindness of your youth, the love and excitement you had for Him, "I remember you. How you use to act from the heart where this use to be all about love." Reminiscence over seasons of our life to where we use to love and worship from the inward where it once flowed, where it once moved forth toward Him, saying I miss Him. God is saying, "I want it as it was in the old days, I want your heart flowing like it was in the old days when you went after me in the wilderness. Those early days of salvation when all you had to hear was the name Jesus and you cried out. I am talking about those days when you slept little, you ate little and you didn't have to think about it, you just did it. WHY? Because there is another service going on, there is another prayer meeting going on". You use to say, "I need to get alone with Jesus!" It wasn't a part of your life; it was the very essence of your life. It was your heart. You had to be with Him, you had to feel His presence. You had to know His kiss of His word. It's all about a yearning again, it's all about His hand coming upon the door latch of our heart, your heart and my heart. Yearn for Him! That's what He is after! It's about a longing and a reaching of the heart, a going after in the heart, it's all about a reaching for, and if we settle for anything else we've lost it all. Reminisce over seasons of our lives when we use to love God, praise God, and worship God from the inward, where it once flowed. Are we saying, "I miss Him, I want it like the way it was in the old days"? God is saying, "I want your heart flowing like it was in the old days. The way it was in the wilderness when you went after me. I remember you, how you went after me from the heart; where this once was all about love." Do you remember the days when you wanted to draw close to God? You cried to him. The days you use to run after God, you were not ashamed. All you needed was one look from the eyes of Jesus and you were captivated. You were searching for His heart, His eyes, you needed to know what He was thinking, what He was feeling. When you hear His voice does your heart still yearn when He says your name? Do you still cry out "I am yours!!"?

I pray you do.

Made in USA - Kendallville, IN
1227725_9781467951135